VOYA's Guide to Intellectual Freedom for Teens

Margaret Auguste

VOYA Press

an imprint of E L Kurdyla Publishing, LLC

Bowie, Maryland

ISBN 978-1-61751-007-6

Copyright © 2012 by Margaret Auguste

Published by VOYA Press, an imprint of E L Kurdyla Publishing, LLC
www.kurdylapublishing.com

LCCN: 2012935469

The paper used in this publication meets the minimum requirements of the American National Standard for Information Sciences-Permanence of Paper for Printed Materials, ANSI Z39.48-1992.

Manufactured in the United States of America

I dedicate this book to Guy, Patrick, Marissa, Tristan, and Julian.

I love you all!!

TABLE OF CONTENTS

Introduction

"Once you learn to read, you will be forever free." This quote is credited to Frederick Douglass, the 19th century American abolitionist and orator. He attributed his escape from slavery and his success in life to his commitment to reading books that he was prohibited access to when he was a slave. In his book, *Escape from Slavery*, he states that overhearing his master discuss his opposition to slaves reading is what inspired him to read. He overheard him say, "Now, if you teach [him] how to read, there would be no keeping him. It would forever unfit him to be a slave. He would at once become unmanageable, and of no value to his master." (Douglass 12) Douglass' inspirational story illustrates the passion that characterizes the centuries-old debate about the control of who can read and what should or should not be read, while demonstrating the innate power that books have to inspire us, take us to new places, and enrich our lives.

The restriction of ideas and the prohibition of thought have flourished in nearly every part of the world throughout history. In ancient Greece, Plato proposed that official government censors monitor and prohibit mothers and nurses from reading stories to their children that were described as being bad or evil. He also wanted anyone who spoke of unorthodox ideas about God to be treated as criminals. Also during that time, the famous poet Ovid and other poets and authors were banished or severely punished for their words. (*Art and Popular Culture Encyclopedia*)

In 1650, William Pynchon published a religious pamphlet, *The Meritorious Price of Our Redemption,* that contained information that opposed the views of the ministers and leaders of his community. The court ordered the book to be destroyed because the religious publication contained "errors and heresies" and the book was burned by the public executioner. This nefarious event became known as the first book burning to occur in the New England colonies. (Paulsen)

Book burnings, however, are not only an archaic part of the past. The battle over who can read has been ongoing and relentless over recent decades. In 1992, the largest book burning in modern history took place in Sarajevo, Bosnia. Serb forces attacked Sarajevo's National Library and destroyed more than one million books and one hundred thousand manuscripts and records during a three-day assault. Librarians and other volunteers risked their lives to save as many books as they could, with one unknown volunteer stating, "We managed to save just a few very precious books. Everything else burned down. And a lot of our heritage, national heritage, lay down there in ashes." (Riedlmayer)

"Book Fuels Debate over 'Objectionable' Content in Richland Schools" read the headline in the Seattle Times. On April 2010, *Extremely Loud and Incredibly Close* by Jonathan Safran Foer was challenged in the city of Richland, Washington. This provocative bestselling book, described as beautiful and heartbreaking, and alternatively, as irritating and manipulative, is about Oskar, a nine-year-old boy whose father died on September 11, 2001, in the World Trade Center. The book was not required reading but was listed as a choice for tenth-grade honors students to read because, as one of the teachers who offered it stated, "literature is meant to provoke discussion and teach the reader about the lives of others." (*Seattle Times*)

Many parents and students believed they learned something from the book, but other parents disagreed because the book contained profanity, sex, and descriptions of violence. They told the school board that they had the right to be informed about the content in the books that their children were exposed to and they felt those books should be flagged. The school board's solution ranged from putting a statement in the syllabus to devising rating systems that would note objectionable material. The teachers worried about how a fair rating system could be developed, when all parents' concerns may not be the same. The students were concerned that some books that would be labeled objectionable could be singled out as being inappropriate. The editor of the student newspaper stated that, "By this point in time, we have to decide for ourselves what's right and wrong."

In modern society, the act of reading is not forbidden and everyone possesses the freedom to read without government control, and yet, book challenges and book bannings still occur on a regular basis. It appears as though books written for young adults seem to have been impacted the most. Since the American Library Association (ALA) began tracking book challenges in 2001, statistics show that 1,720 of book challenges occurred in classrooms and 1,432 occurred in school libraries. Parents, at 48 percent, were the group most likely to initiate the challenges. Deborah Caldwell Stone, a lawyer for the ALA, states that she has also noticed an increased number of organized groups whose sole purpose is to remove books from libraries and schools. (Beale) Even more noteworthy, these statistics only show the number of challenges that were reported. The actual number of challenges combined with those never reported is even higher. The frequency with which censorship occurs today, as well as its negative impact on young adults in particular, attests to the relevance and timeliness of this complicated issue. Librarians, as the leading advocates for the freedom to read, and who posses a unique and extensive knowledge of both teens and the books they love, are well-positioned to take the lead in facilitating the discussion regarding this contentious issue.

VOYA's Guide to Intellectual Freedom for Teens will offer innovative ideas, suggestions, solutions, and new tools that are geared towards addressing the challenging environment that librarians face by enhancing their ability to educate library users about the complicated context in which censorship occurs in today's world. The philosophical and historical nature of censorship will be explored to answer the following questions: Why does the written word still evoke such strong and passionate reactions? Do books purposely contain ideas or actions that are provocative or inappropriate? Is it censorship or common sense to ban them? Or is it just that good books written with thoughtfulness and charm are performing the task they were destined to do, which is to provoke us to expand our thinking, therefore challenging us, and our view of life?

Why censorship occurs will be examined in a new and multifaceted way by exploring the cultural and social influences that demonstrate why books like *The Adventures of Huckleberry Finn* and *The Giver* are considered classics by some and inappropriate texts that have no place in education to others. Censorship will be explored through the eyes of parents, teachers, authors, librarians, and teens to give voice to each group's unique point of view of what censorship means to them, and to examine their thoughts, concerns, and expectations of young adult literature. This should decrease the number of challenges by enabling librarians to develop the necessary insight to tailor services that directly address the needs of each individual groups.

At the center of the storm are young adult authors, who try to write stories for teens that are relevant and true to their experiences and yet, often find their creative vision vilified and denigrated by censors, with one author even finding herself being referred to as "Satan." Through this guide, librarians will be able to explore how this characterization impacts an author's ability to write and sometimes even leads to self-censorship in order to avoid confrontation. Librarians will learn how to articulate how and why young adult authors create their stories so library users will recognize the effort and care that goes into the books written for teens. Finally, the collaboration between public and school librarians is highlighted to show how working together to organize an author visit can bring together teens, parents, and the community to share their personal history, thoughts, values, and opinions about books in a way that can bring potentially controversial subjects into the open.

Parents often feel as though their concern or disagreement over the books their children read is met with condescension or a lack of respect for their role and responsibility as parents. Many parents crave information about the books their children read and firmly believe that the lack of information about these books is the main cause of misunderstandings that develop and spiral out of control. Many of these parents suggest rating books like movies would give them the information they need to make informed choices for their children, while the ALA takes the position that rating books is equivalent to censorship. This guide offers an overview of this debate, as well as many others that impact intellectual freedom by providing ideas and answers that can assist librarians in staying true to their ideals, while continuing to meet the needs of their library users.

With most book challenges taking place in classrooms and schools, it is essential for librarians to understand the unique challenges that classroom teachers face with their book choices so we can offer solutions. Classroom teachers face self-doubt and anxiety when their credibility, and even their livelihood, are threatened by book challenges. Librarians can help alleviate some of this pressure by collaborating with teachers to develop book rationale forms, alternate book choices, and by offering to educate schools, parents, and the community about censorship, the First Amendment, and intellectual freedom.

Librarians can support and assist teens to have their voices heard by listening to what they think about censorship, learning what they have done to speak up for their rights, and learning how to advocate for young adults' right to read. Sexuality, violence, profanity, and religion and the occult have been the main reasons that young adult books have been challenged or banned since the ALA first began collecting the statistics on censorship. Each of these reasons are explored in detail through current research, interviews, and news articles, as well as through new media sources such as blogs and Twitter, in order to offer librarians a thorough background on the history, concerns, and questions regarding each issue. A commanding grasp of the specific areas that are of the most concern is essential for librarians to facilitate open and honest discussion with their library users, which is what parents, in particular, want the most. This information is used to generate activities, ideas, handouts, presentations, and other useful tools that librarians can utilize to actively engage library users in discussion about these difficult subjects.

This guide will assist librarians in this endeavor by exploring the best way to develop a comprehensive selection policy that reflects the library's plan for addressing multiculturalism, sexual orientation, and potentially controversial issues in books meant for young adults, through sample policies and specific examples. This is essential to help librarians develop a flexible plan that reflects young adult literature and that can easily be shared with parents and community members who want to discuss any concerns. A specific selection policy for young adult books that reflects and explains the complexity of the issues that are unique to young adult books is essential in preventing the need for challenges, because it enables librarians to have a clear rationale for the books they choose that can also empower their ability to communicate with parents and community members in an informed and confident manner.

This guide also takes the additional step of encouraging librarians to examine how the "self" is reflected in those selection policies. The common, but rarely discussed problems of self-censorship, anxiety over dealing with challenges, and questions over intellectual freedom are examined to encourage sharing and the need to support each other. Librarians are encouraged to take the difficult, but essential steps to honestly examine their own culture, values, and possible biases in order to design the most objective and user-oriented selection policies.

The commitment that librarians have made to always consider intellectual freedom an integral part of their library's underlying mission is an essential part of any policy that is used to describe the library's commitment to the rights of all library patrons, including children and teens. Many library users, in particular teen library users, are not familiar with these rights; however, through historical research and related activities, librarians will be better equipped to educate library users about this important principal.

Special attention is made to examine how our laws lay the foundation for the best defense against all forms of censorship. The constitution, the First Amendment, and freedom of speech are explored through the examination of notable court cases that reference the connection between the freedom to read and first amendment rights, about which many library users have little to no information. A thorough knowledge of these inalienable rights and the library's historical role in protecting and defending those rights will strengthen the librarian's resolve in advocating against censorship.

Banned Books Week is the worldwide celebration initiated by librarians that promotes the values of the First Amendment and intellectual freedom to the world. The special role that librarians played in developing the observance are examined. Celebrations held around the country and around the world are highlighted, enabling librarians to find many new and exciting ways to celebrate what it means to read freely.

The final chapter highlights the achievements of several librarians who have been advocates for intellectual freedom. For as long as censorship has been in existence, librarians have been at the forefront of the battle against it, speaking up to provide open and free access for everyone, no matter what their race, economic status, or age. The profiles of these champions of intellectual freedom will inspire the librarian reader to appreciate and celebrate our unique role as advocates for the freedom to read.

Librarians have historically acted as leaders in protecting the freedom to read, even in the face of the possible negative impact on their personal and professional lives. They traditionally have taken on the challenge of advocating for the rights of everyone, equally, to read the books that inspire them. Librarians have always, with enthusiasm, defended the right of the words within banned books to exist, even when they are upsetting to some people, because they know that the freedom of the individual is the very foundation upon which our country was founded. In that spirit, librarians continue to honor this proud tradition by leading the charge to educate their communities about the role that censorship plays in their lives. *VOYA's Guide to Intellectual Freedom for Teens* will give librarians the tools that they need to fight against censorship and for intellectual freedom for young people.

Resources

Adler, David. *Frederick Douglass: A Noble Life*. Holiday House, 2010.

Beale, Lewis. "Book Banners Finding Power in Numbers" *Pacific Standard*, 10 February 2010. *http://www.psmag.com/culture-society/book-banners-finding-power-in-numbers-28097*. 05 May 2012.

"Book Fuels Debate over 'Objectionable' Content in Richland Schools." *Seattle Times*. 04 April 2010. *http://seattletimes.nwsource.com/html/localnews/2011585931_schooldebate12.html*. 07 January 2012.

Paulsen, Kenneth. "Book-burning in America: When Wizards Go Up in Smoke." *Freedom Forum*. 13 January 2000. *http://www.freedomforum.org/templates/document.asp?documentID=15610*. 05 January 2011.

"Plato on Censorship." Art and Popular Encyclopedia. *http://artandpopularculture.com/Plato_and_censorship*.

Riedlmayer, Andras. "Libraries Are Not for Burning: International Librarianship and the Recovery of the Destroyed Heritage of Bosnia and Herzegovina." International Federation of Library Associations and Institutions, 1995. *http://forge.fh-potsdam.de/~IFLA/INSPEL/61-riea.htm*. 07 January 2012.

CHAPTER 1
CENSORSHIP TODAY

The Twilight series—*Twilight, New Moon,* and *Eclipse*—has managed to define my personal and professional life for the past few years by opening my eyes to the complex nature of censorship as it exists today. Initially, it never crossed my mind that I would ever have a connection to censorship in any way. Like most people, even though I was a librarian, I rarely thought about censorship being relevant to my life. In my mind, the word called up visceral images of black and white newsreels showcasing fanatics shouting, while they hurled books into a large crackling bonfire. Any discussion of censorship, whether it be with other librarians or other colleagues, seemed to provoke an instantaneous emotional, and yet detached reaction, in that most people are upset about it and know it is wrong, and yet, are absolutely sure that it has nothing to do with them. This misconception is a mistake that librarians, as advocates for the freedom to read, cannot afford to make. Censorship is alive and well; it is just more difficult to recognize sometimes because it takes place in a much more multifaceted and subtle fashion, often occurring under the radar so that even the most well-intentioned people don't realize that it has occurred.

This surprising reality is confirmed by the American Library Association (ALA) Office of Intellectual Freedom who has tracked book challenges that have occurred all around the country since 2001, in an effort to clearly document the reasons that books are challenged and banned. They receive their information from newspapers and reports from individuals and compile the information in a database. According to the ALA website, American libraries were faced with more than 4,660 reported challenges from 2001 to 2010.

Reasons for Book Challenges

- 1,536 book challenges were due to "sexually explicit" material

- 1,231 book challenges were due to "offensive language"

- 977 book challenges were due to material deemed "unsuited to age group"

- 553 book challenges were due to "violence"

- 370 book challenges were due to "homosexuality"

The Twilight series became my wake-up call to this reality. My daughter, who was in the sixth grade at the time, was and is now, a voracious reader who reads above her designated reading level. She was transfixed by *Twilight* and begged for me to get the second book in the series for her. Since my daughter attends school in the same district where I work as a middle school librarian, I checked it out for her from my library after I saw that her school library did not have any of the books. The minute she saw it she screamed with delight, immediately started reading, and decided to take it to school the very next day to show her friends. To my surprise, I received emails that afternoon marked with high importance from her sixth-grade teacher and librarian, both demanding to know why I checked out that book to her when their school had decided that they would not buy any of them for their fifth- and sixth-grade readers because they were, "clearly inappropriate and not suitable to their age group." They also asked me, "What if parents complained and challenged the books?" They felt that I had created a firestorm because now all the other students were insisting that they wanted to read the books as well, and some of the other students, whose parents had either bought them copies or checked out copies from the local public library, were stating that they were bringing their copies to school to read for independent reading.

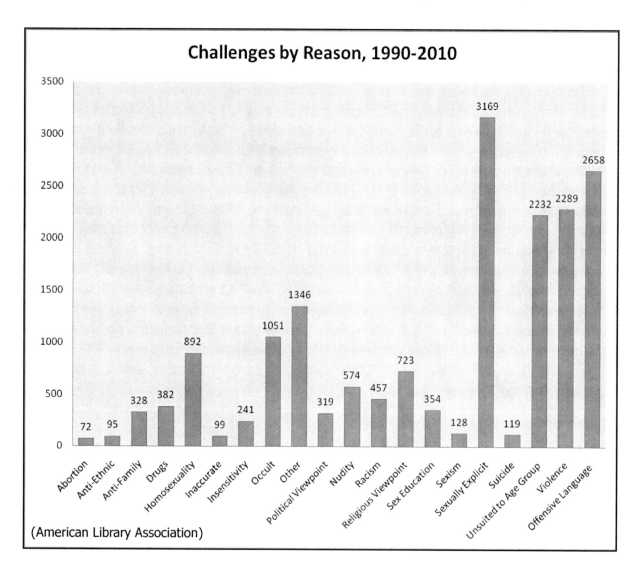

Challenges by Reason, 1990-2010

(American Library Association)

I felt an overwhelming sense of guilt, misgivings, and self-doubt. Was I wrong? Was I exposing my daughter and her friends to obscene or profane literature, or was I providing a great way to encourage my daughter and other students to become excited about what reading could offer them? Was it censorship for the school to not provide the books to the students based on criteria that clearly were not objective or even well thought through? What about my role and rights as a parent? Didn't I have the right to allow my daughter to read whatever I saw fit without having to feel as though I committed a crime?

As angry as I was with them for restricting my daughter's right to read, I began to wonder if I was guilty of the same behavior. The Twilight series was also incredibly popular in my middle school library media center. I had enthusiastically booktalked *Twilight, New Moon,* and *Eclipse* and I can truthfully say that the majority of my students, both male and female, including my reluctant readers, advanced readers, and even my ESL readers, who devoured my Spanish and French copies, were all fascinated with the characters, storylines, and movie versions of each book. And then *Breaking Dawn* was released and I read it, all of it, with all of its sexuality, violence, and blood. As I read it, I felt a growing sense of apprehension and dread. What was I going to do? My students were all enthusiastically waiting for me to me to buy the last book in the series. The old saying of "Be careful what you wish for because you may just get it" came to my mind, as my students did all the things that I had encouraged them to do in the past. Without my prompting, they looked up the release dates and suggested that we should make a countdown clock to put on the library bulletin board where I posted book information and they came to me to put their names on the hold list in the library catalog.

Little did they know that I wasn't sure that I should buy the book. The Twilight series was increasingly beginning to come under fire from various divergent groups who complained that writing a book that put vampires and werewolves in a positive light was anti-religious. Feminist groups alternately complained that the books offered a negative role model for young women because the main character was obsessed with an unattainable relationship instead of forging her own path and because the main characters' chaste relationship was unrealistic and even damaging to young women's burgeoning sexuality. Other complaints were that the book was too sexually explicit, unsuited to any age group, and contained offensive language. These mounting concerns had resulted in the Twilight series joining the American Library Association's top ten list of books that were banned or challenged in the country in 2010. The books also ranked fifth among books for which people have filed formal written complaints.

I had been lucky with the first books in the series, but with *Breaking Dawn,* perhaps my luck had run out. What if this book were challenged? What if my school administrators or the students' parents complained or questioned my judgment in purchasing the book? Would I get a letter in my file, or would they ask me to take the book out of the library? Was the book too violent or too sexually explicit? Most important, I asked myself, is it censorship or selection if I chose not to buy it?

I began to look for excuses to not buy the book. After all, the reviews for *Breaking Dawn* weren't that great, so I could always use that as an excuse to not buy it. Sure, the students could get it at the public library, but my lower income and ESL students often tell me that they cannot get there due to lack of transportation. I could simply pass the problem on to the high-school librarians, and tell my students that, "Oh well, you can read it once you get there in two years," but how could I let their enthusiasm for reading languish by making them wait? Maybe I could have them sign a permission slip like the students use for their literature classes when they do research on controversial issues like abortion or gun control.

I found that other schools, librarians, and teachers were also debating the same issue within their classrooms and libraries. The Capistrano Unified School District's literacy coordinator reviewed the Twilight books after noticing that so many students were requesting them and determined that the books were too mature for middle school students. She requested that all of the Twilight books be sent to the district office where they would be reallocated to the high school libraries. Four days later they were returned to the middle school libraries. The district spokesperson was quick to state that they changed their minds because they were not interested in banning the books, but that the overall feeling was that the books were not suitable for sixth- and seventh-graders. (Martindale)

The Daily Telegraph, a well-regarded newspaper in the United Kingdom, interviewed a number of teachers and librarians about their opinions regarding the debate over the Twilight series and their students. The head librarian at the Sana Sabina College at Starthfield stated that her school decided to not offer the book to students in the junior high school library because they might be too young to deal with the adult themes. She also explained that she and the teachers were concerned that the parents might express some concern as well. At the Balmoral Queenwood School for Girls, the head librarian stated that only senior high school students are allowed to check the books out. At St. Anthony's Catholic primary school, the parents were asked to not allow their children to bring the book to school. The most interesting opinion came, not from the perplexed and confused adults, but from the one student who was interviewed; ten-year-old Emmi Payton from Bellevue Hill secondary school, who stated, "I know it's all just fantasy. I think it's really good, really interesting, and bits of it are really funny." (Dickson)

Censorship Defined

This information added to my confusion. My biggest question became are my problems possibly related to those "misguided people" who wanted to ban books? I asked myself, do I know what censorship really is? In the introduction to Judy Blume's book, *The Places I Never Meant to Be*, in which censored authors share their personal stories of censorship, Blume makes this observation: "If you ask a dozen people to define censorship, you'll get twelve different answers." She used her thesaurus to look up the word censorship and found the following words: "Forbid. Prohibit. Restrict." She posed the following question for reflection on the complexity of censorship: "What do these words mean to writers and the stories they choose to tell? And what do they mean to readers and the books they choose to read?" (Blume)

Others don't believe censorship occurs. According to Jonah Goldberg, the editor of the *National Review Online*, censorship only occurs when the government legally orders the removal of books. His reasoning is that, "How can censorship exist when any citizen can go to a bookstore or Amazon.com and buy any book legally in print—or out of print for that matter." After all, isn't it a parental right to protect children by refusing to allow them to read a book that the parent thinks is inappropriate for them? Others wonder if it is censorship to protect children from being exposed to ideas that they believe can hurt them. Is it censorship if you are an educator or a librarian and you refuse to purchase books containing information that goes against your values and morality, or if you don't buy books that might cause a negative response from your supervisor or the community?

The ALA has the answer to this debate: Yes, censorship does exist today. The ALA, committed to advocating for the right of everyone to read free from restrictions since their inception in 1853, recognized early on that censorship can occur in many different, and sometimes unrecognizable, forms. In 1939, the ALA drafted the Library Bill of Rights to affirm the belief that, no matter when censorship occurs and no matter what the intention, censoring is always an assault against the First Amendment rights that all Americans enjoy. An integral part of their commitment has been to use their extensive knowledge, resources, and experiences to educate librarians, legislators, and the public about what censorship is and how it relates to our First Amendment Rights. In that spirit, the ALA offers the following definition of censorship in order to ensure that everyone understands what censorship is and how it takes place:

1. *Censorship* is when a person or group successfully imposes their values upon others by stifling words, images, or ideas and preventing them from reaching the public marketplace of ideas.

   Example: In 1933, Nazi students, professors, and librarians raided libraries and bookstores, collected more than 25,000 books that they thought should not be read by Germans, and burned them in a large bonfire while they sang songs of joy. The books they choose were by Jewish authors and by famous Americans, such as Ernest Hemingway, Jack London, and even Helen Keller, who said, when she heard of what happened, "Tyranny cannot defeat the power of ideas." (United States Holocaust Memorial Museum)

2. *Book banning* is the actual removal of the book.

   Example: In 2010, Gail Sweet, library director of the Burlington County New Jersey Library system, ordered all copies of the book *Revolutionary Voices*, a book that features gay teens discussing their lives and experiences being gay, removed from the library shelves before a formal complaint was even filed, ostensibly to avoid any controversy, after the book was challenged at the local high school. (Barack)

3. *A book challenge* is an attempt to remove or restrict books or materials at the request of a person or group.

   Example: In 2011, the parents of students in an advanced reading program in the Murrieta Valley High School challenged the book, *The Wedding*. The book is set in Europe and is about a young French couple who want to get married but learn that the woman has AIDS. The story follows their journey in deciding whether or not they should marry. Some parents requested an alternate book and were upset because an alternate choice was not offered initially, however other parents opposed the book and wanted it removed from the curriculum because it used "the f-word and is therefore 'vulgar' and does not represent the values of the community." (Schultz)

   Example: In 2011, in the town of Republic, Missouri, Professor Wesley Scroggins, who had no children in the school district, complained about the local high school offering Kurt Vonnegut's classic *Slaughterhouse-Five* in the school library because it "taught principles contrary to the Bible." The school board voted to keep the book in the school library but restricted the book to parent checkout only. It appears that no one asked the opinions of the parents or the students. One student who was interviewed called the book "fantastic and great" and said, "They're here to teach us and we're here to learn. By taking away our books they're taking away our right to learn." (Riley)

According to Pat Scales, who has written books on censorship and given expert advice for years on the subject, censorship can occur whenever a book is removed from its intended audience. This includes parents who don't agree with an assigned classroom school book and decide that no other children should read it, public libraries who move children's books to the adult section of the library, librarians who move books to restricted areas, or offer excuses like lack of money or shelf space. Scales also states firmly that the often used excuses of "It doesn't fit our curriculum" or "We don't have any gay students" are clear cases of censorship. (Whelan) In addition, if a library's collection policy determines that a book is age appropriate and there is an audience of young adults who wants to read the book and who would benefit from reading the book, removing it is unconstitutional. According to Caldwell Stone, the director of the ALA's Office for Intellectual Freedom, "Students do have a measure of First Amendment rights, and it says that governments can't censor materials unless they're obscene, contain child pornography, or are harmful to minors." (Whelan)

Young Adult Books Targeted

Since 2001, the ALA has been keeping a record of the most frequently banned books. They also track the most banned authors, classics, and the most frequently banned books by the decade. These resources are extremely helpful and relevant because they offer information of the subjects that garner the most attention.

The Top Ten Banned Books of 2010

1. *And Tango Makes Three* by Peter Parnell and Justin Richardson. Reasons: homosexuality, religious viewpoint, and unsuited to age group.

2. *The Absolutely True Diary of a Part-Time Indian*, by Sherman Alexie. Reasons: offensive language, racism, sex education, sexually explicit, unsuited to age group, and violence.

3. *Brave New World* by Aldous Huxley. Reasons: insensitivity, offensive language, racism, and sexually explicit.

4. *Crank* by Ellen Hopkins. Reasons: drugs, offensive language, and sexually explicit.

5. *The Hunger Games* by Suzanne Collins. Reasons: sexually explicit, unsuited to age group, and violence.

6. *Lush* by Natasha Friend. Reasons: drugs, offensive language, sexually explicit, and unsuited to age group.

7. *What My Mother Doesn't Know* by Sonya Sones. Reasons: sexism, sexually explicit, and unsuited to age group.

8. *Nickel and Dimed* by Barbara Ehrenreich. Reasons: drugs, inaccurate, offensive language, political viewpoint, and religious viewpoint.

9. *Revolutionary Voices* edited by Amy Sonnie. Reasons: homosexuality and sexually explicit.

10. *Twilight* by Stephenie Meyer. Reasons: religious viewpoint and violence.

What is notable about the 2010 Banned Book list is that the majority of the books are young adult titles; a consistent trend of the past several years. This seems to suggest that as young adult books have become more popular with young adults and adults, they have also increasingly drawn more attention and scrutiny from society. The *New York Times* bestseller list is dominated by young adult books such as the Twilight and The Hunger Games series and sales of young adult books are up 25 percent, according to the Children's Book Council. (Reno) Movies based on books that depict the lives of teenagers, like *Diary of a Wimpy Kid* and *Precious* based on the book *Push*, have enjoyed incredible success, almost solely due to the interest of young adults. In response to this surge in popularity, every major publisher now has a young adult imprint. The literary world has also taken notice with the National Book Foundation expanding their awards to include young people's literature as a category.

The History of Young Adult Books and Censorship

Although it may be difficult to believe, there was a time when there was no such thing as young adult books. In 1802, Sarah Trimmer, an early advocate of children's literature, was credited with being the first person to publish a magazine that was dedicated to reviewing books that were solely for children and young adults. Trimmer was also the first to use the terms "Books for Children" for children under fourteen and "Books for Young Persons" that focused exclusively on books and stories for those between fourteen and twenty-one, terms that are still popular to this day. The magazine Trimmer began, *The Guardian of Education,* focused on popular books with religious material and quickly became very popular with parents. Trimmer created the magazine because she believed that children should be seen as a natural resource and that they were the ones who would be responsible for bringing out positive social change. She believed that all children, both rich and poor, should receive a good education and those books were the best way to achieve that goal. Trimmer's efforts helped to set the tone and precedent for the young adult novels that exist today. (Notable Biographies)

In the 1950s and 1960s, books like *The Catcher in the Rye, Seventeenth Summer,* and *The Outsiders* began to be popular. These books were darker and dealt with much more serious issues than the previous books that were written about young adults. Authors also, for the first time, began to write from the perspective of the teens themselves, as opposed to writing about them. They began to use more realism in their approach to describing the lives of teens, including their experiences with pregnancy, juvenile delinquency, and substance abuse. Unlike the former depiction of teen characters, such as the dutiful daughters in *Little Women* who were family oriented, sweet, and caring, these new teen characters, their language, and settings were anything but proper and idealistic, and the books featured plots that did not always end happily. This shift to portraying the edgier aspects of teens' lives became known as "problem," or "coming of age" novels.

Teens enthusiastically responded to this focus on realism because the stories were honest and direct and true to how they experienced life and featured characters that they recognized as being like them, not necessarily in deeds, but in spirit. Due to the continuous pushing of boundaries that accompanied writers striving to continue to capture the ever changing evolution of how teens approach life, this form of literature began to feel unsafe to some adults who found this new realism disconcerting. This is attributed to the growing sense of unease and distrust regarding what teens are reading, and is widely felt to have resulted in an increase in book challenges. (Coley)

Censorship Today and Tomorrow

So, what did I finally decide? For my daughter, I held my ground and told her teacher and my colleague that if my daughter wanted to read a book and share it with her friends, then that was her right. The school, which was overwhelmed with other students who brought *Twilight* to school, decided to buy the first book in the series for the school library, but restrict it to the sixth grade. I contacted other parents that I knew on my own and spoke to them to see if they had any concerns. It turns out that most of them had no concerns, or were even unaware of the controversy. We started an informal parent-child book club and read the series along with our children and planned a celebrity movie event for everyone, where we watched the movie *Twilight* and discussed the difference between the movie and the book.

This experience led me to advocate for what I inherently already knew, but before my "trial by fire" was hesitant to say: Teens and even pre-teens are very capable of managing and interpreting the information that they read despite its edginess, because teens benefit from the mental stimulation that complex, issue-oriented books can provide. In addition, at this integral time in their lives, young adults, because of their unique openness and sense of imagination, are especially eager to explore and critically think about the new information and ideas offered in books written especially for them. Their commitment to books, favorite characters, and genres stems from their enthusiasm, and their sense of discovery, which coincides with their natural curiosity and search for self. So what did I learn from my dilemma? I realized the decisions that we make as librarians, teachers, and parents are often made with the best intentions as we try to do what is best for our library users and ourselves and that these decisions are often made under the influence of fear and anxiety and the desire not to upset any one.

Professionally, my personal battle gave me the courage to buy *Breaking Dawn* for my middle school students, to their delight, without them ever knowing my internal dilemma and personal drama that accompanied the purchase. The nervousness and stress that accompanied my decision and the endless questions that I asked myself did not stop with that purchase, however, and will most likely not end anytime soon. Censorship, no matter who engages in it, and how and why it occurs, often occurs under the veil of trying to do the right thing. I realize now that the self-doubt and intense self-questioning that can lead to self-censorship is only one of the issues relating to censorship that challenge librarians on a daily basis. In fact, if you ask most librarians, they would probably say that contending with book challenges and censorship, both internal and external, is the most difficult issue that they have to contend with today. With faith in ourselves and in our library users, and with a with a strong understanding and commitment to the ideals of freedom that our country is founded upon, we can take the lead in teaching others about intellectual freedom and its role in our society.

Librarians Take Action: Teach about censorship.

I have found that the best way to address all of these issues is through discussion, educational activities, and by disseminating information openly, honestly, with sensitivity and respect. This approach offers librarians the opportunity to directly address the issues with young adult literature that cause book challenges to be initiated. A large part of that openness is to accept that, as librarians, we should recognize and work through any fears and concerns that we have by opening a dialogue with our parents, library users, colleagues, and fellow librarians whenever we can. Megan Schliesman, of the Cooperative Children's Book Center, suggests that we need to "encourage one another to talk about barriers that can arise in materials selection openly and honestly, and we need to create environments where these discussions can take place without fear of judgment."

Recognizing our own issues should also encourage us to be more understanding of others who express their doubts and concerns about the books their children read. We should demonstrate a willingness to be receptive to their complaints and concerns, as well as a willingness to answer the questions that they might have. Parents are naturally concerned with the content of their children's books, especially if they discuss subjects that parents feel are provocative or controversial. You can help parents and community members feel more accepting of the literature their teens want to read if you can speak honestly about their concerns by engaging them in conversation. According to Pat Scales, intellectual freedom and censorship expert, parents and community members who question are not censors. Questions should be welcomed, as they give librarians the opportunity to educate the public about the First Amendment, the freedom to read, and how they relate to censorship.

Since young adult literature is receiving most of the criticism and challenges, it is imperative that librarians, educators, parents, and teenagers become informed about their First Amendment rights and how it protects and relates to their right to read. My mission as a middle school librarian is to promote the discussion of censorship and how it relates to all of us by educating my students, colleagues, parents, and community members on what book banning and censorship is, what it has to do with the First Amendment, and most important, why it is relevant to their lives today.

Censorship Education Activity

This activity that utilizes well loved and familiar books, is designed to introduce both students and parents to how censorship is relevant to their daily lives. I surprise the students when they arrive in the library for class with a collection of their favorite children's books displayed on tables to look over and read in small groups. Titles include: *Captain Underpants, A Wrinkle in Time, Junie B. Jones, Little Women, Scary Stories to Read in the Dark,* and *Little Red Riding Hood,* among others. They are always delighted to see the books and immediately start reading them, telling stories about what grade they were in when they read them and how old they were. What I don't share with them right away is that all of these books have been banned at one time or another.

After the students finish reading the books, I ask them what they think the books have in common. They look at each other and at me in confusion as they give me various answers like, they are all fantasies or fairy tales, or they are all fiction books. When I tell the students that what they all have in common is that they have all been banned at one time or another, they invariably look at me and start laughing incredulously. By the end of the two-week lesson plan, they begin to understand why censorship is relevant to their daily lives and have a new appreciation for what it really means to have the freedom to read. Their initial surprise at, and later realization of, how the right of being able to read and enjoy any book they choose can be taken away from them when they don't understand what their rights are within a democracy, becomes a profound experience for them.

A shorter version of this activity is also very popular with parents. I usually use it as a way to get their attention before I give a presentation about censorship. They, too, are absolutely delighted to see the books they either read as a child or enjoyed sharing with their children. They also express much of the same shock and surprise when they realize that their rights, guaranteed by the constitution, are in danger if they remain unaware of the affects that censorship has on their daily lives.

You Are the Investigator!
Why were these books banned?

Your Mission: Find out why each of the books in this list was banned.

1. Sylvester and the Magic Pebble
2. A Light in the Attic
3. In the Night Kitchen
4. In a Dark, Dark Room, and Other Scary Stories
5. Junie B. Jones
6. Captain Underpants
7. Little Red Riding Hood
8. Blubber
9. A Wrinkle in Time
10. And Tango Makes Three
11. King and King
12. The Lorax
13. Where the Sidewalk Ends
14. James and the Giant Peach
15. Little House on the Prairie
16. The Five Chinese Brothers
17. The Three Little Pigs
18. Where the Wild Things Are
19. The Rabbit's Wedding
20. The Stupids Have a Ball

_____

1. What is book banning?

2. What is censorship?

3. What are book challenges?

Answer the following questions about each book.

1. Why was each book challenged? Find two sites that tell about the challenge.

2. If the book challenge went to court, what happened?

3. If the book challenge did not go to court, how was it resolved?

4. Who is the author of the book?

5. Does the author have anything to say about censorship?

Your name _____

Date _____

You Are the Investigator

Why Were These Books Banned?

The word cloud shows several common reasons books are challenged and banned. Can you think of other reasons?

Characters

Occult

Profanity

Racism

Themes

Sex

Violence

Religion

Nudity

Fantasy

Name _____

Date _____

From *VOYA's Guide to Intellectual Freedom for Teens* by Margaret Auguste. Bowie, MD: VOYA Press, an imprint of E L Kurdyla Publishing, LLC. Copyright 2012

References

Barack, Lauren. "NJ Library, Citing Child Pornography, Removes GLBT Book." *School Library Journal*. 27 July 2010: n. page. Web. 22 Feb. 2012. *http://www.schoollibraryjournal.com/slj/home/886066312/ nj_library_citing_child_porngraphy.html.csp*

Blume, Judy. "Judy Blume's Offical Website." 2007. Web. 22 Feb 2012. *http://www.judyblume.com*

Blume, Judy. *The Places I Never Meant to Be: Original Stories by Censored Writers*. Simon Pulse, 2001.

Coley, Ken P. "Moving toward a Method to Test for Self-Censorship by School Library Media Specialists." American Library Association. 27 September 2006. *http://www.ala.org/ala/mgrps/divs/aasl/ aaslpubsand journals/slmrb/slmrcontents/volume52002/coley.cfm*. November 07, 2011.

Dickson, Lauren. "Schools ban racy Twilight books by Stephenie Meyer." *Daily Telegraph*. 12 September 2009, Web. 22 Feb. 2012. *http://www.dailytelegraph.com.au/entertainment/schools-ban-racy-twilight-books-by-stephanie-meyer/story-e6frewyr-1225772090737*

"Frequently Challenged Books of the 21st Century." American Libraries Association. *http://www.ala. org/ala/issuesadvocacy/banned/frequentlychallenged/21stcenturychallenged/index.cfm*. 21 March 2011.

Goldberg, Jonah. "Banned Books Week Is Just Hype." Townhall.com2011. Web. 22 Feb 2012. *http:// townhall.com/columnists/jonahgoldberg/2011/09/08/banned_books_week_is_just_ype/page/full*

Martindale, Scott. "School district briefly bans vampire book from middle schools." Orange County Registrar [Orange] 30 September 2008, Web. 22 Feb. 2012. *http://www2.ocregister.com/articles/ books-school-series-2175239-district-library*

"Nazi Propaganda and Censorship." United States Memorial Holocaust Museum. *http://www.ushmm .org/outreach/en/article.php?ModuleId=10007677*. 5 March 2011.

Reno, Jamie. "Generation R (R Is for Reader)." *Newsweek*. 13 May 2008. *http://www.thedailybeast. com/newsweek/2008/05/13/generation-r-r-is-for-reader.html*. 07 March 2011.

Riley, Cynthia. "Controversial books removed from Republic schools to return to secure section of library." NewsLeader.com [Springfield]. 20 September 2011, Web. 22 Feb. 2012. *http://www.news-leader.com/article/20110920/NEWS04/109200351/Controversial-books-removed-from-Republic-schools-return-secure-section-library*

"Sarah Trimmer, Notable Biographies." *Encyclopedia of World Biographies*. 2012. Web. 22 Feb 2012. *http://www.notablebiographies.com/supp/Supplement-Sp-Z/Trimmer-Sarah.html*

Schliesman, Megan. "Self-Censorship: Let's Talk About It." Wisconsin Library Association Intellectual Freedom Roundtable. Spring 2007. Web. 22 Feb 2012. *http://www.education.wisc.edu/ccbc/freedom/ selfcensorship.asp*

Schultz, Craig. "Parents Protest against Book." Murrieta [Oceanside]. 29 October 2011, Web. 22 Feb. 2012. *http://www.nctimes.com/news/local/murrieta/article_9ea86bae-4031-5087-afe3-2a7ce54422b8.html*

Whelan, Debra Lau. "A Dirty Little Secret: Self-Censorship." *School Library Journal*. 1 February 2009: Web. 22 Feb. 2012. *http://www.schoollibraryjournal.com/slj/home/886066312/nj_library_citing_ child_porngraphy.html.csp*

CHAPTER 2
SEXUALITY AND YOUNG ADULT LITERATURE

Sexuality is a unique subject because our understanding of it is subjective and defined through the prism of our values, ethics, and personal perceptions. As a consequence, this multitude of wide-ranging views, combined with the sensitivity and complexity of the topic, particularly when it involves our children, evokes an intensely personal and passionate debate. The ever-evolving nature of the sexual content featured in young adult literature, along with passionate reactions, both negative and positive, have resulted in more acts of censorship and book challenges than any other reason listed for book challenges. (ALA)

Judy Blume's classic, *Forever*, written in 1971, is widely regarded as the first novel written for teenagers that bravely, and with sensitivity, explored a teenage couple's first sexual relationship. *Forever* tells the story of Katherine and Michael, two earnest and intelligent teenagers who are certain that their love will last forever. "Realistic" and "deeply likable" are just a few of the words used by Sarah Crown, of *The Guardian* magazine, to describe the novel. The book continues to be one of the most popular young adult books of all time, selling over 3.5 million copies worldwide.

Blume explains that when it was released in 1975, *Forever* was greeted with both high praise because of its honesty, and with controversy because it did not promote abstinence and monogamy. Even so, it was widely read and even used in classrooms for discussion. Blume states that beginning in the 1980s, censorship became more common as the religious right became more influential and challenged books that did not meet their worldview. During that time, *Forever* was challenged and banned numerous times because it discussed birth control and encouraged disobedience to parents. (Blume) *Forever*, with its frank descriptions of teenage sexual activity, has since remained a primary target, and as a result, has become one of the most banned books of all time, with Blume becoming one of the most banned authors. (Crown)

Forever ushered in a wave of novels that dared to explore teenage sexuality in its entirety, as new young adult writers were encouraged and inspired to write books that stretched the boundaries of the narrow definition of what issues were considered acceptable for young adults. Formerly taboo sexual topics became commonplace, as stories marketed for adolescents fearlessly depicted the difficult and controversial topics of teen pregnancy, HIV, prostitution, healthy relationships, unhealthy relationships, and sexual abuse, among a wide variety of other sexual issues and problems.

This newly discovered open acceptance of teen sexuality in young adult books was neither welcomed, nor accepted, by those who believed that the sexual topics featured in young adult literature are way too graphic and explicit for teenagers, and are even possibly detrimental to their social, psychological, and emotional well-being. The following opinions represent an overview of the thoughts, concerns and issues that characterize this debate.

Viewpoint: Sexuality in young adult literature is gratuitous and detrimental.

"More *Sex in the City* than *Nancy Drew*," is how Janet Shamlian, a journalist from MSNBC, characterized the current state of young adult literature as she describes the conflict that sexually charged books has caused among families. To illustrate her point, she recounted an incident that occurred between a mother and her two daughters. The dilemma came about because the daughters love to read, however, the choices that that they made caused their mother to feel very uncomfortable. "Fantasy or smut," according to the mother, appear to be the only options available. (Shamlian)

The Reading Teen book review and discussion site hosts a blog where the most relevant topics regarding young adult books are discussed. Sexuality and its place in young adult literature is one of the most commonly discussed topics. One of the reviewers, a parent and person who values young adult literature, has strong feelings about the irresponsibility she feels characterizes the manner in which sexuality is written about in YA books. She wrote a passionate essay that began an intense debate. She questioned the overabundance of sexuality in young adult books, as well as the concern that the sexuality represented actually reflects the reality of what teenagers experience. In her estimation, it appears as though every teenage character in current young adult books is having sex, or wants to have sex if they only had the opportunity. She also believes that with all the sex that teenagers are inundated with through movies, television, and the Internet, that the sex featured in books only adds to the pressure that teens face on a daily basis.

She goes on to say that contrary to what is portrayed in young adult literature, "Not all teenagers are having sex." Statistics show that the rates of teenage sexual activity, while still high, have steadily decreased in the last decade from its high of 54 percent in 1991 to the current rate of 46 percent. In fact, with the exception of teen pregnancy, most indicators of teen sexual activity, including the number of partners, have decreased. She asks the question, "Where are the books for the teenagers who are abstinent or who are trying to make the decision to not have sex?" She wonders if "authors are afraid to write those stories." (Andye)

Viewpoint: Sexuality in young adult literature is essential and beneficial.

"Books are the safest place for them to have sex." This statement, made by author Tonya Lee Stone in her essay, "Now and Forever," reflects the open and welcoming attitude of those who strongly believe that young adult books that explore teenage sexuality have enabled teenagers to have an outlet in which they can safely explore their developing sexuality. (Stone)

Through books, teenagers are allowed to try on new sexual roles, read about characters like themselves who work through issues that concern them, and find experiences that mirror their own in a safe virtual environment where there are no judgments. Teens, who are often embarrassed to talk to their parents or other adults about sex, can find the answers to the questions they have about the physical changes their bodies are going through, the emotional turmoil that they feel, and can sort through the often confusing messages they have about sex through reading books written specifically for them. (Wood)

Furthermore, many believe that young adult literature does mirror the reality of teen sexuality, not specifically regarding who decides to engage in sexual activity, but because of the fact that teens face pressure either to have sex or to embrace abstinence from every direction. They face the external pressure that comes from movies, television, and other media, and from their families and friends, as well, and are constantly thinking about sex, talking about sex, or having sex. Young adult authors recognize this reality, and in an effort to be true to their readers, reflect this reality in their work. (Stone 463) In the article "Pushing the Envelope: Exploring Sexuality in Teen Literature," librarian and researcher Eleanor Wood explains that teens face so many expectations regarding sex from their family and community, as well as the pressure from their friends and peers in regards to sexual experiences, that they need a safe place to explore these feelings and expectations. Books that honestly reflect this reality can assist them in examining this experience.

Statistics tell us that despite the fact that the numbers of teens engaging in sexual activities has seemingly decreased, the number of teens that do engage in sexual activity in some fashion is still noteworthy. According to the National Institute of Health, in 2007, at least 46 percent of teenagers have had sex and at least 14.9 percent of them have had sex with at least four partners. In addition, between 2005 and 2006, the birth rate rose 3 percent for teens aged 15-17 and 4 percent for teens aged 18-19. Teens have expanded their exploration of their sexuality by adding a virtual element, with virtual sexual activities becoming a common theme within their lives. Fifteen percent of teens state that they have received sexually suggestive images or messages via their cell phones and four percent of teens state that they have sent sexually suggestive messages or images to someone else.

Teens are also engaging in oral sex in unprecedented numbers and at younger ages than one would expect; a fact that is surprising and disturbing to many parents. (Jayson) In fact, a study was completed by the *New York* magazine in which one hundred high school students and one hundred unrelated parents who lived in the same vicinity as the students were polled. They were asked questions about teenagers and sexuality. One question that addressed oral sex found that 61 percent of students reported receiving it while 51 percent reported giving it. In contrast, only 10 percent of parents thought their teens had received it and 5 percent thought that their teens gave it. Author Tonya Lee Stone states that, "Closing our eyes to any of these statistics is not helpful to teens," and supports brave authors, who, despite an incredible amount of criticism, have written groundbreaking books that address this controversial issue. A few recent well-regarded and controversial books that tackle these edgy issues are: *Looking for Alaska* by John Green, *Sandpiper* by Ellen Wittlinger, and *Kendra* by Coe Booth.

Viewpoint: Young adult books should show the consequences of sexual activity.

The perception is that there are little to no consequences to the sexual activity that is shown in the young adult books that feature sex. The questions are: How can the relationships portrayed reflect reality when unrealistic storylines feature characters that negotiate love and sexual relationships with an ease that even most adults cannot manage? Where are the characters whose sexual decisions result in STDs, pregnancy, or emotional distress? How can you show teenagers engaging in sexual activity without also showing the potential emotional devastation and the young lives that are irrevocably altered by those often times risky and thoughtless decisions? (The Reading Teen)

Viewpoint: Young adult books should not focus only on the consequences of sexual activity.

The exploration of the risks and consequences of sexual activity are the hallmark of the problem novel. The first novels written about sexuality focused on the dire consequences that resulted from engaging in sex before marriage. In Richard Peck's *Don't Look and It Won't Hurt* published in 1970, the main character is rejected by her parents and sent to a home for unwed mothers. In a *Perfect Family,* published in 1970, the protagonist, Welcome, is forced to leave her house and give her baby away for adoption. This trend has continued with many novelists who feel a sense of commitment to ensure that they do not glamorize teenage sexuality. They emphasize the consequences that can occur and the lessons that the protagonists learn from both the negative and positive decisions that they make. (Wood)

Several recent popular novels address the consequences of teenage sex. *The First Part Last* by Angela Johnson features a single father who decides to raise his baby on his own when the baby's mother is unable. In *November Blues* by Sharon Draper, the main character becomes pregnant and struggles to decide between adoption or keeping her baby. In *After* by Amy Efaw, the main character is arrested and put on trial after she hides her pregnancy, gives birth alone and is accused of killing her baby.

Consequences are a part of reality and are important for teenagers to be aware of and understand, but focusing on *only* that aspect of relationships can sometimes have the unintended effect of generating fear and negativity. Author Tonya Lee Stone states that the positive aspects of sex should not be forgotten. Characters in young adult stories should be allowed to show that it is possible for teenagers to develop into healthy and happy sexual beings that are able to experience sex and intimacy, without the accompanying feelings of shame and guilt. This is particularly true for young women, who are often told through novels that focus on unwanted pregnancies, STDs, HIV, and emotional turmoil, that "The only things that result from sex are negative." (Wood) To push against this negativity, Judy Blume explains that her decision to write *Forever*, where two smart and well-adjusted teenagers make a mutual responsible choice to have sex, was specifically written to contrast the negative portrayals of sexuality in the available young adult novels.

The perils of only focusing on the negatives associated with sexuality were discussed on the online young adult book site, The Book Lantern, where current topics regarding young adult fiction are addressed daily. An interesting post was written by a new writer of young adult fiction who lamented about the lack of positive sex messages in young adult literature. "Sex is the natural and realistic conclusion to healthy relationships and it is very important that teenagers learn this, as opposed to viewing sex as something that should only be characterized by chastity and control." (Vinaya) Sexuality is very important and relevant to teenagers and needs to be validated in the literature they read.

> Judy Blume wrote her classic book, *Forever,* because her daughter asked her to write a book where the teenage couple did not die or suffer other dire consequences for having a sexual relationship.

Many authors seek to achieve a balance that speaks to the reality of the dangers and consequences of sexual activity, while still recognizing the positive and joyful aspects of sex. Judy Blume addresses this new reality, while still staying true to the book's timeless and classic message of positivity, in a special foreword she wrote for the 2009 twentieth edition of her book, *Forever.* In it, she addresses the advent of HIV and the importance of using condoms, issues she acknowledges were not on anyone's radar at the initial time of her book's publication.

Some publishers, who publish books exclusively with teenagers in mind, also strike to balance their messages about sexuality by directly addressing it in their writer's guidelines. Harlequin, the publisher of the popular Kimani Tru series, is one such publisher. In their guidelines for writers, it states that, "Safe sex should be encouraged in all sexually intimate scenes and condoms should be used unless unsafe sex is one of the issues being dealt with in the novel." (Howard)

Viewpoint: Young adult books are only valuable if they teach a lesson.

If authors are going to write about teens and sexuality, do they have a responsibility to only write about sexuality in a way that teaches a lesson? In the 1990s, many novels about rape and sexual abuse began to be published that did just that. One of the most well-known and positively regarded of these books is *Speak,* the award winning novel written in 1999 by Laurie Halse Anderson. This book examines depression, alienation, and sexual abuse through the eyes of fourteen-year-old Malinda, the victim of a traumatic rape that renders her nearly voiceless. This story is an example of a thoughtful, sensitive portrayal of sexuality that carefully addresses the emotional and physical effects of sexual abuse. The connection that readers feel towards Melinda's all-too-common experience, the honest portrayal of teenage life, the authentic depiction of how easily sexual abuse can occur, and the emotional toll it can take have made this book a favorite of teenagers and adults alike. Despite the book's acknowledged literary merit; it has frequently been challenged or banned due to its frank discussion of rape. In 2009, the book was challenged in Temecula, California, after concerns were raised about the book's depiction of rape, although the school board eventually voted to allow the book to be added to class reading lists. As recently as 2010, the book was referred to as filthy, immoral, and as soft pornography in an editorial attributed to Professor Wesley Scroggins in the Gannett's *News-Leader*, a charge that led to a challenge in a Missouri high school. (Scroggins)

The novel *Speak*, which has captivated so many people, came about because of a nightmare. Laurie Halse Anderson explains how one night she had a nightmare about a hysterically crying girl. Nightmares were a regular part of her childhood and she learned that writing them down was the only way to have some control over them. She continued this practice into adulthood. After this particular nightmare that she named "The crying girl," she rushed to her daughters' bedroom in fear that they were upset or sick. When she saw that they were fine, she began to put her nightmare into words and created the character of Melinda Sordino, the protagonist of *Speak*.

Viewpoint: Young adult books do not have to teach a lesson in order to have value.

The idea of teens having sex for the sake of entertainment generated an extremely high level of criticism and concern within many diverse groups, even among those who are steadfast supporters of young adult literature. No young adult novels push the envelope more in this area than the Gossip Girl series by Cecily von Ziegesar. In 2000, *Gossip Girls*, with its elite prep school girls, was marketed to a young adult audience and featured teenagers engaging in casual sex with a lack of regard for any moral uncertainty or emotional turmoil. This series has been uniformly criticized for its portrayal of sexually irresponsible and reckless teenagers. Completely lacking in values, except for the value placed on sex, social status, and money, is how writer Naomi Wolf describes them in her *New York Times* essay. (Wolf) More critics purport that sex portrayed for the sake of sex only, with no consequences or redeeming values, risks encouraging teenagers to view sex as simply another activity like shopping or texting. Casual sex, however, unlike shopping, does have consequences that can have a serious impact on the lives of teenagers. (Biederman)

Not everyone agrees with this conclusion. Librarians were interviewed about this difficult subject by the TeenLitLab, an organization that was founded to research issues within young adult literature. One librarian stated that, "Just like in real life, YA audiences will realize that sex can be both explorative and exploitative, and sometimes both. It all helps with forming an opinion and making life decisions." (Biederman)

When interviewed about her thoughts regarding the criticism of her promotion of a lack of values and consequences in her Gossip Girl series, author von Ziegesar stated: "I always resented books that tried to teach a lesson, where the characters are too good: They don't swear; they tell their mothers everything. I want to be the responsible mother who says, 'Oh, there are terrible repercussions if you have sex, do drugs, and have an eating disorder!' But the truth is my friends and I dabbled in all of those things. And we all went to good colleges and grew up fine. And that's the honest thing to say."

Author Sarah Ockler, whose book *Twenty Boy Summer* is about a girl who tries to recover from a tragedy by engaging in relationships with boys over a summer, was challenged and eventually removed from a Missouri high school because, according to the challengers, the characters showed "a lack of remorse when engaging in sexual activity." In an essay, Ockler, had this to say about their decision: "Not every teen who has sex or experiments with drinking feels remorseful about it. Not every teen that has sex gets pregnant, gets someone pregnant, or contracts an STD. Not every teen that has sex does so while in a serious relationship. Not every teen who has sex outside of a relationship feels guilty, shameful, or regretful later on. And you can ban my books from every damn district in the country — I'm still not going to write to send messages or make teens feel guilty because they've made choices that some people want to pretend don't exist." (Ockler)

The Librarian's Role

The ALA states that reaching out to teenagers and their parents about these difficult issues is the surest way to bring these issues out into the open for discussion and understanding. The following two ideas can help you to communicate about young adult books and their appropriateness in the lives of teenagers.

Librarians Take Action: Initiate discussion with educational activities.

Teen Pregnancy Education Activity

Teen pregnancy is often one of the issues written about in young adult books that generates controversy, as some adults think that the books that depict pregnant teens both glorify and encourage pregnancy, or cast a healthy interest in sexuality as dangerous and negative by vilifying girls who become pregnant. Teens still remain in need of the facts regarding the medical risks to the baby and to themselves, as well as the emotional and social ramifications that can result from pregnancy. Young adult librarians can partner with their local high school or middle school health teachers to collaborate on an activity that educates teenagers about pregnancy through both fiction and nonfiction sources.

Dr. Amy Pattee, in her insightful article, "The Secret Source: Sexually Explicit Young Adult Literature as an Information Source," suggests that, "Young adult literature has the potential to fill in the gaps left by sexuality education curricula by depicting the many ways young people choose to be intimate. These information gaps should be filled by young adult authors so teenagers can understand the entire spectrum of sexual experience in a comforting, non-judgmental format." Another added benefit is that parents, by seeing firsthand how young adult literature can educate as well as entertain, can enable them to feel more comfortable with what they sometimes perceive as needlessly explicit sexuality in the books their children read.

The two titles selected for this activity are *Someone Like You* by Sarah Dessen, and *The First Part Last* by Angela Johnson.

Someone Like You tells the story of two sixteen-year-old girls, Scarlett and Halley, who are best friends. Scarlett is more outgoing and confident and Halley is somewhat shy and reserved. After Scarlett's boyfriend dies in an accident and she finds out she is pregnant, Halley takes on the caretaker role in their relationship to help support her friend. The situation leads both girls to evaluate the decisions that they make with their lives. Scarlett decides whether or not to have an abortion and Halley decides what choices she wants to make in terms of her relationships with boys, drinking, and disobeying her parents, among other issues. I choose this book because, in my experience, teens love anything that Sarah Dessen writes and I knew that they would be immediately intrigued. I also liked how the books show how life can change in an instant and how becoming an adult means learning to take on new roles.

The First Part Last is about Bobby, a sixteen-year-old boy who, after he learns that his girlfriend Nia is pregnant, quickly finds out that his life will never be the same. Bobby plans on helping out with the baby and is prepared for that, but when Nia becomes disabled at the birth of their daughter, against the advice of the hospital social worker, he decides to care for the baby himself. He learns first hand just how much his life changes and will continue to change due to his commitment to his daughter. The people who help him, his relationship with his baby, the sacrifices he makes, all make for a very compelling story told from the unusual perspective of a teenage father. I choose this book based on my experience in knowing that the picture of single fatherhood is often subject to solely negative stereotypes and is still not very well discussed or documented. This is an area of education that is definitely lacking and that teenagers need to have addressed. I taught this lesson this year with a health teacher that I work with frequently and found that when I suggested this book as a part of the lesson, he was surprised and elated to know that books depicting a teen father in a positive role even existed.

The Activity Outline

The activity will take place over a two month time period in a high school health education class where a librarian will collaborate with a health teacher in helping students to explore the issues surrounding teen pregnancy.

1. The students are assigned to read both books over a two month time period, at home and during class.

2. The students will learn about the author's background, purpose in writing the books, and experiences with censorship.

3. The books present perspectives from both a girl and a boy to allow the students to gain a better understanding of the experience from each protagonist's experience.

4. At the same time the books are being read, the subject of teen pregnancy regarding prevention, abstinence, birth control, and medical concerns will be addressed from the perspective of the health curriculum, which is approved by the district and approved of by each student's parents.

The authors' purpose in writing the books

The students will read interviews from both authors to get an idea of what inspired them to write about teenagers and potentially controversial subjects.

The *Teaching Books* website has a wonderful interview with Angela Johnson in which she talks about how she got her start in writing, her writing process, and her experiences and feelings about censorship at *http://www.teachingbooks.net/content/JohnsonA_qu.pdf*. The students read the interview and answer and discuss the following questions:

1. Why do you think that an author would take a chance on writing a book that might get challenged or banned?

2. Johnson thinks that books with sexuality are probably banned more than books with violence in them. What do you think?

Here is an excerpt from Johnson's interview about censorship:

"The majority of parents have said they like *The First Part Last*. But, I have had parents say, 'I'm not letting my kid read this book because it'll give them ideas.' I said, 'Ideas about going into a coma? Ideas about having this baby who's weighed you down and you've lost your childhood?' I mean, which idea? Obviously these people haven't read the book."

"Last year in Michigan, I was speaking to a library reading club, and a couple days before I came, the aide associated with the club decided to call the parents and tell them that in *The First Part Last*, which was one of the books that the kids were reading, I had 'language.' She made calls to the library board, she called the parents, and she got nothing. Everyone felt the book was age-appropriate — what kids don't speak like this? The reasons for banning books are just ludicrous to me. It's interesting to me that the last thing that is banned is always violence. Sexuality, language, and content are banned. Violence is not. You can blow up a few buildings, and you can have people dragged down the street. People will stick guns in their children's hands and send them out in the woods to shoot animals, but they don't want to hear about sex. It's so ridiculous."

 Angela Johnson was inspired to write the book, *The First Part Last*, after she rode the subway and noticed a young man holding a baby around 11:00 a.m. in the morning. She found herself wondering why a young man would be holding a baby at that time of day instead of going to school and immediately went to her hotel room where she began to write the book.

The students also read an interview with Sarah Dessen on *TeenReads.com* at *http://www.teenreads.com/authors/au-dessen-sarah.asp* and a letter written on her behalf by the NCAC (National Coalition Against Censorship) when her book *Just Listen* was challenged. Here is an expert from the letter:

"We urge Hillsborough County school officials and Armwood High School book review committee members to stand by First Amendment principles and keep the book, *Just Listen* by Sarah Dessen, in school libraries. While many parents support the book, some have objected to its sexual themes and language. Without questioning the sincerity of those parents, their views are not shared by all, and they have no right to tell other people what their children may read. In our experience, book challenge controversies are best handled by enriching the array of library materials available, not restricting it, and by including additional voices rather than silencing any. These critical educational goals – the goals that inspire the First Amendment – cannot be achieved by modifying the library holdings to reflect specific beliefs or sensitivities. We urge the book review committee to keep the book in the school library and to uphold the principle that is so essential to individual freedom, democracy, and a good education: the right to read, inquire, question, and think for ourselves."

Questions for Students to Answer and Discuss

Someone Like You deals with the issues of pregnancy, teenager sexuality, drinking, and more.

1. How would you feel if this book were challenged and taken away from the school?

2. Do you think that parents who object to a book should also be allowed to take the books away from other teenagers?

Discussion Questions about the Novels

The students will discuss the books and the issues that the books bring up about the personal experience of being pregnant and the how it alters your life. The following questions will help the students to contemplate the personal and emotional impact of teen pregnancy.

1. Why do you think each character made the decision they did about their child?

2. What kind of father is Bobby to Feather and what kind of mother do you think that Scarlett will be?

3. What do you think is the most difficult thing for Bobby and Scarlett?

4. What impact do each character's friends and family have on their decisions?

5. Predict what happens to each family ten years into the future. Explain why.

6. Write three questions you would ask Bobby and Scarlett.

Explore the facts of pregnancy with these nonfiction resources.

The facts of pregnancy are discussed to see how they do or don't reflect the characters' experiences in the novels. The following are some great sites that can be used by the students to take notes on the facts that they find, that then can be discussed as a group.

- Teen Pregnancy. *http://www.teenpregnancy.com*
  The site covers the issues of teen pregnancy facts, choices, myths, and fallacies and provides resources that can help assist teens in making decisions about pregnancy.

- National Institute of Health. *http://www.nlm.nih.gov/medlineplus/teenagepregnancy.html*
  The site provides information on birth control, how to have a safe pregnancy, statistics and facts, prenatal care, and reproductive information.

- TeenageParent. *http://www.teenageparent.org/english/activity.html* and *http://www.teenageparent. org/english/teach.html*
  These sites give students the opportunity to create a budget for providing for a baby. Students can read the stories of teens, both girls and boys, who became parents at an early age.

- National Campaign for Boys. *http://www.thenationalcampaign.org/resources/pdf/pubs/ThatsWhat HeSaid.pdf*
  This is a great site that describes the experiences and concerns of teenage boys regarding pregnancy, relationships, and issues relating to sexuality.

  1. What medical problems can babies born of teen mothers have?

  2. What medical problems can teen mothers experience?

  3. What is prenatal care?

  4. What are some of the emotional reactions of teens who learn they are pregnant?

  5. How are the emotional experiences of teen girls and boys different when they face the idea of becoming parents?

  6. What does it cost to have a baby? Use the baby budget to find out!

Librarians Take Action: Create a display that features teen sexual issues.

It has happened in my library that a parent or a teenager randomly selects a book out of the collection and reads a passage that, of course, goes right to a sex scene and they come to me upset or perplexed, demanding answers about why I purchased such an inappropriate book. You can try to prevent this scenario from occurring by bringing the books that contain sexuality into the open where they can be seen and discussed.

By pairing the fiction books with their non-fiction counterparts, you can create a context that puts the fictional stories in the real world, and that also serves to create a simple but direct non-verbal rationale that demonstrates why you are proud to have "those types" of books in your library. I have featured teen pregnancy, unhealthy relationships, and books about sexual abuse in a display with current nonfiction books that are geared towards teenagers and parents and basic health information regarding these topics.

- Choose an accessible display space where the books can clearly be seen.

- Locate the display space near your desk where you can answer questions and engage browsers in conversation.

- Rotate the display frequently.

Tips for discussing your display

1. Be prepared.

    - Read all the books you put on display. It is important that you have read every book in the display and are aware of any controversial material that they might contain, so you are prepared to discuss it.

    - Know about as many issues as you can about the topic that you are featuring.

    - Be able to say how the non-fiction books relate or enhance the fiction book.

2. Seize the moment.

    - Even if people don't approach you to ask questions, if you see them reading the books, initiate a conversation about your display.

3. Emphasize with their feelings and thoughts.

    - Don't judge them.

    - Recognize the legitimacy of their feelings, thoughts, and concerns.

4. Be direct.

    - Explain why you have the display.

    - Explain why having books that feature sexuality are so important.

    - Ask them their opinions of your display.

    - Answer any questions they have.

5. Always address censorship.

    - Always include a few books that have been challenged or censored.

    - Mark the censored books in some way.

    - Have a sign that talks about what censorship is.

    - Be prepared to talk about censorship, freedom to read, and intellectual freedom.

    - Invite more discussion by making a brochure that browsers can take away with them. Make up a two page, front-to-back reading guide for the book that includes: author information, book reviews, reading guide questions, website addresses about the topic, censorship information if the book has been censored, and a short overview of what censorship is.

References

Anderson, Laurie Halse. *Speak*. R.R. Donnelly, 1999.

Anderson, Laurie Halse. "Speaking Out." *The ALAN Review*, Volume 27, Number 3, Pages 25-26. 2000 *http://scholar.lib.vt.edu/ejournals/ALAN/spring00/anderson.html*. March 12, 2012.

Andye. "Sex in YA: One Naive Mom's Opinion." *Reading Teen: Book Reviews for Young Adult*. 09 March 2011. *http://www.readingteen.net/2011/03/sex-in-ya-one-naive-moms-opinion.html*. 07 July 2011.

"Author Programs: Angela Johnson." *Teachingbooks*. 06 October 2009. *http://www.teachingbooks. net/athr_upcls.cgi*. (Registration required.) 23 June 2011.

Biederman, Lynn. "Young Adult Literature." TeenLitLab at ALA Annual Conference, 2009.

Blume, Judy. *Forever*. Simon & Schuster, 1975.

———. "Judy's Books: *Forever*." Judy Blume on the Web. *http://www.judyblume.com/books/ya/forever.php*. 02 May 2011.

Booth, Coe. *Kendra*. Scholastic, 2008.

Crown, Sarah. "Teen Spirit." *Guardian*. June 08 2005. *http://www.guardian.co.uk/books/2005/jun/08/booksforchildrenandteenagers.sarahcrown*. 04 March 2011.

Dessen, Sarah. *Just Listen*. Penguin, 2006.

———. *Someone Like You*. Penguin Books, 1998.

Draper, Sharon. *November Blues*. Simon Pulse, 2007.

Efaw, Amy. *After*. Penguin Group, 2009.

Greene, John. *Looking for Alaska*. Dutton, 2005.

Howard, Glenda. "Guidelines: *Kimani Tru*." Harlequin, *http://www.harlequin.com/articlepage.html?articleId=1242&chapter=0*. 04 June 2011.

"Issues & Advocacy: Strategies and Tips for Dealing with Challenges to Library Materials." American Library Association, 1999. *http://www.ala.org/ala/issuesadvocacy/banned/challengeslibrarymaterials/copingwithchallenges/strategiestips/index.cfm*. 15 January 2011.

Jayson, Sharon. "Teens define sex in new ways." *USA Today*. 19 October 2005. *http://www.usatoday.com/news/health/2005-10-18-teens-sex_x.htm*. 09 January 2011.

Johnson, Angela. *The First Part Last*. Simon & Schuster, 2003.

Ockler, Sarah. "Banned, but Never Shamed." Sarah Ockler blog. *http://sarahockler.com/2011/07/26/banned-but-never-shamed/*. 10 April 2011.

———. *Twenty Boy Summer*. Hatchett, 2009.

Oughton, Jerrie. *A Perfect Family*. Houghton Mifflin, 2000.

Pattee, Amy. "The Secret Source: Sexually Explicit Young Adult Literature as an Information Source." *Young Adult Library Services*. 2006. 01 September 2011.

Peck, Richard. *Don't Look and It Won't Hurt*. Henry Holt, 1973.

Scroggins, Wesley. "Filthy Books Demeaning to Republic Education." *News Leader*. 17 September 2010. *http://www.news-leader.com/article/20100918/OPINIONS02/112020001/Filthy-books-demeaning-Republic-education*. 05 March 2011.

"Sex in YA: One Naive Mom's Opinion." Reading Teen: Book Reviews for Young Adult. 09 March 2011. *http://www.readingteen.net/2011/03/sex-in-ya-one-naive-moms-opinion.html.* 07 July 2011.

"Sexual Health of Adolescents and Young Adults in the United States." The Henry J. Kaiser Health Foundation. National Institute of Health, January 2011. *http://www.kff.org/womenshealth/upload/3040_04.pdf.* 11 April 2011.

Shamlian, Janet. "New Trend in Teen Fiction: Racy Reads." MSNBC. August 2005. *http://www.msnbc.msn.com/id/8962686/ns/nightly_news/t/new-trend-teen-fiction-racy-reads/#.Trrlpt5vv1Q.* 02 August 2011.

Stone, Tonya Lee. "Now and Forever: The Power of Sex in Young Adult Literature." *VOYA.* February 2006: 463-465.

Thiel, Stacia. "Everything You Don't Want to Know About Your Kid's Sex Life." *New York Magazine.* 12 November 2005. *http://nymag.com/lifestyle/sex/annual/2005/15079/.* 03 June 2011.

Vinaya. "Testing Positive: On Teen Sexuality and Mixed Messages." *The Book Lantern.* 14 March 2011. *http://www.thebooklantern.com/2011/03/testing-positive-on-teen-sexuality-and.html.* 15 Oct. 2011.

von Ziegesar, Cecily. *The Gossip Girls.* 17 Street Productions, 2003.

Wittlinger, Ellen. *Sandpiper.* Simon & Schuster,2007.

Wolf, Naomi. "Young Adult Fiction: Wild Things." *New York Times.* 12 March 2006. *http://www.nytimes.com/2006/03/12/books/review/12wolf.html?pagewanted=all.* 20 July 2011.

Wood, Eleanor. "Pushing the Envelope: Exploring Sexuality in Teen Literature." *Journal of Libraries & Research on Young Adults.* American Library Association, 2010. *http://www.yalsa.ala.org/jrlya/2010/11/pushing-the-envelope-exploring-sexuality-in-teen-literature/.* 15 May 2011.

CHAPTER 3
VIOLENCE AND YOUNG ADULT LITERATURE

Teen Girl-on-Girl Fighting Goes Online is the startling headline on the 2010 CBS news website that describes the increasing amount of girls-fighting-girls videos that have been posted on YouTube and other online websites. (CBS News) Mental illness in the forms of depression and eating disorders also plague teens in unprecedented numbers and according to the National Institute of Mental Health, "Suicide remains one of the top three leading causes of death for young people ages 15 to 24." (National Institute of Mental Health)

Although these stories are true, they represent only one aspect of the world that teens inhabit. Bullying is a form of violence that has become rampant within the schools that teenagers attend, creating an atmosphere of fear and isolation. Teens across the nation have taken ownership of this problem by raising awareness of the issue, taking anti-bullying pledges and sharing their stories to help empower other teens who have been victims. Jillian Roels is such a student, who, after experiencing cyberbullying in high school, started three nonprofit groups to specifically address the issue. Roels also volunteered to mentor elementary and middle school girls to support them in stopping bullying in their schools. (Story) Katy Butler, another high school student from Michigan, organized thousands of people to protest the R rating given to the movie *Bullying*. This movie, that follows the students at a middle school who bully and are bullied, is dedicated to honestly depicting the reality of teens experience, and yet its R rating ensures that the students who need the see it the most will be restricted from seeing it at schools or through other educational events. (Weinstein) The film's rating was lowered to PG-13 due to public pressure, making it easier for the teens to see the film. (ABC News)

Which story is the true representation of violence both external and internal in the young adult community? The answer is both. Similar to the adult world, teens are alternately happy or sad, and are emotionally vulnerable at various points in their journey through adolescence. They experience abuse, depression, and other issues that threaten to have a negative influence in their lives, and just like adults, many of those same teens are able to rise above those negative experiences and internal problems to help others overcome those same problems through the support of their families, schools, and friends.

Young adult authors struggle to provide an accurate and thoughtful representation of how teens experience and resolve the issues of violence in a way that is sensitive and not exploitative, as evidenced by the words and thoughts of Sapphire and Suzanne Collins, two popular authors who skillfully approach the issues of violence in their work.

Viewpoint: Authors include violence when it is needed to tell their story.

Any story an author writes, when picked apart and examined by its separate pieces, is subject to being seen as being too explicit, violent, or frightening. This is the mistake that censors make when they select certain words, acts, or events in a book that, in their perception, are inappropriate, and overlook the fact that when the disparate provocative pieces come together, the overall theme of the book and its relevancy are then apparent. One of the best ways to combat censorship is to be able to speak about the author's background and reasoning behind the books that they write. It often helps to put what appears to be a provocative or seemingly disturbing book into a context that can be understood.

Sapphire, the author of the critically acclaimed book *Push,* which has been described as unforgettable and yet, truly horrifying, talks about her motivation in writing stories that are alternately praised for their blunt truths and also questioned for their graphic and brutal depictions of physical and sexual abuse. She explains that her motivation was to tell the stories of the unforgettable students she worked with as a remedial reading teacher in Harlem in the 1990s. These students were locked out of the broader culture due to their race, economic status, and social isolation and were essentially struggling for their very survival. The character Precious, who was a stereotype to many: obese, dark skinned, unwed mother, and illiterate, was essentially a compilation of those memorable students. Sapphire hoped that the story would go beyond the stereotype, allowing the character's dreams, hopes, and intelligence to shine through the violence and abuse. Sapphire also explained that it was important to her that the story of this character and girls like her was told—girls who were victims of abuse, with horrific stories to tell that needed to be brought out into the open.

The author's highly anticipated sequel to *Push, The Kid,* is written in the same blunt and hard hitting style. In this story, Precious dies and her son Abdul, at age nine, goes into foster care where he experiences much of the same horrifying abuse as his mother. This story is told in the author's same stark and devastating writing style.

When asked how she keeps such graphic images in her head, she states, "Sometimes I don't even remember what I've written to create the art that I create, I have to compartmentalize. I can't stay in it." Still, when critics press Sapphire about how she can write about such desperation and dire circumstances, she exudes confidence when she states emphatically, "I could choose to write another way; I choose to write this way."

Suzanne Collins' best-selling dystopian science fiction series, The Hunger Games, has received accolades from book reviewers and from readers who love her books and anxiously waited as each sequel was released. Her books have also received criticism based on what some feel is the high level of despair, destruction, and excessive violence. The series has already begun to be the recipient of book challenges. In 2010, a parent in New Hampshire asked for *The Hunger Games* to be removed from school after it was a part of a read-aloud program in a class because it "gave her eleven-year-old daughter nightmares and could possibly numb the other students to the effects of violence." The mother, who did not read the book, felt that the book contained no lesson, other than one child kills other children so that her family can win. The book, she concluded, was simply too violent. (Barack)

Why does The Hunger Games series contain violence? Exploring Collins' background and the thought process she uses to develop her characters and storyline makes the overall context of the books clearer. Collins' father was in the military, as were many of the members of her family. Her father often spoke to her about weapons and military strategy, making warfare very familiar to her. He also took her to visit castles in England as a child, where, she states, it was not about "fairy tale magic," but so he could educate her about where the arrow slits were placed and where they poured the boiling oil.

Collins, who is a critic of violence, made a decision to make the warfare that is the book's foundation as personal as possible so that the reader is forced to not just view the violence as an outsider or a voyeur, but in a personal and more intimate way. (Dominus)

Viewpoint: Today's young adult literature is too dark and damaging to the emotional and psychological well-being of teens.

Before she wrote The Hunger Games series, Suzanne Collins was the head writer for the children's television show *Clifford's Puppy Days*, a show that follows the adventures of Clifford when he was a small puppy before he grew to be Clifford the Big Red Dog. Collins also wrote for the show *Wow! Wow! Wubbzy!*, a children's show for preschoolers about a make believe character who loves to play and have fun adventures all day. In an interview, Collins stated that she continued to write scripts for *Wubbzy* during the time she was writing *The Hunger Games* in order to get some relief from the intensity of writing about characters who may not live to see the light of day.

An essay written in the *Wall Street Journal* by journalist Meghan Gourdan, critical of the dark aspects of young adult literature, ignited a firestorm among parents, journalists, librarians, teenagers, and authors. The essay described young adult fiction today as rife with profane language, as well as lurid and graphic in its depiction of severe physical and sexual abuse, dystopian worlds, and eating and mental health disorders. In particular, she pointed out the hyper violence of the series The Hunger Games by Suzanne Collins and the explicit self-abuse depicted in *Rage* by Jackie Morse Kessler as examples of what is wrong with the books offered to teens. In her opinion, these books are "too dark" and are potentially damaging to the emotional and psychological well-being of adolescents. Gourdan also contends that these disturbing books are not representative of the reality of the majority of young adults and instead, celebrate a desolate and narrow view of life at the expense of more positive stories that promote the joy and hope that embody the true nature of our youth. (Gourdan)

Viewpoint: Violence does not reflect the experience of most teens.

A librarian wrote an opinion essay in the *School Library Journal* in 2003 stating that violence was, for the most part, absent in the lives of her students. They had no experience with corporal punishment at home or in school and that physical fighting was not something that they would witness. She expressed concern over what potential harm reading details of physical and sexual abuse would do to teens that were essentially sheltered from those harsh experiences. (Isaacs)

Viewpoint: The "dark issues" are not new to teens, they just haven't been addressed in young adult literature.

The contrasting view is that these issues are not new to our teenager's lives or to our culture and society as a whole—they have simply not been publicly addressed in such an open and honest manner. Young adult literature, by bravely addressing these painful, but true-to-life issues, has the unique opportunity to improve and strengthen the psyche of our children by bringing these issues out of the darkness and into the light.

Author Sherman Alexie, who wrote the popular and controversial novel, *The Absolutely True Diary of a Part-Time Indian*, is often mentioned when dark books that feature tough subjects are discussed. His award-winning book has frequently been censored and challenged across the country and has become one of the most challenged books in the United States, according to the American Library Association. The book was challenged in 2009 at Antioch High School in Chicago after it was assigned for summer reading and parents described it as "vulgar, racist, profane, and sexually inappropriate." (Fuller) The book was also challenged in Stockton, Missouri, when a parent became upset after learning that the book would be added to the school library and would be studied in class. The parent took offense at the book's sexual explicitness and stated that the book went against their community standards and religion, and, after much debate, the book was banned from the school district. (Penprase)

Alexie wrote an article called, "Why the Best Kids' Books are Written in Blood," which addresses why sometimes violence in young adult novels is necessary and is relevant to all teenagers. Alexie describes those that believe most teenagers can't relate to books like his as condescending and ill-informed about the lives of teenagers today. He cites his many school visits in which he has been warmly received by all the students he meets—many who say that his book was the only one they ever finished—as evidence that the feelings of isolation or loneliness that accompany self-abuse, sexual abuse, or violence towards others are shared and understood by most teenagers. In addition, he cites the many teenagers that tell him their stories or write him letters about events in their lives that are equally as tragic and heart wrenching as Alexie's book.

Viewpoint: Stories about teens with pathologies encourages more teens to engage in self-destructive behavior.

Some people are concerned that stories about self-harm and other pathologies encourage teens to engage in self-destructive behavior. Those who already suffer from mental illness, like anorexia or cutting, might find comfort in reading about others who have the same problems. The concern is that it may inspire them to more desperate acts or to view their behavior as acceptable, even fashionable. What about those teenagers who were previously unaware of these behaviors? Could books that describe these pathologies have the unintended effect of educating and inspiring those teenagers to experiment with the destructive behaviors?

Viewpoint: Exposing these self-destructive behaviors can bring comfort and begin healing.

"Talking about painful issues and experiences is about breaking silence and encouraging healing," says author Cheryl Rainfield. Rainfield's award winning book, *Scars*, candidly explores the issues of self-harm, depression, and rape through the story of a teenage girl who cuts herself in response to sexual abuse that she experienced as a child. The book has been highly recommended to teens because it is comforting, insightful, and informative. (Chen) However, Gourdan, in her "Darkness Too Visible" article, referred to this positive description as "inexplicable." She goes on to criticize the review for not showing concern about the fact that the main character's father is responsible for the past abuse and terrorizes his daughter throughout the book. (Gourdan) *Scars* was also challenged in the Boone County Public Library in Kentucky in 2010, because parents were worried that the cover of the book, which shows a scarred forearm, might encourage those that self-harm to relapse. (Gourdan) However, after a review of the complaint, the book was allowed to remain. (Chen)

 Did you know that the arm covered in scars on the cover of the book *Scars* is the author's arm? She wanted to include it to show that she was no longer ashamed.

Rainfield, who was also a victim of sexual abuse, and used self-harm as a coping strategy, is very aware that those who self-harm are often triggered by experiences or images that remind them of the problems that underlie their disorder. Rainfield does not deny the reality of this possibility and, due to her personal experience, is very aware of this danger and assertively addresses this potential problem in many ways. Her book offers a very thorough and informative guide to self-harm resources. She makes a special effort to educate parents and survivors whenever she can about the dangers of self-harm and how steps can be taken to prevent and resolve these tough issues. Her website also offers tips, advice, and links to articles and organizations that can help those who suffer from this destructive behavior, with a reminder that reading about the issues could cause triggering.

Rainfield explains that in her experience people don't self-harm because they read about it in books. Reading about it helps because those who self-harm often feel ashamed of what they are doing and feel an extreme sense of isolation. Knowing that there are others out there like them who are having the same experiences helps to validate and confirm their experiences.

In the book, her description of self-harm is honest in its depiction of the intense and debilitating pain, both physical and emotional, that accompanies self-harm, leading her to firmly believe that almost anyone who suggests that a book like *Scars* would encourage self-harm, probably has not read the book in its entirety. In the many letters she has received, her readers have told her that reading the book either makes them want to stop or never start. Teens also write to tell her that *Scars* helped them to get into therapy, and now they know they are not alone.

Author Diane Duane, who has worked as a psychiatric nurse with teenagers with mental health disorders, states that what her teenage patients wanted most was the acknowledgment that their problems were real and important. They wanted to know that they were not alone or unique and that others were aware of their issues. Books were often used as an integral part of therapy in order to help the patients explore how others worked through similar problems.

Rainfield, a victim of ritual abuse who was taught to cut herself, states that books were the key to her survival. She read fantasy books that helped her to temporarily escape from the daily torture and abuse that she suffered. Realistic books about other teenagers' problems helped her feel less alone and offered her the opportunity to dream about the future. *Blubber* by Judy Blume was one of her favorites because she could relate to the bullying. *Annie on My Mind* was also significant because it addressed her sexuality. She wished she could have found a book that represented her particular struggle, but at the time there were none. It was for that reason that she decided to write *Scars*.

Wintergirls, by Laurie Halse Anderson, addresses the subject of anorexia. Anderson was also concerned about the possibility of encouraging or inciting those with the propensity for self-destructive behavior to either increase or engage in even more self-harming behaviors. She spoke to those who had survived eating disorders, researched them through medical journals, and interviewed many psychiatrists to thoroughly investigate the facts before she embarked on her novel. She then submitted her book to other experts in the field before the book's publication.

The experts she spoke to stated that it is possible that reading about anorexia in her book could interest teens in trying to lose weight unsafely, or if they already had the propensity toward eating disorders, perhaps initiate some destructive feelings. But that anything, images on magazines, billboards, other teenagers, as well as information that is readily available on the Internet, could also encourage those who are vulnerable. The experts agreed that a book like *Wintergirls,* with its stark and brutal depiction of the horrendous realities and aftermath of eating disorders, would most likely deter participation in this destructive behavior.

Anderson states that she did not pursue the idea of writing about anorexia lightly. Although she was not anorexic, she had body image issues while growing up that made her very aware of the negative influence these At least ten to twenty percent of boys also have eating disorders, but often go untreated because people assume that only girls have eating disorders.

problems could have in the lives of others. She hesitated to write about anorexia at all, but did so at the urging of her many young readers who specifically asked her to write on the subject. (Horning)

The Librarian's Role

Young adult librarians are advocates for the rights of their young readers to choose whatever literature speaks to their experiences or interests, however, we also have to acknowledge that at this stage of their lives, the interest or concern of their parents and the community regarding any issue that affects them should also be a concern of ours as well. The challenge that remains is how we can acknowledge the questions and concerns, while still adhering to our commitment to intellectual freedom and the rights of our young readers.

The dangers of book banning are always the most imminent concern for librarians who recognize how fear and lack of knowledge can often encourage censorship. However, it is not censorship to acknowledge positive or negative perceptions about literature or to address the questions and concerns that exist about any books that are in your collection. Proactively leading the discussion can better prepare you, as the librarian, to have the tools you need to reassure a nervous parent or to properly guide your readers into choosing books that best fit their needs and is your best defense against book challenges.

Librarians Take Action: Give a presentation on young adult books and eating disorders.

Many parents are understandably concerned about these issues and want as much information as they can find about the subjects. The library acts as a partner with parents by providing them with the information they are seeking to help their teens. Fiction books that mirror the concerns that parents have also show them how the books can provide assistance and support for their children.

According to the ALA, community outreach is essential to the prevention of censorship. Opportunities to provide information to the young adults, parents, and community members about what young adults are reading and how it ties into issues that impact their lives are educational and provide a sense of open communication between the library and the library users. (ALA)

Educate yourself.

1. You should know everything you can about the issue so that you are informed and can speak easily about the topic.

    - What questions do you have?

    - Research your local newspapers to see if eating disorders have been a local issue.

    - Research websites and journals.

    - Interview an expert.

    - Contact a local pediatric group.

    - Contact a local hospital or eating disorder facility.

    - Ask a parent or library user who is an expert.

    - Contact the local university.

2. Collaborate with others to encourage the sharing of information and resources which will help to facilitate the creation of activities and events that would be difficult to accomplish alone.

Find speakers, handouts, and information.

1. Contact:

    - Local mental health information center

    - Pediatric groups

    - Community hospital

    - Local public schools

    - Health teachers and guidance counselors

    - Local university and college health centers

- The National Federation of Families Children's Mental Health at *http://ffcmh.org.* They offer links to local organizations in your area across the United States. They offer workshops, speakers, and information on all mental health issues related to children.

- The teenagers that frequent your library or that are in your teen advisory group

- The parents of those teenagers might also know someone

- The director of your library

- Local librarian's organization, especially the young adult division

- Ask the members of your teen advisory group to help out with the presentation. Get permission forms first.

Asking for collaboration among the people that frequent your library and live in your community has the benefit of enabling them to choose topics to present that are relevant to their particular needs and concerns. It also empowers them because they know that their viewpoints, knowledge, and skills are appreciated and needed. Finally, it allows them to feel a personal ownership of the event, making them more likely to participate and encourage their family, friends, and neighbors to join in as well.

Plan the presentation

- Decide what roles you and your co-presenter will take.

- Will your co-presenter take the lead on medical questions?

- Act as the media expert and focus, perhaps, on body images in the media.

- Draw on your own experience.

- Most librarians have a wealth of experience that they bring to librarianship. For example, I have a MA in psychology and worked as a family therapist in the past, giving me an interest and foundation in mental health issues.

Introduction

- Ask the audience what drew them there.

- Ask the audience what experience or information they have to offer.

- Let them know when they can ask questions.

- Start with something startling, interesting, and informative.

Example introduction when speaking about eating disorders

Pro Ana is a term used to describe people who believe that engaging in anorexia-like behaviors in order to lose weight is a positive idea. Beginning your presentation by discussing this idea that is not well known to most parents is a way to inform them of the depth of your knowledge about this subject. Teenagers access this information primarily through websites and blog sites. These online sites offer support and promotion of medically unsupervised and approved weight loss techniques and ideas. Many of these sites also will state that anorexia is not a disease or mental health disorder and will claim that they are merely offering support. Parents should also be aware of the following terminology that these sites use, such as Thinspiration, Thinspo, Pro ana (pro anorexia), Pro mia (pro bulimia), or just Ana (the personified version of "pro-anorexia").

The Presentation

1. Basic information of the symptoms, etiology (causes), treatment, medications, statistics, history of problem, and the future outlook, such as new treatments and theories.

2. Book talks on fiction books regarding eating disorders. This is your chance to proactively present the books in your collection that address anorexia and other eating disorders. Explain their purpose, content, and the author's background. Tell how often the books circulate and read teen book reviews.

3. Always mention censorship and explain how books that contain upsetting or controversial information can be disturbing to some people and cause them to want to have the books removed from the library. Explain that if they have any questions about any books that they feel uneasy about, that they can speak to you about them.

4. Special tips on presenting medical or health information

   • Always mention that you are not a therapist or doctor.

   • If you are not sure, say that and offer to get the information later.

   • Have a list of definitions available.

   • Present the information in chunks. For example, after you present the symptoms of eating disorders, offer to answer questions and discuss.

   • Try to avoid medical jargon.

   • Use stories about people to explain each reference.

Conclusion

• Give audience members a handout with the following information:

   • Websites on the topic.

   • Local information, hotlines.

   • Books that you book talked.

   • Other books in your library.

   • Movies on the topic.

• Offer your phone number or email for follow-up books.

• Ask parents what other information sessions they would like.

• Ask for an email address for further contact.

References

ABC News. "'Bully' Film Rating Lowered to PG-13 After Public Pressure." 06 April 2012. *http://abcnews .go.com/blogs/entertainment/2012/04/bully-film-rating-lowered-to-pg-13-after-public-pressure/*

Alexie, Sherman. *The Absolutely True Diary of a Part-Time Indian*. Little, Brown, 2007.

Barack, Lauren. "New Hampshire Parent Challenges 'The Hunger Games" *School Library Journal*. 19 October 2010. *http://www.schoollibraryjournal.com/slj/newslettersnewsletterbucketextrahelping/887280443/ new_hampshire_parent_challenges_the.html.csp*. 12 May 2012.

CBS News. "Teen Girl-on-Girl Fighting Goes Online" 07 July 2010. *http://www.cbsnews.com/2100-500202 _162-6165570.html*. 14 May 2012.

Chen, Diane. "Book Challenges Made Visible: Scars by Cheryl Rainfield challenged." *School Library Journal*. 26 February 2011. *http://www.ufollow.com/authors/diane.chen/sources/practically.paradise/5*. 14 May 2012.

Collins, Suzanne. *The Hunger Games*. Scholastic Press, 2008.

Dominus, Susan. "Suzanne Collins: War Stories for Kids." *New York Times Magazine*. 08 April 2011. *http:// www.nytimes.com/2011/04/10/magazine/mag-10collins-t.html?pagewanted=all*. 12 March 2012.

Duane, Diane. "The Eyes in the Peacock's Tail." Out of Ambit blog. 07 June 2011. *http://www.dianeduane. com/outofambit/2011/06/07/the-eyes-in-the-peacocks-tail/*. 10 February 2011.

Fuller, Ruth . "Some parents seek to ban *The Absolutely True Diary of a Part-Time Indian*." *Chicago Tribune*. 09 June 2011. 17 August 2011.

Gourdan, Meghan. "Darkness Too Visible." *Wall Street Journal*. 04 June 2011. *http://online.wsj.com/article/ SB10001424052702303657404576357622592697038.html*. 15 July 2011.

Horning, Kathleen T. "Fearless: An Interview with Laurie Halse Anderson." *School Library Journal*. 01 June 2009. *http://www.libraryjournal.com/article/CA6660876.html*. 17 Oct. 2011.

Isaacs, Kathleen T. "Reality Check: A look at the disturbing growth of violence in books for teens" *School Library Journal*. 10 January 2003. *http://www.schoollibraryjournal.com/article/CA326326.html*. 14 May 2012.

National Institute for Mental Health. "Suicide in America: Frequently Asked Questions." *http://www.nimh. nih.gov/health/publications/suicide-in-america/complete-suicide-in-america-frequently-asked-questions. shtml*. 12 May 2012.

Penprase, Mike. "Stockton book ban upheld 7-0 in packed public forum." Newsleader.com. *http://www. news-leader.com/article/20100909/NEWS04/9090375/Stockton-book-ban-upheld-7-0-packed-public- forum*. 09 September 2010.

Rainfield, Cheryl. *Scars*. WestSide Books, 2011.

———. "*Scars* Is Being Challenged." Cheryl Rainfield blog. *http://cherylrainfield.com/blog/index.php/2011/ 02/22/scars-is-being-challenged/*. 17 October 2011.

Sapphire. *The Kidd*. Penguin Press, 2011.

———. *Push*. Vintage, 2009.

"Sapphire's Story: How 'Push' Became 'Precious'." NPR Books: All Things Considered. 06 November 2009. *http://www.npr.org/templates/story/story.php?storyId=120176695*. 09 April 2011.

Story, Karen. "Redmond Teen's Passion for Helping Others is More Than Just Talk." 06 March 2012. *http://redmond. patch.com/articles/redmond-teen-s-passion-for-helping-others-is-more-than-just-talk*. 05 May 2012.

Weinstein, Harvey. "Weinstein Co. to Release 'Bully' Documentary without MPAA Rating" LA Times Blog. 26 March 2012. *http://latimesblogs.latimes.com/movies/2012/03/weinstein-co-to-release-bully-docu- mentary-without-mpaa-rating.html*. 12 May 2012.

CHAPTER 4
PROFANITY AND YOUNG ADULT LITERATURE

The use of profanity around young adults, whether it's spoken or written in books, is shocking to many people, especially parents, because it is unexpected and is therefore very disconcerting. It can be especially shocking to learn that these words are sometimes used in the context of the school classroom; a space that parents consider to be safe and nurturing. The immediate reaction that most parents have is to shield their children from anything that the parents deem as harmful or that might have a negative affect on them.

Profanity and censorship in young adult books has been a topic for debate as far back as the 1950s, when *The Catcher in the Rye*, the classic young adult book by J. D. Salinger, was published to the delight of teens for its ability to precisely channel the angst of adolescence, and to the objections of many adults, who disliked its profane language and worried about the book's negative influence on teenagers.

Before *The Catcher in the Rye* was published, J. D. Salinger seemed to like attention and was very proud of his work, but after it came out, he found he hated fame. He subsequently asked to have his picture removed from any of his book covers, refused to be interviewed, and moved to an isolated estate where he had a high fence build around his property. He even sued and won against someone who wanted to write a biography about him in a case that went all the way to the Supreme Court.

The book, published in 1951, tells the story of Holden Caulfield, a troubled boy, who after being expelled from yet another prep school, travels to New York and spends three days in the city. The book was originally intended for adults, but teens rapidly embraced its themes of alienation, loneliness, and the search for identity enabling the book to become a worldwide symbol of teenage rebellion.

The Catcher in the Rye also became one of the most censored books in the history of the United States. It was the most censored book between the years of 1961 and 1982, and was the most challenged book in the United States from 1990 to 1991. In 1981, *The Catcher in the Rye* was both the most-censored book *and* the second-most-taught book in U.S. public schools, according to University of Maryland Professor Herbert Foerstel's book, *Banned in the USA*, because of its depiction of sexuality, blasphemy, immorality, alcoholism, and lack of family values. Profanity remains the reason that the book has been banned the most often. (Turner) In fact, in 2004, profanity and obscenity were the reasons behind its being challenged by a parent who complained that the book shouldn't be in school, much less discussed in school. The parent stated that, "We want students to use appropriate language. So why should they study inappropriate language?"

Viewpoint: Giving children the permission to read books that have foul language is the same as giving children permission to use the same language and the more teens read or hear profanity, the more they will feel that it is a normal part of life.

Parents are concerned with instilling values into their children's lives. Many parents feel that reading books that contain profane language goes against the values that most children are taught at home. As a result they feel that it is inappropriate for children who are under the age of eighteen to have access to these books without the permission of their parents.

The usage of profane language seems to be more widespread among teenagers, states Dr. Francis Compton, a psychology professor who has conducted many studies regarding cursing and behavior, who has discovered in one of his studies "that 87 percent of children (ages twelve to nineteen) used curse words or foul language and that 74 percent of eighteen- to thirty-four-year-olds admit to swearing in public." He concluded from the study that "Sometimes harsh or graphic words used by the participants were verbalized to make them feel older or more mature." (Francis)

These statistics concern parents and teachers alike who spend much of their time either disciplining their children for swearing or trying to figure out ways to decrease their desire to curse. Parents also wonder about their children who curse becoming violent or menaces to society. (Aubrey) Pediatricians like Monika Walters attempt to ease the minds of anxious parents regarding this issue. She states that the idea that cursing leads to violent behavior has been put into a greater context today, with the common thought being that if the offensive behavior is linked or associated with a pattern of violent behavior, there is a problem, however, in most cases, it really is just the way that teenagers express themselves or they think it makes them seem older and more like adults. (Aubrey)

Viewpoint: Profanity is a form of free expression protected by the First Amendment.

An understanding of the constitution will help to resolve the debate about profane speech and young adults in regard to community standards. Free speech is one of the most important rights recognized by the First Amendment and is guaranteed under the U.S. Constitution. This right states that beliefs through speech can be expressed both verbally and symbolically without government restriction. According to the Supreme Court, profanity is considered free speech and is considered a form of expression like any other that deserves protection. The question is: How does profanity with its provocative nature fit into the context of free speech when it comes to young adults?

Cohen vs. California (1971)

The Supreme Court ruled that profane words, even though they could be construed as off-putting, are still deserving of protection under the First Amendment. During the 1960s and 1970s, the Vietnam War elicited strong emotions and debate whenever the subject was raised. Everyone had a strong opinion about it, expressed with songs, books, and many articles. On April 26, 1968, nineteen-year-old Paul Robert Cohen went into the Los Angeles Courthouse carrying a jacket that said "F the Draft" on it. He put the jacket on when he was leaving the courthouse and was promptly arrested. He was convicted of violating section 415 of the California penal code that prohibits disturbing the peace in a malicious or willful manner and received thirty days in jail.

The conviction was upheld by the California Court of Appeals which said that offensive conduct was an act of violence meant to disturb the peace. The Supreme Court overturned their opinion because four-letter words alone should not put the person's use of free speech into a category that should be subject to greater regulation. The words also could not be considered "fighting words," which are prohibited by the Supreme Court because the words on the shirt could not be considered a personal attack on anyone. (Thomas and Herbeck 2009)

Viewpoint: The government should regulate speech that borders on obscenity or that could cause violence.

Since the constitution was written, people have struggled to come to an agreement about whether or not all speech is protected by the First Amendment. These concerns and disagreements have resulted in a few instances in which free speech has been regulated by the government.

Chaplinsky vs. New Hampshire (1942)

The "fighting words doctrine" was established by this case in which the precedent was set that there were some limitations to free speech and that these limitations have to do with words that are clearly intended to incite violence. (First Amendment Schools)

Chaplinsky was a Jehovah's Witness and street preacher who was attempting to give a sermon on a New Hampshire street corner. A town marshal asked him to stop preaching. Chaplinsky was arrested when he told the sheriff that he was a racketeer and a fascist. He was charged with violating New Hampshire's law that states that it is illegal for anyone to use "intentionally offensive speech being directed at others in a public place and to address any offensive, derisive or annoying word to anyone who is lawfully in any street or public place . . . or to call him by an offensive or derisive name."

The Supreme Court unanimously upheld the decision and allowed the arrest to stand. The decision stated that there was a narrow category of speech that was not protected because they did not have social value or contribute to the expression of ideas. Fighting or insulting words, similar to the ones used by Chaplinksy, fit this description.

Viewpoint: Children and young adults require special protection that can legally result in some of their rights being restricted for their safety.

The Supreme Court places the most restrictions on free speech when it effects young adults, with most of the restrictions concerning free speech in the public school setting. The courts have consistently ruled that there is a difference between private student's speech and speech that occurs in a school setting. While students do have the right to receive information, educators have a greater authority to control student speech because student speech falls under the "the imprimatur of the school," or the rights of educators to have final approval over what students are allowed to say in a school setting. According to First Amendment Schools, "Educators do not offend the First Amendment by exercising editorial control over the style and content of student speech in school-sponsored expressive activities so long as their actions are reasonably related to legitimate pedagogical concerns." In addition, "A school must also retain the authority to refuse to sponsor student speech that might reasonably be perceived to advocate drug or alcohol use, irresponsible sex, or 'conduct otherwise inconsistent with the shared values of a civilized social order,' or to associate the school with any position."

Bethel School District No 404 vs. Fraser (1986)

Public school students are subject to have greater restriction on their First Amendment rights than are guaranteed to adults. On April 26, 1983, respondent Matthew N. Fraser, a student at Bethel High School in Pierce County, Washington, delivered a speech nominating a fellow student for student elective office in front of 600 high school students, many of whom were under the age of fifteen. The assembly was part of a school-sponsored educational program in self-government and students were required to attend or go to study hall. During the entire speech, Fraser referred to his candidate in terms that were graphic and explicitly sexual.

Two of Fraser's teachers told him that the speech was inappropriate and recommended that he not give it because he would most likely be disciplined. During the speech, a school counselor observed the reaction of the students and found that it upset and embarrassed the students and caused some to repeat the obscene words and to misbehave in general.

The student, with the help of the ACLU, filed a lawsuit against the school stating that his first Amendment rights had been violated. The U.S. district court ruled in his favor. The school district then appealed to the U.S. Ninth Circuit Court of Appeals which also ruled in Fraser's favor after the school appealed the decision. The school district asked the U.S. Supreme Court to review the case.

The Supreme Court ruled that the school was correct in disciplining the student and that their school policy against profanity did not violate the First Amendment because the words used could be considered disruptive to the educational process and that certain styles of expression in a school setting with minors could be considered vulgar and obscene. (Linder)

Viewpoint: School officials can remove books from the school library or classroom that they feel contain profanity or other obscene material.

School officials cannot pull books off library shelves because they disagree with what they contain according to the Board of Education vs. Pico case. The ruling also stated that school officials *could* remove books from library shelves if they proved that the books were "pervasively vulgar" and violated educational standards set by the school.

Viewpoint: The usage of adult terms in children's literature might expose children to language they are not developmentally ready to comprehend.

When children's librarian and author Susan Patron wrote her 2007 Newberry award-winning book, *The Higher Power of Lucky*, she had no idea a simple reference to a male body part that occurs early on in the book would serve to ignite a firestorm that would lead to a national debate on appropriate word choice in children's books with the *New York Times*, the *Today Show*, and *Publishers Weekly*, as well as numerous librarian list-servs and other online discussion groups. (Bosman) Offensive language, she found, is not always about profanity, but can also center on language that some feel is not appropriate or necessary for children.

"Scrotum sounded to Lucky like something green that comes up when you have the flu and cough too much. It sounded medical and secret, but also important." Profanity is expected to offend some people, but when correct anatomical terms were used in a children's book, and was challenged by librarians, the unexpectedness of it all was surprising. The controversy began when a group of elementary school librarians felt strongly that the word was ill-chosen and not appropriate for the elementary school audience, resulting in their decision to not buy the book for their libraries. The varied opinions stated that "I think it's a good case of an author not realizing her audience," and "I didn't order it for either of my schools, based on 'the word,' " while other librarians supported the book in full.

When interviewed about the controversy, Patron spoke of her disappointment that anyone would think that she used a word just for shock value or to get attention. She stated that she saw her ten-year-old self in the character of Lucky, a child who is bright and curious about the world around her. She said that she believes strongly that children are intelligent and that they can handle the naming of a body part. She also imagined that perhaps their curiosity, like that of Lucky's, might inspire them to ask their parents, librarians, or teachers about the word's meaning if they were not familiar with it. (Reading Today)

Viewpoint: Authors use profanity because the character's personality and situation call for it.

Chris Crutcher's book *Whale Talk* is often used in classrooms across the country and is challenged frequently due to the fact that it contains what many feel to be an excessive amount of profanity. The book was banned in March 2005 at the Limestone County School in Alabama due to its language. Some of the board members recommended banning it totally because, as they stated, "We can't allow students to go down our halls and say those words, and we shouldn't let them read it." (Stancil) In fact, PABBIS (Parents Against Bad Books in Schools) went so far as to count the variety and number of curse words by page number. The book, which is extremely popular among teenagers, is about a group of misfits who are led by J.T, a natural athlete who hates the restrictions of teams and rules. Crutcher, who visits schools and libraries often and interacts with students, teachers, and librarians, usually responds personally when his books are challenged. He wrote a letter to the Limestone County School, describing his reasons for the use of profanity. In the letter he describes the main scene that seems to ignite the complaints, when a biracial girl, who, one day in a fit of anger, screams the racially derogative words that her bigoted stepfather calls her when he is berating her. Taken out of context, he agrees, the words do sound terrible, but when you read the book, you realize that she is finally freeing herself by repeating the terrible words that he says to her. In fact, Crutcher, who in addition to writing also works as a therapist, remembers a young girl who was working through a similar situation. (Crutcher)

Viewpoint: Authors use profanity to authentically represent the lifestyle and vernacular of the characters.

Coe Booth is the author of *Tyrell*, a Los Angeles Times Book Prize winner and gritty urban drama about a fifteen-year-old Bronx teenager who faces some major challenges; his father is in jail, he is homeless, he takes care of his seven-year-old brother, and he is desperate to find a legal way to earn money. Booth paints a realistic depiction of Tyrell's world that includes street slang, drugs, alcohol, and sexuality, all of which are controversial, but it is the character's repeated use of profanity that has drawn the most criticism and caused the book to be challenged.

Tyrell was recently removed from an elementary library in Gary, Indiana, after a fourth grade student brought the book home and his mother objected, describing her child's reading the book as being like "a molestation of his mind." The superintendent subsequently reviewed the book and decided that the book would only be available to high school students. (Gonzalez)

The profanity and street slang that characterize the South Bronx is not for everyone. Booth expected this when she wrote the book and agrees that the language in *Tyrell* is offensive for some. This reality was clear to her from the numerous letters she has received from sixth and seventh grade teachers who tell her that they would love to have their students read the book, but cannot because of the student conduct codes regarding profanity that exist in their schools.

Despite the challenges and criticism, she remains committed to her honest portrayal of Tyrell's world based on her experience as a former social worker who worked extensively with teens who were in gangs, homeless, addicted to drugs, or victims of sexual abuse. She credits their personal challenges and resilience in face of such a rough environment with her inspiration to write *Tyrell* because "inner-city kids are near and dear to my heart." She also wanted to make sure that through *Tyrell* she told their stories through their vernacular, whether it was received positively or negatively, with respect and honesty. (Booth)

Viewpoint: Authors use profanity to express themselves.

On her blog, Justine Larbalestier spoke extensively about her appreciation of profanity, why she chooses to use it in her books, and its impact on YA literature at a conference on banning and censorship. For herself, she explains that she loves the feel of the words as she speaks them and that they allow her to convey her true feelings in a way that no other words can. She told a captive audience that she would love to write a book that solely captured the profane vernacular of teenagers that they use on a daily basis, but knows that it would never get published. (Larbalestier)

Her thoughts on the idea that profanity could be offensive to some are this: "I hate stories about unicorns and girls that wait to be rescued because they offend me." She would not want to ban those books from others because they enjoy them. She states that she wishes fervently that she could write a book that was dramatic and moving that did not offend anyone, but she wonders, "What would that look like?"

Viewpoint: The possibility of censorship due to profanity has an affect on new authors.

Authors who write specifically for young adults strive to have their stories reflect the reality of their subject's world. The use of curse words to depict the choice of vocabulary of many teens seems to be the most appropriate selection; however, because of the controversy, this choice is often a difficult one. Many author discussion sites focus on this dilemma. Jordan Sonnenblick wrote the successful book, *Drums, Girls, and Dangerous Pie*, a book he describes as clean and appropriate for conservative groups. When he decided to write a sequel to it he ran into trouble. The problem was with one character who is angry and bitter and who would clearly use cursing as self-expression, and yet Jordan agonized and sought advice from other writers on the popular Barnes & Noble online group for authors about his concerns over possibly offending anyone. (Sonnenblick)

The authors seem to distinguish between middle school readers and high school readers when making the decision to use profanity. Writers who are writing specifically for middle school age—children ages ten to thirteen, or "tweens"—take care to use as few curse words as possible and then only "mild" ones. This is particularly true if they want to appeal to school libraries or reading clubs such as Scholastic. One writer suggests, "Beware of strong language in your middle grade novel. You may wish to use profanities because a particular character demands it, but at this age, parents and teachers are still very protective." Those writing for high school students were somewhat more relaxed, as the general advice was that they had much more freedom to curse. Even with the clearer sense of freedom, those writing for high school age teens professed their discomfort; a writer offered a warning about not using profanity on the first few pages because it might turn readers away. (Jensen) New writers also believed, regardless of the age they were writing for, that by adding profanity, they were running the risk of limiting their audience. Teens might appreciate it, but parents, librarians, and teachers, who usually purchase the books, might refuse to purchase them. (Klaassen)

Susan Patron, after her experience with being the center of controversy, has this advice for writers and readers. "The use of controversial elements for shock value, or because of a perception that doing so will enhance sales, disrespects readers and shows a lack of integrity." (Reading Today) A direct and honest approach to addressing parents and community members concerns is the best way to resolve issues surrounding profanity in the content of your library collection. "As long as your work is honest, has integrity, and respects the reader, you should never let the fear of censorship enter your creative process. (Reading Today)

The Librarian's Role

Librarians and teachers, along with parents and community members, also struggle with maintaining their commitment to their teen readers' right to read, while also addressing how to determine what type of language is suitable for a young adult audience who, like adults, share different expectations about what language is appropriate for them.

The issue of the use of profanity in young adult books can be volatile and provocative, with parents struggling to ensure that the values they stress at home are reinforced by the books their children select from their public and school libraries. Authors also struggle to find a balance between what language is the best fit for their characters, in contrast to what language is appropriate to use to match the wide range of experiences, needs, and expectations of their readers.

Confronting these issues directly is necessary and beneficial for everyone involved in order to ensure that freedom to read is not infringed upon. Librarians should begin this process by being aware of all the viewpoints and discussions that characterize profanity so that they can empathize with the complaints that parents and community members feel and use this knowledge to lead conversations about this complex issue.

Librarians Take Action: Unlock the secrets of your character through a language activity.

Librarians should:

1. Become knowledgeable about the First Amendment and free speech and how it relates to young adults.

2. Recognize and share with parents and others the dilemma that young adult authors face over their choice to use or not use profanity or other controversial language in their books.

3. Strive to understand why books with profanity are challenged so frequently and understand what objections parents have to profane language in books.

4. Collaborate with classroom teachers to educate students, parents and the community about the place of language and dialogue in literature in order to provide them with a complete understanding of why certain text are chosen.

I believe that most challenges to books containing profanity take place in the classroom because even parents who are accepting and understanding of the place that language has in literature, even when that language is disagreeable, are nevertheless unsure about their children being exposed to language that they find unacceptable.

Because of the impact this conflict has on increasing the number of book challenges, collaborating with classroom teachers and working directly with parents is essential. Students will learn how and why characters in books use certain types of dialect and language, as well as how the words shape the character while propelling the story. Parents might not feel the need to challenge when they are aware of what their children are reading and how it is necessary to their education and will then feel more of an equal partnership with their teachers and the schools.

Character Study Activity

This character study can be used with students in classroom groups who are reading an assigned book, with parent book clubs or even as a parent activity with a selected short story that offers them a look at the experience that students have in the classroom.

The language that is used to represent the unique viewpoint of individual characters can sometimes be disturbing. Language is used to reflect a wide variety of issues that can include recklessness, confidence, anarchy, violence, excitement, and loneliness, among a multitude of other emotions that can sometimes, when used to accurately represent young adults, include profanity. Looking at the usage of these words through the context of the character's experiences, values, and choices can help to place those words into a venue that makes them no less disturbing, but can serve to teach us about the lives and experiences of others.

Discussion Questions

The following questions are asked of the participants in order for them to use their critical thinking skills to look through words that may seem offensive or shocking in order to explore how these words define and draw the character out. The participant will either be assigned or select a character or group of characters from the book or short story where their language is clearly integral to how they negotiate the world around them. The participants can utilize this activity as a long term assignment where they read a few chapters each week and use the form to track the character's development or a selection from a book or read a short story to complete the activity in one session.

1. Why does your character use profanity?

   Knowing why your character chooses to use profanity to express themselves gives you clues to determine what emotions, thoughts and ideas shape the character. Are they doing on purpose to draw attention away from their real problems and as a way to mask their real feelings or do they just enjoy it because it makes them feel confident and cool?

2. What emotions do you notice when they use profanity?

   How does the character behave when they are using a great deal of profanity? Do they seem excited and happy as if they are finally addressing their deepest feelings or do they appear to feel depressed and as though they are giving up when they speak?

3. When do they use profanity?

   What situations seem to cause the character to use profanity? Is it usually in the presence of certain other characters, or when they anticipate that certain events or actions are going to take place?

4. How do they feel after they have used profanity?

   Does the character seem to feel a sense of relief after they use profanity or do they feel like they have lost control or even embarrassed? Or do they maybe feel a sense of empowerment or strength?

5. What setting does the character primarily reside in and how does it affect their language and use of profanity? Does their language change depending on what setting they are in?

   Many authors make a great effort to reflect the unique dialogue and language that represents the place that their character resides in. Whether the character lives in the deep South or a remotely rural setting, the language they use paints a realistic picture of what influences and teaches the character to use certain language.

6. What time period does your character live in and how does it affect the language they use?

   The time period the character lives in has a great deal to do with how they use language to express themselves. For example, if they were African American they might not be able to express their true feelings through their direct use of words but may express their thoughts through internal dialogue in order to express frustration.

Character and Language Activity

Name: _____

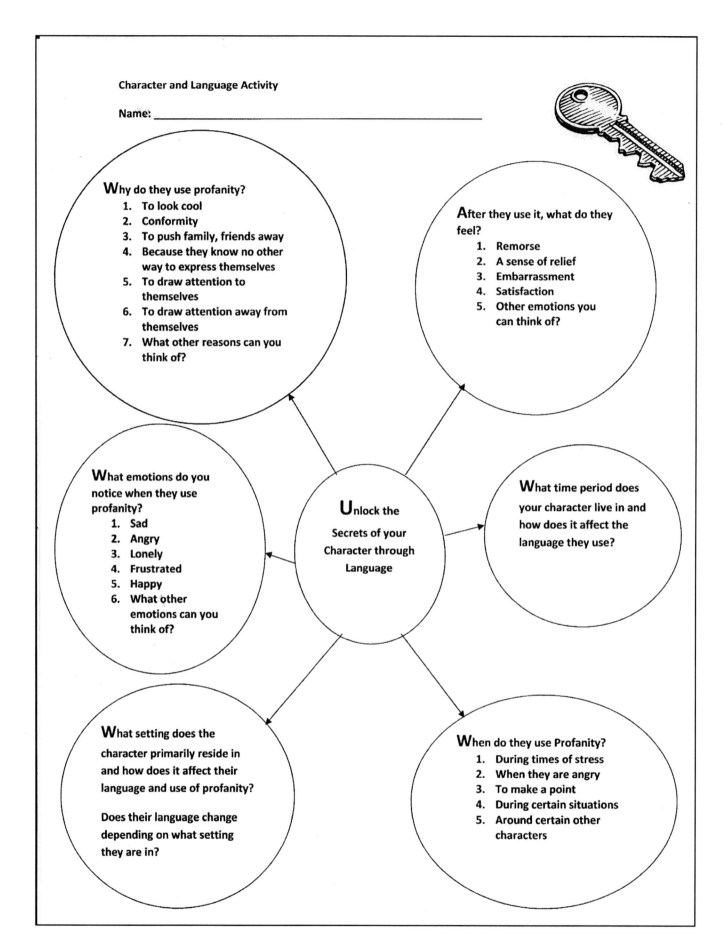

Why do they use profanity?
1. To look cool
2. Conformity
3. To push family, friends away
4. Because they know no other way to express themselves
5. To draw attention to themselves
6. To draw attention away from themselves
7. What other reasons can you think of?

After they use it, what do they feel?
1. Remorse
2. A sense of relief
3. Embarrassment
4. Satisfaction
5. Other emotions you can think of?

What emotions do you notice when they use profanity?
1. Sad
2. Angry
3. Lonely
4. Frustrated
5. Happy
6. What other emotions can you think of?

Unlock the Secrets of your Character through Language

What time period does your character live in and how does it affect the language they use?

What setting does the character primarily reside in and how does it affect their language and use of profanity?

Does their language change depending on what setting they are in?

When do they use Profanity?
1. During times of stress
2. When they are angry
3. To make a point
4. During certain situations
5. Around certain other characters

References

Aubrey, Allison. "Your Health: Why Kids Curse." NPR. 27 March 2008. *http://www.npr.org/templates/story/story.php?storyId=89127830*. 18 September 2011.

Bosman, Julie. "Books: With One Word, Children's Book Sets Off Uproar." *New York Times*. 18 February 2007. *http://www.nytimes.com/2007/02/18/books/18newb.html*. 05 August 2011.

"Coe Booth." The Brown Bookshelf. 22 February 2008. *http://thebrownbookshelf.com/2008/02/22/coe-booth/*. 02 September 2011.

Crutcher, Chris. *Whale Talk*. Harper Collins, 2000.

Foerstel Herbert. *Banned in the USA*. Greenwood, 2002.

Francis, Compton. "Teen Swearing: What Parents Can Do." Scott Counseling. *http://www.scottcounseling.com/wordpress/teen-swearing-what-parents-can-do/2009/11/03*. 12 December 2011.

Gonzalez, Michael. "Gary Takes a Closer Look at 'Tyrell'." *Post-Tribune*. 04 August 2011. *http://posttrib.suntimes.com/news/3742086-418/gary-takes-closer-look-at-tyrell.html*. 18 October 2011.

Jensen, Jennifer. "Writing Fiction: Middle Grade Novel Guidelines: Writing for the Tween Market." Suite 101. 30 November 2007. *http://jenniferjensen.suite101.com/middle-grade-novel-guidelines-a36689*. 07 March 2011.

Klaassen, Mike. "Deciding if one should use profanity in young adult fiction." *Helium*. 05 March 2005. *http://www.helium.com/items/197281-deciding-if-one-should-use-profanity-in-young-adult-fiction*. 05 September 2011.

Larbalestier, Justine. "The F-Bomb." Justine Larbalestier blog. 25 June 2007. *http://justinelarbalestier.com/blog/2007/06/25/the-f-bomb/*. 18 October 2011.

Linder, Doug. Bethel School District No. 403 Et Al. v. Fraser, a minor, et al. University of Missouri-Kansas City. 2012. *http://law.umkc*. 14 May 2012.

McGrath, Charles. "J. D. Salinger, Literary Recluse, Dies at 91" *New York Times*. 28 January 2010. *http://www.nytimes.com/2010/01/29/books/29salinger.html?pagewanted=all*. 12 March 2012.

"Reading Today: Newbery Winner Spawns Controversy." International Reading Association, June 2007. *http://www.reading.org/General/Publications/ReadingToday/RTY-0706-newbery.aspx*. 02 August 2011.

Salinger, J. D. *The Catcher in the Rye*. Little, Brown, 1951.

Sonnenblick, Jordan. "Should characters curse in young adult novels?" 07 September 2008. B & N Community Blog. *http://bookclubs.barnesandnoble.com/t5/Family-Room/Should-characters-curse-in-young-adult-novels/td-p/199057*. 10 June 2011.

Stancil, Clyde L. "Banned author coming here to defend his work." *Decatur Daily*. 22 September 2005. *http://legacy.decaturdaily.com/decaturdaily/news/050922/banned.shtml*. 18 August 2011.

Thomas, Dale, and Herbeck Tedford. *Freedom of Speech in the United States*. 6th ed. Strata Publishing, 2009. eBook. *http://www.stratapub.com/TedfordHerbeck6/contents.htm*.

Turner, Randy. "School Censorship Continues in 2010." The Turner Report. 25 April 2010. *http://rturner229.blogspot.com/2010/04/school-censorship-continues-in-2010.html.* 18 October 2011.

"*Whale Talk.*" Parents Against Bad Books in Schools (PABBIS). *http://www.sibbap.org/whaletalk.htm.* 9 November 2011.

CHAPTER 5
RELIGION AND THE OCCULT AND YOUNG ADULT LITERATURE

Spiritual growth is a process of learning and then letting go, of losing our religion and finding it again. In *Losing Your Religion, Finding Your Faith: Spirituality for Young Adults,* among Millennials:

- 40 percent say religion is very important in their lives, similar to 39 percent of Baby Boomers at the same ages.

- 41 percent report praying daily, like 42 percent of Gen Xers as young adults.

- 53 percent are "certain God exists," like 55 percent of Gen Xers were certain at the same ages.

Jill Carroll, a professor of religious studies at Rice University, has extensively studied religion and how it interacts with culture and social issues, including book censorship. She explains that religions that exist in the world are founded on the basis that what they believe is the absolute truth and that what they believe "is divinely revealed, recorded accurately in their sacred text, and delivered in its most complete form to their religion alone." This belief gives them the confidence to dictate what they believe are the proper values and morals for their children and others. (Carroll) When books are written that challenge their religious beliefs by promoting ideas that they don't feel are acceptable, historically these believers have sought to destroy the books or imprison the authors.

Viewpoint: Religious groups have the right to restrict or remove books from classrooms, schools, and public libraries.

Today, some religious groups and religious individuals actively use the media to personally petition for books that they feel reject religion to be restricted or removed from classrooms, schools, and public libraries. Christian groups, like the American Family Association and the Kjos Ministries, feel it is their duty to protect children from books that they believe promote anti-Christian ideals. The American Family Association supports such endeavors as stopping radio and television indecency. They are also outspoken critics of books that feature gay characters or storylines. In a statement on their human events news website, they state that they have "good news" because the book, *And Tango Makes Three,* a book about "homosexual parenting" has made the ALA's most banned book list. They are also outspoken critics of the American Library Association and describe the organization's commitment to advocate against censorship as false.

"This is false hysteria created by the American Library Association. It's all fantasy land. Just because you remove the book from the school library because you deem it inappropriate for children to read does not mean that the book is banned in America." Censorship by definition they believe, is only government imposed. The group says that the American Family Association does not support "censorship of ideas." What they do support is responsibility. (American Family Association)

Viewpoint: Books with occult themes are anti-Christian and should be banned.

The Kjos Ministries, as an advocate for Christianity, encourages parents and children to reject the *Harry Potter* books and movies because they promote an anti-Christian agenda and, instead, promote the occult. They blame the entertainment industry for introducing the books to children and describe their behavior as shameless. The group quotes this scripture to describe the role of the entertainment industry. "They hold fast to deceit, they refuse to return. . . . No, they have no shame at all; they do not even know how to blush." (Jeremiah 8:5,12) They also believe that the *Harry Potter* books reinforce this anti-Christian agenda because they "reinforce a global and occult perspective," where people are encouraged to reject Christianity and to instead embrace fantasy and wizardry. Schools, they believe, are the main perpetrators of this effort, by introducing a multicultural and environmental agenda and by promoting books like *Harry Potter*, that help to indoctrinate children away from Christian values, toward the occult. (Kjos Ministries)

Harry Potter has been the focus of book challenges since the books were first published with J.K. Rowling, the author of the Harry Potter series, having frequently been referred to as the author that most Americans would like to see banned. According to the American Library Association, there were more than three thousand attempts to have her books banned from American libraries between 2000 and 2005 because these groups believe that the books promote the occult and Satanism.

In 2000, to celebrate the release of *Harry Potter and the Goblet of Fire*, a public library in Jacksonville, Florida, sought to increase children's interest in reading by inviting local children to the library for a party where they read their favorite passages from the book and were awarded the "Hogwarts' Certificate of Accomplishment" if they finished reading the book. The Christian group, The Liberty Council of Orlando, complained and threatened to file a lawsuit against the library, with one parent stating that, "If they are going to pass out witchcraft certificates, they should also promote the Bible and pass out certificates of righteousness." The issue was settled before it could be taken to court when the library voluntarily stopped handing out certificates after several parents complained. The library director stated, "We decided that discretion was the better part of valor." (Associated Press)

The Harry Potter books have been banned in several countries. In July 2000, Birkenhead Primary School in Auckland, New Zealand, banned the Harry Potter novels being read aloud by teachers in class after parental complaints regarding the books' supposed occult content. However, the ban was lifted after a number of students and parents complained. (Middlebrook)

J.K Rowling speaks: "On censorship: The *Harry Potter* books have frequently been challenged in public schools and libraries. Some parents feel the books promote witchcraft and are anti-Christian. I really hate censorship. I find it objectionable. I personally think that they're very mistaken. I think these are very moral books and I think it's a very short-sighted thing. Short-sighted in the sense that if you try hard to portray goodness without showing that the reverse is evil and without showing how great it is to resist that . . . well, that's always been my feeling about literature.

"You find magic, witchcraft, and wizardry in all sorts of classic children's books. Where do you start? Are you going to start with *The Wizard of Oz*? These people are trying to protect children from their own imagination." (Baker)

The Witch of BlackBird Pond was also banned because it was allegedly anti-Christian and glorified the practice of witchcraft, as well as referred to evil spells and magic. The book is set in 1687 and is about a teenage girl from the Caribbean, who goes to live with her Puritan relatives in Massachusetts after her guardian dies, where she befriends a lonely Quaker woman who is accused of being a witch because she is different.

Book sales of the classic *Wuthering Heights* reached an all time high as a result of being mentioned in the Twilight series, endearing it to its large base of teenage readers. In fact, the latest copy of the *Wuthering Heights* has a redesigned gothic style cover similar to the Twilight series covers.

Supporters of the book, however, point out that the book is actually about tolerance, and shows how prejudice and hysteria can uproot a town, and in a large sense, a society. The book portrays religion in a positive light, as the Puritans are portrayed as sensible, solid people, who teach Kit what it means to be a part of a family as well as the value of community. (Grogan)

The Twilight series is the latest series of books to become censored due to complaints that the books promote anti-Christian values. (Hickerson) This debate surrounding the Twilight series has led to the series becoming the fifth most requested books to be banned by public libraries. (Mantyla) The Twilight series, written by Stephenie Meyer, who is of the Mormon faith, are about the adventures of Bella Swan, a girl who befriends vampires and werewolves. However, the book also promotes abstinence, with the main characters deciding to wait to begin a sexual relationship until they are married. This has led to a quandary with the Christian Coalition groups who want the book banned even though it is pro-abstinence, because it is also pro-vampires. The spokesperson for the Christian Coalition explains that vampires are definitely not good role models, and she blames Hollywood for promoting the controversial subject.

"We can let our voices be heard, and anytime you do that you have an effect, one way or another . . . These Twilight books are very disturbing books for family values. Teen marriage is not the standard, but the part that is more troubling is the vampire; it's just not normal for young people to idolize a vampire." (Mantyla)

Viewpoint: The First Amendment upholds the freedom of and for religion, and freedom from religion.

Courts have consistently held that for freedom of the press and speech to be meaningful, people must have the right to receive information: That is, to read, view, hear or access what they choose. In addition, the freedom of (and for) religion has been understood to include both the right of individuals to believe and practice their religion (the "free exercise" clause) and the right of individuals and the state to be free from religion (the "establishment" clause).

In most cases involving religion and libraries, these latter freedoms of, for, and from religion are not an issue. The constitutional principles at stake are usually freedom of expression and the corollary freedom to access the expression of others. For instance, most challenges to materials with religious content infringe on the rights of persons to access constitutionally protected speech rather than limit the practice of religion or one's beliefs.

The Librarian's Role

Librarians have a professional responsibility to be inclusive rather than exclusive in collection development. Libraries serve all members of their communities and within their budgetary constraints should address all information concerns of all members—including religious information needs. Collections should reflect those needs by providing access to diverse religious thought without becoming a proponent of any of them. Articles I and II of the Library Bill of Rights are clearly inclusive regarding audience ("all people of the community the library serves") and materials ("all points of view on current and historical issues").

With the strong emotions and intense debate that religion evokes, it might seem as though it is best to avoid offending anyone by simply not selecting any books that refer to religion or spirituality. This is a mistake because the exclusion of religious materials goes against our commitment as librarians to offer information on diverse subjects despite any potential controversy. It is also a violation of the Library Bill of Rights, which stresses a commitment to inclusivity, and states that materials should not be excluded because of their origin.

In addition, avoiding religious issues does not serve our teen library users, who are actively questioning and seeking answers everywhere. Religion and spirituality are often an essential part of their development that librarians should be prepared to address.

Two guidelines will help in the selection process:

1. Have a working definition of what religion or spirituality is. The ALA's Intellectual Freedom manual is a great resource for answering this question and others regarding this sensitive subject. The ALA states that, "religion" refers to all that touches on the ultimate—God, the gods, or one's understanding of the ultimate foundation of life. It includes formal organized systems of belief and practice and informal individual spiritualties. It also refers to adherents of older religions (i.e. the major world religions), newer religions (i.e. those designated cults by some), and no religion (i.e. agnostics and atheists).

2. The next step is to design a collection policy that meets the religious needs of the community that you serve, while also addressing the different viewpoints that represent a wide variety of ideas. For example, my first library job in a public library was in a predominantly Jewish community. The collection development librarian worked with the community and together, they put together a very extensive collection of contemporary and historical resources that became so expansive, many library users from surrounding towns utilized the resources. However, in addition to those materials, the librarian also made sure she collected a variety of other resources that reflected differing religious views and needs.

Librarians Take Action: Develop a diverse religion collection.

Providing a comprehensive collection of books that address the entirety of spiritual experiences has the effect of clearly demonstrating your library's commitment to inclusivity and diversity.

Christian Book Sources

Christian Books. *http://www.christianbook.com/teens*
> This is an online store that provides Christian clothes, bibles, music, and books. A teen webpage specifically focuses on resources that are designed for teens and tweens. It is a great place to explore Christian materials that are current and relevant today.

Faithful Reader. *http://faithfulreader.com*
> Faithful Reader is a Christian faith book review website that is offered by the same organization that provides the Teenreads.com website. The site offers book reviews, author interviews, and blogs where Christian books can be discussed and explored.

Black Expressions. *http://www.blackexpressions.com*
> This site concentrates on books and resources that are relevant to the African-American community. A section focuses on Christian living where books and other resources can be explored and purchased.

Popular Series and Titles for Teens

The Divine series by Jacquelin Thomas. Pocket Books.
> Divine Matthews-Hardison, a privileged teen, wears designer clothes and attends awards ceremonies and parties. Her mother is a famous singer, and her father is in serious trouble with the law. To shield Divine from the scandal, she is sent to live with her uncle, a Georgia pastor. In Georgia, Divine must share a room, do chores, and attend church regularly. At first she hates it, but as she becomes accustomed to the values of love and faith, she begins to appreciate her new life. The series focuses on Divine and her friends as she grows in her faith and learns to apply that faith to the issues, pressures, and difficult choices that accompany being a teenager.

Does My Head Look Big in This? by Randa Abdel-Fattah. Orchard.
> Amal is a typical teenager and devout Muslim. She loves to watch *Sex in the City*, shopping, and has a crush on a boy at school, who is not Muslim. Amal decides, without any pressure from her parents, that she wants to start wearing the hijab; the Muslim head covering. The reactions of her friends, family, teachers, and classmates make for an interesting, serious, and very funny story as Amal explores how to balance her commitment to her religion with her desire to live an everyday teenage girl's life. She realizes that, "Putting on the hijab isn't the end of the journey. It's just the beginning of it."

A Friend at Midnight by Caroline B. Cooney. Delacorte Books.
> Lily's parents have divorced and her eight-year-old brother has gone to live with their father. One night her brother calls with the news that their father has abandoned him. Lily is a Christian who strongly believes in the role that God plays in her life, however, her anger and bitterness towards her father tests her faith that makes her question just how strong her commitment is to her beliefs.

The God Box by Alex Sanchez. Simon and Schuster.

Paul wonders how he can choose between his spirituality and his sexuality, placing his prayers into a "god box," so that some of his feelings will go away. Then he meets an openly gay Christian who discusses a broader view of Biblical passages.

Godless by Pete Hautman. Simon and Schuster.

Jason, who is agnostic and leaning towards atheism, decides to start his own religion and invents a new god—his town's water tower. His idea takes off and grows beyond his control, and now, what was initially exciting, threatens to become dangerous to himself, his friends, and the townspeople.

Good Girlz series by ReShonda Tate Billingsley. Gallery Books.

Four teenage girls meet when they join a community service group run by a minister's wife, called the Good Girlz. Camille is a teen who is forced to join the group after a boyfriend involves her in a crime. Jasmine, Angel, and Alexis also join the group after mistakes they have made in their lives. Despite their reluctance to participate, the girls eventually become friends, learn how to depend on others, and how to take responsibility for themselves.

If the Witness Lied by Caroline Cooney. Delacorte Books.

Three orphaned teenage siblings, separated by the tragic supposed patricide of their father by their two-year-old brother, reunite a year later to save this same brother from the clutches of their evil aunt, who wants to sell them out on a tell-all television show. A Christian theme shapes their response to their dysfunctional family, as the siblings each question their relationship with God, as well as with one another, and inevitably resolve both issues simultaneously.

The Lost Books by Ted Dekker and J.S. Earls. Thomas Nelson.

Teens who love fantasy will enjoy this series that explores the adventures of teenagers who are selected for a special quest. Their world is threatened by evil and they are selected to fight against the Horde, disfigured evil beings who are led by a dark lord. The teens must successfully locate the seven lost Books of History that have power over the past, present, and future and are sought by the Dark One.

Miracle Girls by Anne Dayton and May Vanderbuilt. FaithWords.

Ana Domingues, a teenage girl moves to Half Moon Bay, California, after her father opens a law practice there. The first book deals with many teenage issues, including popularity, boys, friends, and clothes, within the context of the main character's commitment to her Christian faith. Other books in the series focus on Ana's friends and their continued friendship.

Perry Skky Jr. series by Stephanie Perry Moore. Dafina.

Perry Skky, popular student, football player, and devout Christian, tackles the issues and decisions that adolescent boys face at school, with their friends, and on the football field. Through each book Perry confronts tough choices and sometimes makes mistakes that invoke consequences. His commitment to his faith helps him to try his best to make positive decisions that support his values and ideals.

Sam I Am by Ilene Cooper. Scholastic.

Twelve-year-old Sam Goodman's father is Jewish and his mother is Christian. Sam is accustomed to the difficulty that surrounds the holidays, especially Christmas, as his parents try unsuccessfully to compromise on the proper way to celebrate. Finally, on this Christmas, when everything that could go wrong does, his family has to openly express their feelings and find a way to come together.

Ten Things I Hate About Me by Randa Abdel-Fattah. Orchard.

Jamilah Towfeek, or "Jamie" as she is known at school, hides her Lebanese-Muslim background from her classmates by dying her hair blonde, wearing blue contacts, and by remaining silent when others make racist jokes and remarks. Her lies begin to overwhelm her and eventually she has to make a decision about who she is and her place in her community as a Muslim.

The Weight of the Sky by Lisa Ann Sandell. Viking.

Sarah Green is one of two Jewish students at her small Pennsylvania high school. Sarah is somewhat of a band nerd and is teased by the popular crowd. She is also overwhelmed by the impact that being Jewish has on her every day existence. When she gets a chance to go to Israel for the summer, she jumps at the chance to assert her independence, reinvent herself in a new place, and live and work on a kibbutz.

What Momma Left Me by Renee Watson. Bloomsbury.

After her mother's death at the hands of her abusive father, Serenity Evans and her younger brother are sent to live with grandfather, who is a minister, and grandmother, a church volunteer. Serenity has many worries that include coming to terms with what happened to her parents, a crush on boy, her brother's poor choices, and the various temptations that teens face on a daily basis. With the support of her grandparents and her growing appreciation for the role that faith plays in her life, she begins to slowly heal and embrace the support of her family and church as she begins a new life. Throughout the book each chapter contains poems and quotes from the Bible that help her along the way.

Library Booklists of Spiritual Fiction

Many libraries compile booklists that feature religious or spiritual titles that are popular with young adults. The following are spiritual booklists that will be helpful for book selection.

1. Ocean County Public Library, Ocean County, NJ: "Journeys: Teens and Spirituality," *http://the-oceancountylibrary.org/teens/booklists/Journeys%20booklist.pdf*

2. Hennepin County Public Library, Minnetonka, MN: "Christian Reads," *http://www.hclib.org/teens/booklistaction.cfm?list_num=90*

3. Carnegie Library, Pittsburgh, PA: "Believers and Doubters: Teen Fiction about Religion," *http://www.clpgh.org/teens/books/showbooklist.cfm?catid=6&list=spirituality* and "Christian Fiction," *http://www.clpgh.org/teens/books/showbooklist.cfm?catid=6&list=christian_fiction*

4. Louisville Free Public Library, KY: "Faith Fillers: Great Christian Fiction," *http://www.lfpl.org/teen/booklist-faithfillers.htm*

5. Corpus Christi Public Libraries, TX: "Religion," *http://librarybooklists.org/fiction/ya/yadiverse.htm#rel*

6. Brigham Young University, Provo, UT: Mormon Literature & Creative Arts: "Mormon Young Adult Fiction," *http://mormonlit.byu.edu/lit_search_results.php?fields[0]=w_subgenres&compares[0]=LIKE&values[0]=Young%20Adult%20Fiction*

7. Monroe County Library, IN: "Inspirational Fiction for Teens," *http://www.monroe.lib.in.us/fiction/xian_ya.html*

8. Edmonton Public Library, Canada: "Spiritual Questioning for Teens," *http://richmondhill.bibliocommons.com/list/show/70924580_eplpicks_teen/71560541_epl_picks_-_teen_-_spiritual_questioning*

9. Temple Israel Libraries & Media Center, IL: Contemporary Jewish Fiction for Teens, *http://www.jewishlibraries.org/ajlweb/resources/bib_bank/contemporary_fiction_for_teens.pdf*

10. Berkeley Public Library, CA: "Ineffable Fiction for Teens About Religion, God & Spirituality," *http://www.berkeleypubliclibrary.org/teens/religion.php*

References

Adams, Stephen. "Stephenie Meyer's vampire pushes *Wuthering Heights* to top of Waterstone's classics chart." *The Guardian*. 28 August 2009.

American Family Association. "Does AFA Support Censorship?" *http://www.afa.net/FAQ.aspx?id=2147483678*. 14 May 2012.

American Library Association. "Religion in American Libraries." *Intellectual Freedom Manual 8th Ed.* *http://www.ifmanual.org/religionqa*. 15 December 2011.

Baker, Jeff. "Harry Potter: Need she say more? J.K. Rowling talks about her wildly popular books," *The Oregonian*. October 22, 2000. *http://www.accio-quote.org/articles/2000/1000-oregonian-baker.htm*. 14 May 2012.

Carroll, Jill. "Religion & Banned Books Week." *Houston Chronicle*. *http://blog.chron.com/talkingtolerance/2010/09/religion-banned-books-week*. 17 September 2010.

Grogan, David. "Connecticut Residents Seek to Ban Two Newbery Medal Winners from School." American Booksellers. 29 July 2002. *http://news.bookweb.org/news/connecticut-residents-seek-ban-two-newbery-medal-winners-school*. 10 March 2011.

Hickerson, Mike. "Survey Finds People Want '*Twilight*' Books Banned." Slice of Scifi. 15 April 2010. *http://www.sliceofscifi.com/2010/04/15/survey-finds-people-want-twilight-books-banned/*. 06 January 2011.

Kjos Ministries. "It's Only Fantasy and Other Deceptions" 2003. *http://www.crossroad.to/articles2/2003/phoenix.htm*. 14 May 2012.

"Library's 'Witchcraft' Certificate Endorsed Religion, Group Says." *Associated Press*. 13 September 2000. *http://www.freedomforum.org/templates/document.asp?documentID=3740*. 18 August 2011.

Mantyla, Ken. "Christian Coalition Wants *Twilight* Books Banned." Right Wing Watch. 07 July 2010. *http://www.rightwingwatch.org/archive/201007*. 23 August 2011.

Middlebrook, Libby. "It's wizard: Harry Potter's spells can be spoken in class." *New Zealand Herald*. 03 August 2000. *http://www.nzherald.co.nz/nz/news/article.cfm?c_id=1&objectid=146558*. 14 May 2012

"Religion Among the Millennials." *http://pewforum.org/Age/Religion-Among-the-Millennials.aspx#ixzz1dKmCnQnG*. 15 December 2011.

Chapter 6
Censorship in the Eye of the Beholder

Our definition of censorship is directly shaped by the essence of what makes us who we are: Our values, our historical perspectives, culture, age, life experiences, and what we believe our community expects from us. Our individuality and differing views can make finding common ground difficult, if not impossible. Our established laws provide a way for us to come together. Our laws, set forth in our constitution, celebrate our individuality, while offering us a clear and established path to follow that reminds us of our shared commitment to our First Amendment rights and intellectual freedom. The First Amendment, which protects and ensures that everyone equally has the right to express themselves freely in our society, provides a solid foundation that can help to establish an understanding of the harmful effects that the practice of censorship has on those rights. A librarian's best defense against censorship is knowledge of the laws that protect us all and how those laws impact libraries.

The First Amendment

Congress shall make no law respecting an establishment of religion, or prohibiting the free exercise thereof; or abridging the freedom of speech, or of the press; or the right of the people peaceably to assemble, and to petition the Government for a redress of grievances. (The First Amendment)

The First Amendment and Libraries

The First Amendment establishes the right for the public to have access to discussion, debate, and free and open dissemination of information and ideas.

1. The First Amendment establishes the right to distribute and receive information.

2. The right of free speech and the freedom of the press are extended to public and school libraries.

3. School boards and other officials may remove books from libraries based on educational suitability, but they cannot do so based on their personal opinions or because they believe that certain ideas or content is inappropriate or controversial.

The following resources can help to generate ideas for lesson plans and activities, provide information that can assist you in planning workshops for your colleagues or local organizations, and help you to educate your teen library users about how the First Amendment is relevant to them.

- First Amendment Center (*http://www.firstamendmentcenter.org/*) has information, videos, and lesson plans, as well as many other resources regarding the First Amendment that are great to use with both students and adults.

- First Amendment for Schools (*http://www.firstamendmentschools.org/*) provides educational resources for the First Amendment. Included are lesson plans and activities that highlight the five freedoms that the First Amendment protects: Freedom of religion, speech, press, assembly, and petition.

- Libraries and the First Amendment (*http://www.freedominlibraries.org/Children.aspx*) ties together the link between the First Amendment and libraries so that teens understand why the freedom to read is so important. This website offers questions that you can use to stimulate questions about what rights are protected under the First Amendment.

The First Amendment and School Libraries: Pico vs. Island Trees

The Pico case, in particular, is important to libraries because it reaffirms why we are committed to the freedom of everyone to read. Pico vs. Island Trees was a landmark case that established a clear relationship between our First Amendment rights and the right to read without being censored, while setting precedence that helped refute the legality of book censorship throughout the United States. It also set precedence for the idea that children, as well as adults, have the right to read freely. This frequently cited and famous case was initiated by teenagers, who were not afraid to speak out about the books that they believed were important to them and their fellow students; an important fact that should always be remembered. Their participation speaks to the influence of censorship in the lives of everyday citizens.

Recently, the First Amendment Center interviewed Russel Rieger, one of the teenagers who challenged the removal of the books in 1976, about his memories regarding his participation in one of the most famous Supreme Court cases in the history of the United States. Rieger states that he first learned about the removal of the books from one of his teachers while at a school assembly. It upset him because he had read and enjoyed several of the books on the banned list, including *Slaughterhouse-Five.* "I loved Kurt Vonnegut and his work," Rieger said. He explains that although he was shocked at their decision to remove the books from the school library, he did not think the school board members were bad people, only that they were very conservative. At the time, Rieger was only fifteen years old when he and his fellow classmates—Steven Pico, Jacqueline Gold, Glenn Yarris, and junior high school student, Paul Sochinski—filed the lawsuit. Rieger states that the case shaped him personally because it showed him that in this country there is a process in which an individual can make a difference and protest against injustice and win. (Hudson)

In 1975, the members of the school board in Island Trees, New York, attended an educational conference that was sponsored by the Parents of New York United, a politically conservative group concerned about education legislation. After the school board attended the conference, they determined that ten books in the high school library and junior high school library were inappropriate for young adults and subsequently removed them from the school library and delivered them to the board office. The books were:

- *Slaughterhouse-Five* by Kurt Vonnegut

- *The Fixer* by Bernard Malamud

- *The Naked Ape* by Desmond Morris

- *Down These Mean Streets* by Piri Thomas

- *Best Short Stories of Negro Writers* edited by Langston Hughes

- *Go Ask Alice* by Anonymous

- *Laughing Boy* by Oliver LaFarge

- *Black Boy* by Richard Wright

- *A Hero Ain't Nothing But a Sandwich* by Alice Childress

- *Soul on Ice* by Eldridge Cleaver

The school board released a press release about their decision stating that the books were "anti-American, anti-Christian, anti-Semitic, and just plain filthy," and concluded, "It is our duty, our moral obligation, to protect the children in our schools from this moral danger as surely as from physical and medical dangers." (Hudson)

The school board then appointed a book review committee that consisted of four parents and four school district employees to read the books and give an opinion. The committee recommended retaining five of the books and removing two of them. One book they said should require parent approval and the others they could not decide upon. The school board rejected the recommendations and removed the books causing a group consisting of students and parents to file a law suit against the school board. (Hudson) Their filing said this, "The school board ordered the removal of the books from school libraries and proscribed their use in the curriculum, because particular passages in the books offended their social, political, and moral tastes, and not because the books, taken as a whole, were lacking in educational value."

A lawsuit was filed in 1977 in New York state. However, the case was moved to federal court, in part because of the constitutional issues involved. In 1979, a federal district court ruled in favor of the school district and dismissed the lawsuit.

In 1978, the Second U.S. Circuit Court of Appeals reversed that ruling, finding that, "The students should have been given the opportunity to prove that the school board's justifications for removing the books were 'simply pretexts for the suppression of free speech.'"

In 1982, the Supreme Court ruled that school officials are limited in their ability to remove books from the school library just because they don't like the material. The material has to be shown that it lacks educational value. Justice William Brennan's written opinion stated that: "We hold that local school boards may not remove books from school library shelves simply because they dislike the ideas contained in those books and seek by their removal to 'prescribe what shall be orthodox in politics, nationalism, religion, or other matters of public opinion.'" Justice Brennan also said, "The freedom of speech was designed to allow Americans to discuss, debate, and share information and ideas. Authors could not share information in books if people were not allowed to read them. That means the freedom of speech also includes the right to receive information and ideas. Students must always remain free to inquire, to study and to evaluate, to gain new maturity and understanding." (Education for Freedom Lesson 5)

Intellectual Freedom

Everyone has the right to freedom of opinion and expression; this right includes freedom to hold opinions without interference and to seek, receive and impart information and ideas through any media and regardless of frontiers. (The Universal Declaration of Human Rights)

Intellectual Freedom and Libraries

Intellectual freedom is the right to freedom of thought and of expression of thought. The concept of intellectual freedom involves protecting the rights of all individuals to pursue the types of information they want and to read anything that interests them. Attempts by a member of the community to remove materials from a library collection or to restrict access to them may be the most common challenges to intellectual freedom that a small library will face. Libraries embrace the concept of intellectual freedom as the foundation by which we ensure that all library users—whether they are adults, children, or teens—have the right to pursue any information that interests them, unrestricted. (The International Federation of Library Associations and Institutions)

E-Books and e-readers are becoming the newest frontier for the debate of censorship and the First Amendment. Apple's decision to censor a new graphic novel version of *Ulysses* on the iPad because it contains nudity has drawn fire from authors and iPad users alike. Amazon has reportedly removed several books that have controversial wording after receiving complaints from users about the content of objectionable books in their database.

The Universal Declaration of Human Rights and the History of Intellectual Freedom

After the end of World War II, an international coalition of several countries came together to make sure the atrocities of the Holocaust never occurred again. To ensure the continued commitment of all countries involved, they adopted the Universal Declaration of Human Rights on December 10, 1948. This declaration consisted of nineteen rights or articles that all citizens of the world should be guaranteed. Intellectual freedom was the nineteenth human right that was adopted. Since that time, most countries of the world, including those in Eastern and Central Europe, have wholeheartedly adopted all of the articles of the Universal Declaration of Human Rights. The capacity and right to access information has become a key concept of those rights with the nineteenth amendment becoming one of the most universal of all the human rights.

Librarians Take Action: Introduce the Universal Rights activity.

Read about how the United States adopted our intellectual freedom policy by exploring how the idea of intellectual freedom came about at The Universal Declaration of Human Rights Organization website. This organization provides information about each of the thirty human rights articles, including number 19, Intellectual Freedom. In this activity, teens can explore each human right and read about the founders.

Students Explore the Site

In groups of two, the students explore the site and visit the links at The Universal Declaration of Human Rights Organization website: *http://www.un.org/en/documents/udhr.*

- *History*: Read through the history and write down at least six facts.

- *Human Rights Law*: Read through the page and write down at least six facts.

- *Drafters*: Read the biography of Eleanor Roosevelt at *http://www.udhr.org/history/Biographies/bioer.htm* and write at least five facts.

- *Resources*: Students explore the resources and write a paragraph about what they found.

Concluding Activity

Eleanor Roosevelt was one of the most prominent Americans to sign the Universal Declaration of Human Rights. Search YouTube, School Tube, and Teacher Tube for videos of Eleanor Roosevelt speaking about the Declaration and addressing the United Nations. Watch videos of her speaking about her feelings towards being involved in the Declaration to personalize the historical event for teens who love to see a visual representation of the information they learn about.

Librarians Take Action: Introduce the intellectual freedom activity.

This activity will help teens understand what intellectual freedom is. Students understand a concept more when they can read about it themselves and explore it.

1. Define Intellectual Freedom.
    - "Intellectual Freedom and Censorship Q & A" by the American Library Association (*http://www.ala.org/Template.cfm?Section=basics&Template=/ContentManagement/ContentDisplay.cfm&ContentID=60610*) gives a great overview of intellectual freedom by offering questions and answers that are direct, clear, easy-to-read and understand.

    - "Article 19: Intellectual Freedom" (*http://www.article19.org/pages/en/what-we-do.html*), "The right to freedom of expression plays a critical role in tackling the underlying causes of poverty and is the most potent force for the strengthening of peace and the pre-emption of conflict. Once freedom of expression is lost, all other freedoms fall." This website is dedicated towards the exploration and education about Article 19 and intellectual freedom. The site explores, investigates, and advocates for people around the world who experience censorship, defamation, or discrimination for freely expressing themselves. This resource gives teens a sense of the international need for intellectual freedom.

    - *The First Freedom, VOYA* magazine (*http://www.voya.com*): Cathi MacRae, librarian, former editor of *VOYA* magazine, and book reviewer for the past twenty years, has a new column in *VOYA* magazine that teaches librarians and teenagers about intellectual freedom, how it applies to them, and how they can learn to advocate for themselves and others. Discussing the issues that are raised in this column is a great way to have an ongoing and current conversation about intellectual freedom.

- "Intellectual Freedom for Youth: Social Technology and Social Network" (*http://www.pbs.org/ teachers/librarymedia/aasl/lamb.pdf*) can assist in educating teenagers about how intellectual freedom is relevant to their lives in ways they may not expect. Anne Lamb, school librarian and information specialist, has provided information that enables teens and librarians to understand the complicated relationship between their love of social networks and intellectual freedom. The research she has provided helps librarians assist teens with social networks. It addresses the positive values of this media, contrary to the sense of danger and negativity that adults sometimes feel about this venue.

2. Read about how other countries define intellectual freedom. The International Federation of Library Associations and Institutions (IFLA) (*http://www.ifla.org/*) is the international voice of libraries and librarians everywhere. To teach teens about evaluating and knowing something about the websites that they are using, they should read through the "About Us" part of the website, so they have an idea of what IFLA is. Then the students can take a look at the countries listed and read a little about how other countries have adopted intellectual freedom policies.

The Freedom to Read Statement

The freedom to read was adopted in 1953 by the Westchester Conference of the American Library Association and the American Book Publishers Council. The freedom to read is guaranteed by the Constitution. "Those with faith in free people will stand firm on these constitutional guarantees of essential rights and will exercise the responsibilities that accompany these rights." (ALA)

1. *It is in the public interest for publishers and librarians to make available the widest diversity of views and expressions, including those that are unorthodox, unpopular, or considered dangerous by the majority.*

    Creative thought is by definition new, and what is new is different. The bearer of every new thought is a rebel until that idea is refined and tested. Totalitarian systems attempt to maintain themselves in power by the ruthless suppression of any concept that challenges the established orthodoxy. The power of a democratic system to adapt to change is vastly strengthened by the freedom of its citizens to choose widely from among conflicting opinions offered freely to them. To stifle every nonconformist idea at birth would mark the end of the democratic process. Furthermore, only through the constant activity of weighing and selecting can the democratic mind attain the strength demanded by times like these. We need to know, not only what we believe, but why we believe it.

2. *Publishers, librarians, and booksellers do not need to endorse every idea or presentation they make available. It would conflict with the public interest for them to establish their own political, moral, or aesthetic views as a standard for determining what should be published or circulated.*

    Publishers and librarians serve the educational process by making available knowledge and ideas required for the growth of the mind and the increase of learning. The people should have the freedom to read and consider a broader range of ideas than those that may be held by any single librarian or publisher or government or church. It is wrong that what one can read should be confined to what another thinks proper.

3. *It is contrary to the public interest for publishers or librarians to bar access to writings on the basis of the personal history or political affiliations of the author.*

    No art or literature can flourish if it is to be measured by the political views or private lives of its creators. No society of free people can flourish that draws up lists of writers to whom it will not listen, whatever they may have to say.

4. *There is no place in our society for efforts to coerce the taste of others, to confine adults to the reading matter deemed suitable for adolescents, or to inhibit the efforts of writers to achieve artistic expression.*

    To some, much of modern expression is shocking. But is not much of life itself shocking? We cut off literature at the source if we prevent writers from dealing with the stuff of life. Parents and teachers have a responsibility to prepare the young to meet the diversity of experiences in life to which they will be exposed, as they have a responsibility to help them learn to think critically for themselves. These are affirmative responsibilities, not to be discharged simply by preventing them from reading works for which they are not yet prepared. In these matters, values differ and values cannot be legislated, nor can machinery be devised that will suit the demands of one group without limiting the freedom of others.

5. *It is not in the public interest to force a reader to accept the prejudgment of a label characterizing any expression or its author as subversive or dangerous.*

    The idea of labeling presupposes the existence of individuals or groups with wisdom to determine by authority what is good or bad for others. It presupposes that individuals must be directed in making up their minds about the ideas they examine. But Americans do not need others to do their thinking for them.

6. *It is the responsibility of publishers and librarians, as guardians of the people's freedom to read, to contest encroachments upon that freedom by individuals or groups seeking to impose their own standards or tastes upon the community at large; and by the government whenever it seeks to reduce or deny public access to public information.*

    It is inevitable in the give and take of the democratic process that the political, the moral, or the aesthetic concepts of an individual or group will occasionally collide with those of another individual or group. In a free society, individuals are free to determine for themselves what they wish to read, and each group is free to determine what it will recommend to its freely associated members. But no group has the right to take the law into its own hands, and to impose its own concept of politics or morality upon other members of a democratic society. Freedom is no freedom if it is accorded only to the accepted and the inoffensive. Further, democratic societies are more safe, free, and creative when the free flow of public information is not restricted by governmental prerogative or self-censorship.

7. *It is the responsibility of publishers and librarians to give full meaning to the freedom to read by providing books that enrich the quality and diversity of thought and expression. By the exercise of this affirmative responsibility, they can demonstrate that the answer to a "bad" book is a good one, the answer to a "bad" idea is a good one.*

   The freedom to read is of little consequence when the reader cannot obtain matter fit for that reader's purpose. What is needed is not only the absence of restraint, but the positive provision of opportunity for the people to read the best that has been thought and said. Books are the major channel by which the intellectual inheritance is handed down, and the principal means of its testing and growth. The defense of the freedom to read requires of all publishers and librarians the utmost of their faculties, and deserves of all Americans the fullest of their support.

We state these propositions neither lightly nor as easy generalizations. We here stake out a lofty claim for the value of the written word. We do so because we believe that it is possessed of enormous variety and usefulness, worthy of cherishing and keeping free. We realize that the application of these propositions may mean the dissemination of ideas and manners of expression that are repugnant to many persons. We do not state these propositions in the comfortable belief that what people read is unimportant. We believe rather that what people read is deeply important; that ideas can be dangerous; but that the suppression of ideas is fatal to a democratic society. Freedom itself is a dangerous way of life, but it is ours.

Library Bill of Rights

The Library Bill of Rights enables the concepts of intellectual freedom to be put into a set of principles that librarians can follow in order to ensure that their library users' First Amendment rights are protected. The Bill of Rights was originally written by Forest Spaulding in 1938 and has been revised many times since then. When it was adopted, it was introduced by this statement, "Today indications in many parts of the world point to growing intolerance, suppression of free speech, and censorship affecting the rights of minorities and individuals."

The Library Bill of Rights is a set of principles that were developed based on the library's mission to support and provide for the information needs of all people no matter what their age, origin, background, or views. The American Library Association affirms that all libraries are forums for information and ideas, and that the following basic policies should guide their services.

I. Books and other library resources should be provided for the interest, information, and enlightenment of all people of the community the library serves. Materials should not be excluded because of the origin, background, or views of those contributing to their creation.

II. Libraries should provide materials and information presenting all points of view on current and historical issues. Materials should not be proscribed or removed because of partisan or doctrinal disapproval.

III. Libraries should challenge censorship in the fulfillment of their responsibility to provide information and enlightenment.

IV. Libraries should cooperate with all persons and groups concerned with resisting abridgment of free expression and free access to ideas.

V.   A person's right to use a library should not be denied or abridged because of origin, age, background, or views.

VI.   Libraries that make exhibit spaces and meeting rooms available to the public they serve should make such facilities available on an equitable basis, regardless of the beliefs or affiliations of individuals or groups requesting their use.

Adopted June 19, 1939, by the ALA Council; amended October 14, 1944; June 18, 1948; February 2, 1961; June 27, 1967; January 23, 1980; inclusion of "age" reaffirmed January 23, 1996.

Librarians Take Action: Introduce the Pico vs. Island Trees activity.

The following activity is designed to use with teenagers. Teens will appreciate the fact that teens like themselves were crucial in advocating for their rights, and it will also help them to understand how the case relates to their First Amendment rights. This activity can be done in schools, or as a part of an educational seminar offered by a public library.

1.   To learn about the 1970s, and the time the case took place in, the teens research the:

    • Culture

    • Lifestyle

    • Issues of the day

    • Clothing

    • Popular music of the day

    Learning about the time period puts the information they are researching into some perspective and enables the teenagers to understand the lifestyle and experiences of the teens who were affected by the case.

2.   The teenagers read about the case itself to understand the facts of the case and what happened to be prepared to answer questions. Use the following summary.

    • *Pico vs. Island Trees Case Summary for Students*

    In 1975, the members of the school board in Island Trees, New York, attended an educational conference that was sponsored by the Parents of New York United, which was a politically conservative group that was concerned about education legislation.

    After the school board attended the conference, they determined that ten books in the high school library and one in the junior high school library were inappropriate for young adults and removed them from the school libraries. They stated that the books were, "anti-American, anti-Christian, anti-Semitic, and just plain filthy," and concluded that, "It is our duty, our moral obligation, to protect the children in our schools from this moral danger as surely as from physical and medical dangers." Students who learned of the book removal sued to have the books returned. In 1983, the case went to the Supreme Court where the final decision was made.

3. For more information about the Pico Case, the teens can read a longer summary of the case by using these resources:

    -   *U.S Supreme Court Media: Oyez, Chicago-Kent College of Law* (*http://www.oyez.org/*) is a great resource to research prominent cases. For the Pico case and other notable cases, it offers an overview of the questions that go along with the case, the arguments, and the conclusions, and you can sort the Supreme Court decisions by ideology, seniority, and by vote.

    -   *Findlaw* (*http://www.findlaw.com*) offers detailed information about court cases: the facts, the conclusions, and other important and relevant facts of court decisions.

    -   *First Amendment Schools* (*http://www.firstamendmentschools.org*) is dedicated towards helping teens understand their First Amendment rights and offers detailed accounts of relevant court cases like Pico that also include inquiry questions, lesson plans, and Supreme Court opinions.

4. Lead a discussion with the following questions:

    -   The board wanted to protect the students from books that were inappropriate. Is that censorship or not?

    -   What were the books that were challenged?

    -   Why did the students decide to protest the books removal?

    -   Did the students win the first case in federal court?

    -   Did the court find that the students' First Amendment rights were violated?

    -   In 1982, what was the court's opinion regarding the case?

    -   In 1983, what was the Supreme Court's ruling?

    -   Justice William Brennan wrote the opinion about the case. What did he say?

5. Assignment: Read the opinion of both cases and write a persuasive essay choosing one side or the other based on the issues stated in the opinions and the research completed on the case.

    -   What does each side say about the responsibility and rights of the school board?

    -   Is it the students' right to have access to books at the school library when they can just as easily access them through bookstores and the public library?

    -   Were the students' free speech rights violated?

    -   What is the purpose of the school library?

Justice William Brennan

"Does the First Amendment impose limitations upon [a local school board] to remove books from the Island Trees High School and Junior High? . . . As the case is presented to us, it does not involve textbooks, or indeed any books that Island Tree students would be required to read . . . the only books at issue in this case are library books, books that by their nature are optional rather than required reading.

"The First Amendment rights of students may be directly and sharply implicated by the removal of books from the shelves of a school library. Our precedents have focused 'not only on the role of the First Amendment in fostering individual self-expression but also in its role in affording the public access to discussion, debate, and the dissemination of information and ideas.' . . . In keeping with this principle, we have held that in a variety of contexts 'the Constitution protects the right to receive information and ideas.'

"In sum, just as access to ideas makes it possible for citizens generally to exercise their rights of free speech and press in a meaningful manner, such access prepares students for active and effective participation in the pluralistic, often contentious society in which they will soon be adult members. Of course, all First Amendment rights accorded to students must be construed 'in light of the special characteristics of the school environment.' . . . But the special characteristics of the school library make that environment appropriate for the recognition of the First Amendment rights of students. . . . Students must always remain free to inquire, to study and to evaluate, to gain new maturity, and understanding. The school library is the principal locus of such freedom. . . . A student can literally explore the unknown, and discover areas of interest and thought not covered by the prescribed curriculum. In brief, we hold that local school boards may not remove books from school library shelves simply because they dislike the ideas contained in those books and seek by their removal to 'prescribe what shall be orthodox in politics, nationalism, religion, or other matters of opinion.'" (First Amendment Schools)

Connect Yesterday to Today

The success of the Pico case allowed for other cases of censorship to be successfully challenged in court. The ALA website is a great place to locate these current and relevant cases that offer support in the fight against censorship. Teenagers or other library users can research these cases to find out more information about them as an educational activity.

A Few Notable Cases Directly Influenced by Pico vs. Island Tree

Annie on My Mind: 1995, the Olathe, Kansas, school board, was sued in federal court after students and parents filed a lawsuit over the removal of the book *Annie on My Mind*, which is about the romantic relationship between two teenage girls, from junior and senior high school libraries. The school board said that the book was educationally unsuitable, but the court found that the book was removed because the school board disagreed with its ideas. The court also found that the school board violated its own materials selection and reconsideration policies. *Annie on My Mind* was returned to school library shelves. (Censorship Free Libraries)

Heather Has Two Mommies: In 1999, the books *Heather Has Two Mommies* and *Daddy's Roommate* were challenged by the members of a church in Wichita Falls. The church members objected to the fact that the books, which depicted the lives of gay families, were placed in the children's section of the public

Chief Justice Warren E. Burger

"The states and local elected school boards should have the responsibility for determining the educational policy of the public schools. . . . School boards are uniquely local and democratic institutions. [They] have only one responsibility: the education of the youth of our country. Apart from health, no subject is closer to the hearts of parents than their children's education in those years. For these reasons, the governance of elementary and secondary education traditionally has been placed in the hands of a local board, responsible locally to the parents and citizens of the school district.

"It is fair to say that no single agency of government at any level is closer to the people whom it serves than the typical school board. . . . Although I would leave this educational decision to the duly constituted school board, I certainly would not require a school board to promote ideas and values repugnant to a democratic society or to teach such values to children.

"In different contexts and in different times, the destruction of written materials has been the symbol of despotism and intolerance. But the removal of nine vulgar or racist books from a high school library by a concerned local school board does not raise this specter. . . . Students are not denied books by their removal from a school library. The books may be borrowed from a public library, read at a university library, purchased at a bookstore, or loaned by a friend. . . . Indeed, following the removal from the school library of the books at issue in this case, the local public library put all nine on display for public inspection. Their contents were fully accessible to any inquisitive students.

"In this case, the students' rights of free speech and expression were not infringed and no ideas were suppressed. . . . If the school can set curriculum, select teachers, and determine what books to purchase for the school library, it surely can decide which books to discontinue or remove from the school library, so long as it does not also interfere with the right of students to read the material and to discuss it. It is not the function of the courts to make the decisions that have been properly relegated to the elected members of the school boards. It is the school board that must determine educational suitability, and it does so in this case." (First Amendment Schools)

library. The city council voted that if three hundred library card members signed a petition agreeing to the books restriction that the books would be taken out of the children's section of the library and placed on a locked shelf in the adult section. The church group succeeded in collecting the signatures and the book was removed and placed in the adult section. However, other community members disagreed with this restriction and filed a federal lawsuit, which they won. The books were ordered to be placed back in the children's section. (Censored Books)

Harry Potter: In Cedarville, Arkansas, in 2002, the *Harry Potter* books were put on a restricted borrowing list after one parent objected to the implication that "there are 'good witches' and 'good magic,'" and because the *Harry Potter* books taught that "parents/teachers/rules are stupid and something to be ignored." The parents of a fourth grade student disagreed with the restriction and filed a federal lawsuit on their daughter's behalf.

The parents and student, who objected to the restriction, won the case, with the judge stating that the First Amendment rights of the students were violated by restricting the books. The judge said, ". . . regardless of the personal distaste with which these individuals regard 'witchcraft,' it is not properly within their power and authority as members of the defendant's school board to prevent the students at Cedarville from reading about it." The judge ordered all the books returned to the library and that the students should be allowed full access to the books. (Kidspeak)

References

CBS News. "A Publishing Tradition: Apple Censors Joyce's *Ulysses*—a Century after the U.S. Did the Same." *http://www.cbsnews.com/8301-505123_162-33248534/a-publishing-tradition-apple-censors-joyces-ulysses----a-century-after-the-us-did-the-same/*. 9 June 2010.

Censored Books. "Wichita Falls loses lawsuit over censorship of Daddy's Roommate, Heather Has Two Mommies." June 1998. *http://www.cnsrdbks.com/news/wichita-falls-loses-lawsuit-over-censorship-of-daddy-s-roommate-heather-has-two-mommies*. 14 May 2012.

Censorship Free Libraries. "Annie on My Mind." 17 September 2009. *http://censorfreelib.blogspot.com/2009/09/annie-on-my-mind-2.html*. 14 May 2012.

Cole, Tony. "Amazon on the 'Clean up the world' track again. Ebook censorship rampant." The Digital Reader. 3 January 2011. *http://www.the-digital-reader.com/2011/01/03/amazon-on-the-%E2%80%9Cclean-up-the-world%E2%80%9D-track-again-ebook-censorship-rampant*. 12 March 2012.

Education for Freedom Lesson 5. Case Study: Board of Education, Island Trees Union Free School District v. Pico (1982). *http://www.freedomforum.org/packages/first/curricula/educationforfreedom/supportpages/L05-CaseStudyIslandTreesUnion.htm*. 14 May 2012.

First Amendment Schools. "Board of Education, Island Trees Union Free School District v. Pico (1982)" *http://www.firstamendmentschools.org/resources/handout1a.aspx?id=13965*. 14 May 2012.

"Freedom to Read Statement." American Library Association, July 26, 2006. *http://www.ala.org/ala/aboutala/offices/oif/statementspols/ftrstatement/freedomreadstatement.cfm*. 13 December 2011.

Hudson, David. "Participant in famous book-banning case looks back." First Amendment Watch. 30 September 2010. *http://archive.firstamendmentcenter.org/analysis.aspx?id=23438*. 14 May 2012.

The International Federation of Library Associations and Institutions. *http://www.ifla.org/*. 13 December 2011.

Kidspeak. "Harry Potter Wins His First Censorship Courtroom Battle." 23 December 2003. *http://www.kidspeakonline.org/harry_potter_news.html*. 14 May 2012.

"Library Bill of Rights." American Library Association, June 30, 2006. *http://www.ala.org/ala/issuesadvocacy/intfreedom/librarybill/index.cfm*. 13 December 2011.

"The Universal Declaration of Human Rights." United Nations. *http://www.un.org/en/documents/udhr/index.shtml*. 13 December 2011.

CHAPTER 7
AUTHORS AND CENSORSHIP

Satan Is on the Rampage, and His Name Is Lauren Myracle!!!!
–Virtue Alert

Lauren Myracle, author of two popular series, TTYL and LuvYa Bunches, is one of the most banned authors of the last few years due to her open and honest depiction of teenage sexuality, as well as her inclusion of gay characters in her novels. Because of the controversy caused by her work, she is often personally vilified and was once memorably referred to as, "Satan." The Satan email or, "un-fan mail" as she refers to it, was sent out via email alert through a website called Virtue Alert. The owner of the site is a Christian author and parent, who agreed with and supported the efforts of parents in her neighboring town of Round Rock in their efforts to remove the TTYL books from their middle school library. (Courtney) The books were subsequently removed from the middle school after it was determined by the school district that the books depiction of pornography, drinking, and an inappropriate student-teacher relationship was not appropriate for middle school students, although the books were allowed to remain in the high school. Throughout the years, Myracle has also been told through emails that she is a, "pedophile, a sick money grubbing pervert, has loose morals, is corrupting young adults, and is sick in the brain." (Corbett)

Lauren Myracle has the ability to turn adversity into positivity. In 2011, Myracle was thrilled to learn that she was a finalist for the National Book Foundation award, then she was informed that her nomination was actually a mistake and she was asked to withdraw her name. The book she was nominated for, *Shine*, was very important to her as it depicted the story about a gay teen who was bullied mercilessly. Myracle was very disappointed, but was happy when the organization volunteered to donate $5,000 to the Matthew Shepard Foundation, an organization that was formed to educate others about the lives of gay teenagers.

"I don't think I am depraved, and I know I am not Satan," was her reply in an interview where she talked about the effects of censorship on her personally. Nevertheless, she strives to get past her feelings of anger by dialoging with her detractors through exchanging emails with them so that they can get to know her as a person; something she feels is very important. She states that by doing this, she and the parents often found out that they share some common ground as parents and readers.

Judy Blume, in her essay *Places I Never Meant to Be,* tells the story of how she gave copies of her award winning book *Are You There God? It's Me, Margaret* to her local elementary school and was turned down because the book features characters who discuss menstruation. She then received a phone call from a parent who called her a communist. She states that she never figured out if the woman, "Equated communism with menstruation or religion." Judy Blume has since reached out to her readers and other authors by sharing her feelings about being censored. She encourages them to share their feelings as a method of communicating with others about who the person is behind the banned books.

John Green, who wrote the Printz award winning book, *Looking for Alaska,* was called a pornographer for his work. He eventually resorted to making a video to explain the motivation behind his writing and to emphatically state that he is not a pornographer. (Green)

Similar stories are shared by many banned, challenged, or censored authors that have been disparaged and labeled as personally corrupt, and even dangerous, due to certain words and scenes that, selected solely for their perceived shock value, give an unrealistic and false interpretation of their work. This sets a dangerous precedence, as the words that are chosen by authors are at the forefront of the censorship battle. Yet, in the midst of the intense battle to shield our children from what some believe to be language that is provocative and controversial, the author's individuality and values, as well as their intent and motivation that give their words context and meaning, are too often forgotten. Educating and informing your readers, parents, and community about the motivation and personal experiences that inspire writers to explore the subjects that they choose to write about helps to enlighten a questioning and uneasy audience.

The Motivation behind Provocative Writing

Why do authors write books that cause such uproar? Do writers purposely write about subjects or use words that are guaranteed to get parents and other concerned citizens upset? Answering these questions openly and honestly is an essential part of educating young adult readers, their parents, and the community. Explaining where an author's motivation comes from, why certain topics interest them, or what they hope to offer their readers helps to prevent censorship by providing information that contrasts with the perception of authors who write books with which some may not agree.

The *School Library Journal* interviewed many young adult authors and asked them to define their purpose for writing. They found that most of the authors they spoke to feel a moral obligation to their readers to write honestly and openly and felt that they had a special responsibility because they were writing for kids. (*School Library Journal*)

Judy Blume writes that if anyone had told her when she began writing that she would be the most censored author of her day, she would have laughed in disbelief. She goes on to explain that her intent was never to purposely cause controversy, but that she wrote based on what was honest and true to her childhood experiences. Her goal was only to write books she would have liked to have read when she was a child. (Blume)

Author Chris Crutcher, the author of *Whale Talk* and many other popular young adult books that have been challenged, often talks about his motivation for writing about topics such as poverty, abusive parents, racial and religious prejudice, and mental and physical disability that are loved by teenagers and yet, are unsettling to some adults. In an interview, he was asked why he writes for teenagers. He replied that his memories of his own adolescence combined with his experiences working as a therapist with young adults and families provides the foundation for his stories. In particular, his familiarity with adolescents and their problems encouraged him to want to write about the unique experiences of teens, who for various reasons, perceive themselves as outsiders, to explore how they negotiate life. Crutcher was also asked about why he writes about dark or violent experiences and if any topic is taboo. He replies that he sees value in writing about dark subjects so that they are "brought into the open where they aren't so dark." (Crutcher)

Ellen Hopkins, the author of the popular Kristina series, including the books *Crank* and *Glass,* addresses drug addiction and many other tough issues, such as teenage prostitution and sexual abuse. Hopkins weaves the story of her own daughter's problems with drugs into her work through prose and verse which appeals to teenagers and gives a greater context to her writing. To some who challenge her books, her choices seem to be promoting controversial issues, but a closer look shows that through her focus on these issues, teens can visualize how one wrong choice can affect their lives forever. Hopkins states that, "Teens often have this idea that, 'It's my life. I can do what I want with it.' They have a certain sense of immortality." (Higgs-Coulthard)

Hopkins realizes the subjects she chooses to address and the words she uses to depict those stories are hard hitting and disturbing, but she encourages her detractors to look beyond the words and scenes to realize these issues are a reality that needs to be addressed by adults who care enough to address the issues accurately and with sensitivity.

Why Do Authors Write about Explicit Issues?

Author Tonya Lee Stone is very conscious of her young adult readers when in the process of developing her characters and writing their stories. She explains that the title, *How a Bad Boy Can Be Good for a Girl,* came to her first, and the thoughts on what that phrase would mean to a girl followed. Her main character, Josie, came to her mind and how Josie would deal with a boy who was unlike any other she had ever known. (Stone)

Stone says that some writers write to specifically address issues that drive the scenes they write. She referred to fellow writer, Laura Ruby, who states that themes often develop on their own as a writer writes. For example, she wanted to address the damage that sexual rumors could have on young girls. The main character that she created seemed to want to concentrate more on friendships and self-discovery, so that was the direction the novel took.

One of the most controversial decisions a writer for young adults has to make is how to present sexuality in a way that respects the varying levels of maturity of the audience, while still honestly reflecting the life styles of the characters. An author who writes for the writer's blog, Crowe's Nest, describes how she negotiates this difficult task. She states that she has learned that the best way to write for young adults is to not to think or worry about "what is appropriate, but what is appropriate for the story I am telling." Before she adopted this method, the scenes she wrote that involved sexuality were awkward and clumsy, because instead of concentrating on the characters, she was she was worrying about censorship and parents accusing her of corrupting their children. Now she relies on respecting the characters, along with their right to make mistakes, to take risks, and to hopefully learn from those mistakes. (Baer)

Effects of Censorship on Authors

"It's not just the books under fire now that worry me. It is the books that will never be written; the books that will never be read, and all due to the fear of censorship. As always, young readers will be the real losers." This statement written by Judy Blume underscores the wide-ranging rippling effect that censorship can have, not just on the authors, but on the young readers who will miss on the opportunity to be inspired or changed by a book that they might never get to read.

In today's climate, where the experience of censorship can feel so personal and disheartening at times, authors can feel pressured to write books that they hope won't offend anyone. The danger of this is that the spontaneity, individualism of the author, and the characters' voices might not ring true to the reader.

Brent Hartinger is the writer of *The Geography Club*, an award winning book about a gay high school sophomore who has a crush on a fellow classmate. He discovers that his crush is also gay after they meet in person, following a virtual meeting in an Internet classroom. The book was banned in Hartinger's hometown of Tacoma, Washington, due to parent complaints. The principal agreed with the ban and was particularly concerned about the references to meeting strangers on the Internet; references the principal believed were dangerous and risky to impressionable students.

Hartinger responded in a letter stating that the reason for the book banning just felt wrong to him after receiving so many accolades and positive feedback from readers with no mention of the singular Internet scene. When asked about the experience, he states that, "It's hard not to take it personally when a school district bans your book, and it is even more difficult when you become repeatedly challenged and censored, as I have been. The next time around you're asking, do I need this headache?" (*School Library Journal*)

Carolyn Mackler, whose Michael L. Printz honor book *The Earth, My Butt, and Other Big Round Things* was one of the most challenged books of 2006, admits that "the fear of censors can sometimes have a paralyzing effect." She remembers questioning herself about possibly controversial scenes in her new book, *Guyaholic*. "Do I put it in? Do I not? If I put it in, will I get challenged again?" she says she remembers thinking. "I have to tell myself, don't listen. Don't worry." (*School Library Journal*)

Censorship from Above and Beyond

Censorship can manifest in many different and surprising forms that are more understated and yet, in many ways are more insidious and damaging than when the intent to censor is clear and unmistakable. This subtle execution of censorship is the hardest type to detect and combat because of the lack of overt action and overall passivity that characterizes it.

Publishers and Censorship

Many authors talk about the pressure from publishers, who, in trying to help their authors avoid book challenges and personal attacks, often encourage authors to self-censor for their own good. Lauren Myracle, who wrote the popular tween series Luv Ya Bunches, experienced similar pressure. Her book centered around four girls who become friends because they are all named after flowers. Scholastic wanted to sell her books through their book fairs, but they wanted her to change some offensive language such as "geez," "crap," and "God." Myracle agreed to change the language. They then asked her to change the gay parents of one character into a heterosexual couple. Myracle refused to make the final change, stating that there was nothing wrong with showcasing gay parents.

She had a similar experience with another publisher who asked her to change the title of her book from *The Bitches* to *Rhymes with Witches*. After much consideration, she made the change, which resulted in a whole new set of problems as people complained that the book must be about occult.

Judy Blume writes that when she was writing *Tiger Eyes*, she had written a potentially controversial scene regarding Davey, the main character in her story. The publisher objected to a few lines in a passage. The publisher posed a question to her: "What is more important, to keep the scene, or to be able to get the book out there to your intended audience who might not be allowed to read the book if anyone objected to that one scene." Blume hesitated and felt uncomfortable, but eventually took the lines out as requested.

Nonfiction writers have the same sort of experiences. Tracy Barrett tore up her contract with one publisher when they asked her to tone down her criticism of Andrew Jackson and his treatment of Native Americans in *The Trail of Tears: An American Tragedy*. She ended up going with another publisher. (*School Library Journal*)

Uninvited Authors

Author Rachel Vail had a similar incident late last year—but this time the censor was a librarian. After being invited to speak at an elementary school in Woodbury, New York, Vail says she was shocked to find out that her latest picture book, *Jibberwillies at Night,* would be banned from the library and that copies would not be available for sale in conjunction with her visit. She was told by the librarian that since the book deals with children's nighttime terrors, it might make kids develop fears or worries that they otherwise didn't have. (*School Library Journal*)

Ellen Hopkins was the victim of a recent "uninviting." The Humble Book Festival in Texas is one of the largest and most well-attended book festivals for teenagers. Hopkins, who was previously invited in 2009 but could not attend, was invited again in 2011 and was looking forward to attending the event. A middle school librarian, who felt uneasy with her middle school students being presented with the edgy content of Hopkins's books, expressed her misgivings to the school superintendent who decided to remove Hopkins from the event. Other authors declined to attend the event in support of Hopkins, and the event was eventually canceled.

Hopkins had a similar experience when a school in Norman, Oklahoma, stopped Hopkins from appearing, and she ended up speaking in a nearby church. When asked her opinion about what happened, she stated that, "They're not pulling the plug on my books, but on me. It's censorship when you don't let somebody give voice to their ideas." (Galehouse)

Censorship Under the Radar

Barry Lyga, who wrote the popular book *The Astonishing Adventures of Fan Boy and Goth Girl*, wrote a second novel, *Boy Toy,* that focuses on the sexual relationship between a twelve-year-old boy and his teacher. Lyga anticipated angry letters from parents and letters of protests, but instead received silence. Lyga soon discovered the reason why. Many librarians would tell him they enjoyed the book but refused to buy it for their libraries for fear of complaints. Bookstores, he found, either carried it in the adult section or did not carry it at all. Subsequently, although the book received good reviews, it had disappointing sales.

Authors who write books with gay characters or themes are very accustomed to the subtle censorship that keeps their books off the shelves, even when the books merely feature a character that is gay without any overlying sexual scenes or words. John Coy, who wrote the book *Fall Out* which contains one lesbian character who is not the main character, found that his book was not being carried in libraries because of that character, which surprised him because he thought that the book's focus on school prayer would be the issue to cause problems.

David Levithan, who wrote the book *Boy Meets Boy,* states that he purposely wrote the book to be as "clean as possible," so that if he was challenged, it could only be because people were opposed to happy gay characters in love. (Whelan)

Labeling

On the opposite end of the spectrum, authors who choose to write about Christian themes also report that they have a difficult time having their work judged on the basis of their writing and storytelling ability.

Mable Singletary is a new author who visited my school to speak to my students about the writing process. She writes stories of preteens and how their Christian faith shapes their approach to the issues that they face. She states that it is common to be denied shelf space in book stores like Barnes and Noble or to be shelved in the Christian/Religious section. She feels this is unfortunate, because information that could be helpful to people is often overlooked as a result of the marketing that portrays Christian books as not being useful for the general population.

Labeling affects edgy authors as well. Coe Booth explains that she resents the limitation that accompanies having her work being labeled "street lit" because she feels the label immediately paints a picture of her work that limits her appeal to a wider teen audience. She feels it also gives librarians a reason to not purchase her books despite their stellar reviews because of the perception that they are inferior and controversial. (Whelan)

New Authors Discuss Self-Censorship

I have had the privilege of working with two new writers: Kekla Magoon and Bethany Hegedus, who traveled around the country talking about their books—depictions of segregation and the Civil Rights Movement and how these events impact the lives of teenagers today—when they visited my school and local public library. After the event, I interviewed them about their thoughts and feelings about their choice to write about potentially controversial topics for their first published works.

Magoon wrote *The Rock and the River* in 2009. The novel won the Coretta Scott King/John Steptoe Award for New Talent and was nominated for a NAACP new author award. This book explores the Black Panthers in a coming-of-age story, focusing on two African American brothers growing up in the late 1960s. The two boys, who are participants in the growing civil rights movement, struggle over the dilemma to continue to follow nonviolence as a path or to embrace the burgeoning Black Power movement as an alternative.

Choosing to delve into this sensitive subject matter, due to its racial elements and potential for violence, as a new writer was risky in terms of possible censorship challenges, but Magoon did not shy away from it. She states that her experiences as a multiracial child growing up with the daily challenge of "straddling race and class divisions," inspired her to write about characters that experienced the same struggles. She also felt that there was a lack of fiction stories available that told the story of the Black Panther party and that explored how young men and women experienced the movement from their unique perspective. (Magoon)

Bethany Hegedus wrote *Between us Baxters,* which was named one of the Best Books of 2009 by the Bank Street Awards Committee. The book tells the story of the friendship between two Southern girls, one black and one white, who grew up in the 1950s at a time and in a place where such friendships were deeply frowned upon due to the unwritten rule that blacks and whites should remain segregated at all times. She explains that her inspiration came, not from a desire to court controversy, but from her past experience growing up in both Chicago and Georgia, where she found that friendships between people of different races were viewed in very contrasting ways. She finished college and began a teaching position in rural

Georgia where she was shocked to discover that in 1996, although the laws have changed, the feelings that she thought were in the past, continued to exist. She also realized the impact of race on friendships, as she taught in a district where the Ku Klux Klan was still active and influential; she knew she had to tell the story. (Hegedus)

I asked her if the potential for censorship conflicts with what motivates her as a new writer. She replied that she knows the potential exists but that she does not let that stop her from writing about what moves her, keeps her up at night, or calls to her. She states that she believes that books are made to cross boundary lines, when those boundary lines and the reason for crossing them are carefully considered and investigated. She says as long as her books do that with respect and dignity, and investigate the human experience--whether they get censored or not—"I will be proud to have told the story that I was called to tell."

Librarians Take Action: Host an author visit.

Alleviate the need for book challenges by inviting an author to speak directly with teens and the community as a whole. Books that feature issues like segregation, racism, and violence are often the recipients of book challenges because parents are afraid that reading about these difficult and painful issues will expose teens to adversities for which they aren't emotionally ready. However, being able to personally interact with the writer, who is responsible for conceptualizing thoughts, ideas, and emotions on paper, can be an eye-opening and comforting experience. Offering your library users, parents, and community the opportunity to personally meet an author is a fantastic way to alleviate some of the doubt that exists about who authors are as people and what inspires their writing.

After I met Hegedus and Magoon and read their books, I knew that bringing them and their message to my students and community would be a great way to introduce the students to a more personalized and relevant picture of the Civil Rights Movement. I also wanted to involve the community as a means to alleviate any hesitancy or unease that parents might have about introducing their children to a sometimes uncomfortable subject.

The authors visited my school during the day, and met with parents and other community members in the evening at the local public library. They presented their two novels that feature interracial friendships, segregation, and the Black Panther movement through a presentation entitled The Civil Rights Movement. The day event consisted of a presentation that contained music and images of the Civil Rights Movement, along with information about the writing process and what inspired them. The students also participated by presenting a reader's theatre interpretation written by the authors of two pivotal scenes that took place in each novel. The evening event consisted of the presentation, discussion, and a question and answer session.

Collaboration Is Key

Author visits can seem to be complicated and overwhelming because of the amount of details and people that have to be managed. Sharing the responsibilities with others can lessen the amount of stress that can accompany the planning and the event, and enable the event to be offered to a greater number of people. I collaborated with my local public librarian with whom I work with on many different events and activities. She agreed to help me pay for part of the authors' fees, promoted the author visit with the parents and community, as well as planned and hosted the evening event. I also collaborated with a few literature and social studies teachers who helped me to organize the students and the day activities.

Before the Author Visit

Prepare the teens for the event by making sure that as many teens as possible read either both, or at least one of the books, so that they were as familiar as possible with the themes, characters, and events. I never require reading the book as the only way to gain access to the event. As a part of ensuring access for all readers, I also make sure to include those teens that are interested in the topic but may not be able to read a book that they lack the reading skills to complete. For those students, I made copies of one chapter, or for some, one scene. I also put together a reader's guide that featured the characters and explained some of the themes for them.

I then encouraged the students to think of questions they wanted to ask the authors and had them write them down. I collected the questions and distributed them to the students the day of the visit so they would not forget what they wanted to ask.

I mailed letters to all the parents to inform them about the books, the authors, and what they would be presenting to the students, and invited them to attend the evening event in order to participate in what their children were reading and learning. The authors' publisher supplied me free copies of the books to have the authors sign and give away as prizes to parents and students who participated in a raffle.

Teen Participation

Encourage teens to participate during the author visit. Teens really enjoy getting involved and not just listening and asking questions. My teen advisory group put on a skit based on the reader's theatre activity that the authors wrote from their books. The teens also set up the chairs and helped the teen librarian organize the evening visit.

Discuss Censorship

It is important during these events that you ask the author about book challenges and censorship. They can discuss if they have ever felt apprehensive about the subjects they choose to write about, and if they have experienced challenges, make sure that they discuss the experience with the audience.

A Wonderful Experience

Members of the community, parents, and teens joined together to discuss potentially controversial issues in an open and informative arena. Older community members, who had lived through segregation and who had personally participated in the Civil Rights Movement, told of their experiences, parents spoke of their experiences reading the same book as their children, and teens drew from history and put it into the context of their experiences with race and culture today.

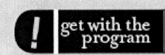

It Takes a Village

Author Visits as Community Events   ▶ MARGARET AUGUSTE WITH SHARI FESKO

In order to keep her connection with the literary world outside of her media center at Franklin Middle School in Somerset, New Jersey, Margaret Auguste began writing book reviews. Little did she know that one of these book reviews would lead to an incredible opportunity for her students, fellow staff members, and the general public. The book, Between Us Baxters by Bethany Hegedus, a story of two girls who are best friends yet have to hide their friendship because of time and place, truly struck a chord with Auguste. After giving it a favorable review, she was contacted by the author's publisher and then eventually began e-mailing back and forth with Hegedus.

Through their conversations, Hegedus introduced fellow writer Kekla Magoon to Auguste. Magoon's book Rock and the River takes place ten years after Between Us Baxters, and concerns father/son relationships and how it felt to grow up during the turmoil and energy of the civil rights movement in the 1960s. Auguste was again left speechless by the powerful message of the story.

AN UP-CLOSE-AND-PERSONAL EVENT ENABLES STUDENTS TO SPEAK WITH AUTHORS KEKLA MAGOON (RIGHT MIDDLE) AND BETHANY HEGEDUS (LEFT BACK).

When she discovered that these authors did joint presentations about their books with a focus on promoting racial diversity and harmony, Auguste was quick to suggest that her school would be perfect for their visit. She was determined to involve as many of her students and members of the community as possible, so a variety of large and small group activities were developed.

Auguste asked the eighth grade teachers to participate and invited the students and teachers to the library to attend the presentations, which gave the authors a manageable forty to fifty students per program. Auguste also wanted the students to have some involvement in the presentations so after talking with the authors, a readers' theatre component was added to the program. Both authors wrote scenes based on their novels for the students to perform. Auguste worked with a few teachers and students who were interested. The

READERS THEATRE BRINGS THE CIVIL RIGHTS MOVEMENT VIVIDLY TO LIFE.

MARGARET AUGUSTE (STANDING) ASSISTS STUDENT NICOLE TONEY AT ONE OF THE WRITING WORKSHOPS.

students worked very hard perfecting their parts and creating costumes and props to go along with the scenes. By planning ahead, students were able to personalize and feel ownership of the program. It also intensified the entire school's anticipation of the event, knowing their fellow classmates would be involved.

In addition to the two presentations, Auguste arranged smaller writing workshops and book discussion groups for students she knew were passionate about writing and learning more about the writing process. She kept these groups small so that students could have one-on-one contact with published writers.

The capstone event was giving the entire community a chance to meet these two gifted authors. Auguste immediately contacted Amanda Decker, the young adult librarian at Franklin Township Public Library. Auguste and Decker had talked often of doing a joint program and finally they had the perfect opportunity to combine forces. They planned a relaxed, informal reception at the public library for the authors after their school visit. There they could answer questions and have a chance to greet parents, students, and other people whom they did not meet during their school visit. Decker's goal was to make teens aware of the library and hoped this reception would draw in young adults and turn them into returning patrons. Auguste wanted to use the reception as a way to educate the entire community on what libraries, both school and public, can offer their children.

The entire event was a huge success. Students learned a great deal not only about the writers and their process but about the subject matter at the heart of both books, that all human beings have value regardless of their gender, race, or religious beliefs. Many of these students were able to be directly involved with some aspect of the day's event, making it even more memorable for them. The icing on the cake was the cooperative event with the public library that allowed the two authors a chance to spread the message of their books to an even wider audience.

Auguste was able to do the entire event for a very reasonable $1,050. Thanks to the fact that her school was the first stop on a joint tour of schools, she was able to book both authors for $900. An extra $150 was charged for the evening reception. In the end, the public library contributed $450 of the costs, leaving Auguste to cover $600. Their collaboration proves that not only do partnerships between school and public libraries strengthen the community, but they also allow both organizations to do more financially than they ever could on their own. ∎

Margaret Auguste has worked for the past fifteen years as a university and public librarian, juvenile court advocate, software trainer, and writer. She currently works as the Library Media Specialist for seventh and eighth grade students at Franklin Middle School in Somerset, New Jersey.

Shari Fesko is the Teen Services Librarian at the Southfield Public Library in Southfield, Michigan.

FOCUS   Winter Edition 2009–2010 School Year

Interactive Program Engages Franklin Middle School Students

Last fall, Franklin Middle School (FMS) students participated in an interactive educational program about the Civil Rights Movement. The program was conducted by Bethany Hegedus and Kekla Magoon, authors of two highly regarded historical fiction novels about segregation, family and friendship. Highlights of the daytime, in-school activities included a student writing workshop, a presentation and several students performing a scene from the books for their peers. The program concluded with an evening session for parents and community members at the Franklin Township Public Library.

This opportunity was made possible through the efforts of FMS Media Center staff, teachers, administrators and the community.

Students participate in workshop discussion. Left to right:

References

Baer, Marianna. "Marianna: Let's Get It On—Sex Scenes in Young Adult Novels." Crowe's Nest. 08 December 2008. *http://acrowesnest.blogspot.com/2008/12/marianna-lets-get-it-on-sex-scenes-in.html.* 14 December 2011.

Berk, Bret. Q&A: National Book Award Un-Nominee, Lauren Myracle, Felt "Gutted and Ashamed." *Vanity Fair.* 18 October 2011. *http://www.vanityfair.com/online/daily/2011/10/-i-vanity-fair--i--exclusive--a-conversation-with-national-book-.* March 12, 2012.

Blume, Judy. *Places I Never Meant to Be.* Simon & Schuster, 1999.

Corbett, Sue. "This Generation's Judy Blume." *Publishers Weekly.* 21 February 2011. *http://www.publishersweekly.com/pw/by-topic/authors/profiles/article/46197-lauren-myracle--this-generation-s-judy-blume-.html.* 25 March 2011.

Courtney, Vicki. "The Rants and Raves of the Author Mom." Virtue Alert. 22 September 2009. *http://vickicourtney.com/2008/10/is-ttyl-on-your-school-library-book-shelves.* 20 January 2011.

Crutcher, Chris. *"Whale Talk* Interview." Harper Collins, 2010. *http://www.harpercollins.com/author/ microsite/readingguide.aspx?authorID=16156&isbn13=9780688180195&displayType=book interview.* 14 December 2011.

Galehouse, Maggie. "Censorship Cloud over Cancelled Teen Lit Fest." Bookish: A book blog with Maggie Galehouse. 28 August 2010. *http://blog.chron.com/bookish/2010/08/censorship-cloud-over- cancelled-teen-lit-fest/.* 14 December 2011.

Green, John. "I Am Not a Pornographer." John Green Official Website, 30 January 2008. *http://johngreenbooks.com/i-am-not-a-pornographer.* December 2011.

Hegedus, Bethany. Personal Interview. 05 April 2010.

Higgs-Coulthard, Kathy. "Channeling the Voice of Youth: An Interview with Ellen Hopkins." Women on Writing. 2010. *http://wow-womenonwriting.com/38-FE3-EllenHopkins.html.* 14 December 2011.

Lau Whelan, Debra. "Dirty Little Secret: Self-Censorship." *School Library Journal.* 01 February 2009. *http://www.schoollibraryjournal.com/article/CA6703349.html.* 02 May 2011.

Magoon, Kekla. Personal Interview. 05 April 2010.

Singletary, Mabel. Personal Interview. 04 April 2010.

Stone, Tonya Lee. "Now and Forever: The Power of Sex in Young Adult Fiction." *Voices of Youth Advocates.* February 2006: 462-465.

Whelan, Debra Lau. "A Dirty Little Secret: Self-Censorship." School Library Journal. 1 February 2009. *http://www.schoollibraryjournal.com/slj/home/886066312/nj_library_citing_ child_porngraphy. html.csp.* 22 February 2012.

CHAPTER 8
TEACHERS AND CENSORSHIP

The educational goal literature should serve in the classroom is at issue when censorship in the classroom is discussed today. Should teachers only choose literature that supports the values and morals that are deemed important to the school's mission and reflect the values of parents and the local community? Should they ensure that everything they choose for their students to read adhere to a strict school, parent, and community sanctioned set of standards regarding appropriate language and behaviors? Or, is the role of a classroom teacher to utilize literature as a tool to expose their students to issues, ideas, and new ways of life that may be controversial in terms of vocabulary, behavior, or lifestyle, in order to challenge them and expand their worldview?

The National Coalition of Teachers Education (NCTE) states that the goal of all teachers should include a commitment to ensure that students "build an understanding of texts, of themselves, of the cultures of the United States and the world; so that they can acquire new information; respond to the needs and demands of society and the workplace; and find personal fulfillment." (NCTE) This is the standard that the majority of teachers are committed to today. Teachers use their professional training in literature and literacy education to meet this standard by choosing texts that enable students to think, to learn, and to increase their knowledge of the world around them.

Viewpoint: Classroom literature should reflect the values of the community.

Diane Ravitch, research professor of education at New York University, does not agree with NCTE's mission. She believes that striving toward this goal has led to the novels that are chosen for classroom use to be essentially joyless and uninspired. She states that, "Teachers have persuaded themselves that their job is not to promote excellent literature, but to promote depressing problem novels." (Ravitch) The parent group Parents Against Bad Books in School (PABBIS) criticizes the classroom literature that is chosen today because they believe that it is too mature for the majority of students. In fact, they caution parents to be constantly on guard and aware of what their children are reading in school, because "They might be shocked at the sensitive, controversial, and inappropriate material that can be found in books in K-12 schools, both in the classroom and school library." (PABBIS)

Viewpoint: Teachers fear choices.

The struggle over integrating the ideals and expectations that teachers set for themselves, along with the varying expectations insisted upon by administrators, school board members, community members, and parents create an internal struggle that invariably affects teachers' self-confidence, their ability to shape their classrooms, has a harmful impact on the parent-teacher relationship, and can negatively affect their ability to instruct their students. The school classroom, according to the ALA, is the place where the most book challenges occur, with parents and community members making most of those challenges. This contentious environment has resulted in many teachers feeling apprehensive about choosing any texts, despite the context, that contain any words, scenes, or ideas that could invite a challenge, even though they personally feel as though the books could offer a great deal to their students. In the article, "The Ripple Effect of Censorship: Silencing in the Classroom," the author, Elizabeth Noll interviews several teachers who discuss just how their fear of complaints and challenges negatively influences their choice of classroom texts. Noll refers to this as the "ripple effect," which she explains as occurring when teachers who witness the devastating after-effects of censorship, become hesitant and timid in their book choices. For example, Carole Marlowe was fired for teaching the Pulitzer Prize winning play *The Shadow Box*, even though her principal initially approved her choice. However, the district superintendent disapproved of the play and cancelled it because it contained homosexuality and offensive language. Marlowe was accused of violating district obscenity standards and was forced to resign.

The widespread publicity directly affected the other teachers within the district as they reported that it definitely led to their hesitation to use any type of literature that might be perceived as offensive. Clair, an experienced teacher, discusses her experience in scanning for the "offensive passages" in what she called a "fabulous book" that she had hoped to use in her classes. Her disappointment and sense of regret when she discovered a singular "inappropriate" scene that she knew would cause her to not choose the book, was so strong that when she saw it, she screamed, causing her colleagues next door to hear her and think that something was wrong. (Noll) Another teacher who was interviewed asked his students to bring in novels from home to read for reader's workshop, with the idea of giving students a choice to read what they liked. However, he immediately had misgivings when he realized that many students were bringing in Stephen King novels, because he began to worry about the parents and his principal objecting. Without being directed by his principal, supervisor, or any parents, he decided only to allow them to read books that were already owned and approved by the school. (Noll)

In my experience in working with teachers, I can attest to this common sense of stress that classroom teachers share. Teachers that I work with felt decidedly uneasy about choosing books for summer reading after a parent complained about one book on the list. Other teachers white out potentially offending passages in books or never ask to teach any new or current texts, instead choosing to teach the same books every year that they hope are safe from challenge.

The NCTE has established an Anti-Censorship Center to provide teachers with information on teaching strategies and lesson plans to help teach controversial books, as well as a place to find support and assistance when books are

The NCTE has historically recommended that students read texts that were unconventional, but interesting and relevant to students, as evidenced by a 1946 NCTE meeting when member Mildred C. Schmidt and other teachers argued that comics and other texts of popular culture were relevant and teachable texts.

challenges or censored. They also provide a place to report book challengers so that they can be documented and can offer teachers legal advice as well as emotional support.

Self-censorship

The result is that many teachers don't wait for a public rebuke of their book choices but instead, self-censor out of fear for their jobs or community retaliation. They are also very cautious and selective about what texts they choose in order to strike a balance they hope will please everyone, while still remaining true to their training and commitment to student growth and learning.

This is true for many teachers like Natalia, who, when interviewed about her experience with censorship, states that even though she uses books sanctioned by the school, whenever she has to teach *The Scarlet Letter, The Lord of the Flies,* or other books with a hint of controversy, she inwardly cringes at the thought of possible parent or community complaints. She reports that she frequently whites out offensive passages or deletes the names of the magazines she get articles from if she feels that they could be thought of not appropriate for students. (Noll)

Censorship and Students

This climate of fear has had a negative effect on students as well. Students are being denied the opportunity to develop intellectually because they are not allowed to hear and experience different vocabulary, problems, and values that offer them the ability to think in a broader context beyond their usual world. They are unable to have the opportunity to question and challenge what they think they know by reading about other viewpoints and integrating the new knowledge with what they already know, thus losing the ability to increase their awareness.

Censorship and the Teacher-parent Relationship

Perhaps the greatest negative impact of censorship is the eroding of the trust and good will that should characterize the relationship between teachers and parents. Parents have to feel a sense of trust with the people that they entrust with their children, and teachers need to feel as though parents are confident in their professionalism and commitment to their students.

The complicated nature of this parent-teacher relationship is showcased by a contentious and unfortunate book challenge that took place in 2008, at the Renton High School, in Renton, Washington, over the novel *The Adventures of Huckleberry Finn. Huckleberry Finn,* which according to the ALA, is one of the most frequently contested books in the classroom. It is widely regarded as a classic, however, its usage of racial epitaphs has pitted educators and parents against each other as they strive to make each other understand their point of view.

The novel, written by Mark Twain in 1885, depicts the adventures of Huck Finn, who is a penniless uncultured boy, and his unlikely companion, Jim, a runaway slave, who traveled together on a raft down the Mississippi River. While on their journey, the two develop a close relationship and learn to respect each other. Twain wrote the book with a satirical and scathing depiction of racism and social attitudes in the South. The book caused uproar at the time it was first published and was banned by a library in Massachusetts that described it as tawdry and coarse. Other libraries also banned it, and in general, the book was considered trash that was only good for the slums.

The book has remained controversial since that time and has constantly been the subject of challenges. One of the most recent challenges took place in 2008, when Calista Phair, a high school student, reported to her grandmother, Beatrice Clark, that she was assigned to read the book and that she was upset about it. She stated, "I was humiliated and horrified that this book was being taught, when it has the N-word 215 times." (Roberts)

Clark supported her granddaughter's opinion after attending her granddaughter's class, where Clark was shocked and disappointed to hear the teacher discussing the N-word with her students. She stated that, "It's not just a word. It carries with it the blood of our ancestors. They were called this word while they were lynched; they were called this word while they were hung from the big magnolia tree." (Roberts)

The teacher, Ms. Anderson, who had taught the class for years and used the book repeatedly, reported that she felt a passion for the book and that led her to select it as a classroom selection year after year. Before reading the book, she took care to carefully and respectfully present the controversial language by leading the class in discussions about its usage of the N-word and its complicated portrayal of African Americans and Native Americans. After reading the book, she asked her students to write an essay about whether or not the book should be banned from classrooms and each year, not one student ever recommended that it be banned. She recognized the controversy surrounding the book but strongly felt that reading the book served to open a dialog among the students about who we are, where we come from, and what our language means to us. She believed that to ignore the book was equitable with ignoring history, which would send a negative message to young adults everywhere.

Nevertheless, Clark viewed the decision to teach a book that used the N-word numerous times as completely inappropriate, no matter what the literary merit. In the end, Clark's granddaughter was excused from reading the book and read an alternate book instead. She and her grandmother continued their protest of the book with Clarks filing a written request for the book's removal from the language arts courses and agreeing that it should remain in the library. The book was included in summer reading lists, but was removed from the classroom until a panel consisting of teachers and outside advisors developed procedures and guidelines on how best to present the book in classrooms.

Librarians Take Action: Write a great book rationale.

When researching this story about the New Renton challenge, it appears that the teacher made every effort to prepare the class as thoroughly as she could before beginning the novel. It is not clear from the newspaper article, however, if she informed the parents and students about the book she had chosen and why before she initiated any discussion about the book.

Parent groups like PABBIS, teachers, and librarians may not agree on many things, but what they do agree on is the need for parents to be completely and thoroughly informed in order for them to feel more comfortable and understanding of the choices that schools are making for their children. Writing a book rationale that explains your reasons for your book choices is a great way to communicate with parents about the motivation behind book selection. This is a useful tool that can be used for classroom teachers and for young adult librarians in both public and school settings. In my opinion, it is also a wonderful way for young adult librarians to collaborate with classroom teachers by working on common book rationales that can be shared by both groups.

What Is a Book Rationale?

A rationale is a reasonable or sound plan that justifies the need to do something. Book rationales are used to explain what elements make a book special, inspirational, or simply the perfect fit for your classroom or library use. A well-written rationale can put parents at ease when it is informative, honest, and comprehensive. As a classroom teacher or librarian, it is also one of your best defenses against possible book challenges, because your reasons behind your choice are in the open for all to see. Teachers and librarians alike can write rationales for use in the classroom or in libraries. They can write them to meet their individual needs or can combine resources and ideas to work collaboratively to develop them as a team.

The best time to give the book rationales to parents is a few weeks before the students begin to read the book, so that the students and the parents have time to decide if they choose to read the book or would like an alternate. This allows the parents have enough time to contact you if they have any questions and concerns and to decide against it and request an alternate book.

What I do is collaborate with the classroom teachers ahead of the book's assignment to put together rationales and present them at our Back to School Night that occurs in September. This event occurs at least a month before any reading is assigned, giving the parents plenty of time to make their decisions.

I present the rationale as a quick book talk and then give the parents the book rationale to take home to go over it on their own time. The classroom teacher and I also provide the parents with our contact numbers, so they can contact us if they have any questions or want to discuss the book further.

The elements of a well-written rationale

A great rationale should be informative and clear and provide interesting and insightful descriptions of the book. In addition, issues that are potentially controversial and have past censorship history should be disclosed so that parents have a complete picture of the book.

- A summary of the book. Give an overview of what the book is about, not a list of every event and do not describe the ending. Instead, you want to give the overall themes and idea of the book.

- Important characters. Provide a list of the characters with the ages, if possible. This gives the parents the idea that the age of the characters is in sync with the students who are reading the book.

- Descriptions of the themes of the book. This takes the book beyond the facts to let the reader or parent know what issues will be discussed and why these issues are important to the readers.

- Personal awards won by the author. This gives an idea of how the person is received by the public, and that the author is respected as one of merit.

- Awards the book has won. This shows how well-regarded the book is by experts on literature, journalists, or others whose opinions are respected

- Reviews of the book. Include professional book reviews and reviews by your library users--both adults and teens. Including a combination of professional and library user reviews give a realistic picture of what various types of people with different interests have to say about the book.

- Possible controversies. This is probably the most important aspect of your rationale. You do not need to count each swear word or risqué scene, but you do want to write openly and honestly about what issues have been noted as controversial and then let the parents be the judge.

- Quotes from the author about censorship or anything else. Including some personal statements about the author's experiences or thoughts about censorship is another good way to bring this discussion to the open.

- Interesting facts about the book. This is the place to include fun or quick facts that add to the reader's knowledge of the author and the book.

Biography

Born on April, 1928, in St. Louis, Missouri, Dr. Angelou was raised in St. Louis and Stamps, Arkansas. In Stamps, Dr. Angelou experienced the brutality of racial discrimination, but she also absorbed the unshakable faith and values of traditional African-American family, community, and culture.

I've learned that make a 'living' is not the same thing as making a 'life.'"—Maya Angelou

Book Reviews

"Simultaneously touching and comic" —New York Times

"It is a heroic and beautiful book." —Cleveland Plain Dealer

"Maya Angelou is a natural writer with an inordinate sense of life and she has written an autobiographical narrative . . .A beautiful book—an unconditionally involving memoir for our time or any time." —Kirkus Reviews

Book Summary

Poet Maya Angelou chronicles her early life, focusing on her childhood in 1930s rural Arkansas, including her rape at the age of five, her subsequent years of muteness, and the strength she gained from her grandmother.

First published: 1970

Type of work: Novel

Genre: Autobiography

Subjects: 1930s, segregation, prejudices, child abuse, southern prejudice, small town life

Librarians Take Action: Offer the students an alternate version of the book.

This controversial choice for the book *The Adventures of Huckleberry Finn* became available in January 2011, when an alternate version of *Huckleberry Finn* was published. The new altered version was written by Alan Gribben, an English professor from Auburn University, who replaced the N-word with the word slave and the word "Injun" with Indian. He did so because he worried that the continued and relentless controversy surrounding the language would force schools to continue to take it off of the reading lists. He also felt that the focus on the offensive words made it difficult for students to feel comfortable reading the book. In the introduction to the book, he wrote, "Even at the level of college and graduate school, students are capable of resenting textual encounters with this racial appellative." He also thought that his version would be, "Welcomed by teachers and spare their readers from a racial slur that never seems to lose its vitriol." (Kakutani) Gribben clearly had the best intentions in mind with his adaptation, however, his provocative idea has created an incredible amount of passionate discussion about race, history, culture, and of course censorship.

In the essay, "Light Out, Huck They Still Want to Sivilize You," the author, Michiko Kakutani, states that this adaptation is only offering a censored version of a literary classic that should be read as it was written. The author's words are an intellectual property that should remain original and true, no matter how they are are perceived by modern day ideas about what is acceptable and what is not. What is inappropriate and wrong is that the author's words and their intent should have to be rendered inoffensive and palatable to satisfy everyone.

In the blog The Social Justice Librarian, many controversial topics that librarians face are honestly and personally discussed to address the internal dilemma that accompanies these issues. The *Huckleberry Finn* adaptation and the controversy surrounding it was discussed through a blog entry entitled "Modernizing vs. Censoring: Where's the Line?" The librarian who wrote the blog admits that the alternate version of the book did not bother her as much as it probably should and she asks the question, "What do we do with a classic when the connotation of some of the language shifts over time?" The example of Shakespeare is used to make the point that few students actually read most of his works in their original text without some kind of translation. Without the realization of the need to make classic texts more palatable for students' emotional and intellectual abilities, how would they ever be able to at least get an appreciation to historical and classic novels? The question is also asked, what should be done when the words are clear but the connotation behind them has changed so much to make it very offensive to many people. The culture of harassment and bullying is also addressed in the blog when it is asked if it is really fair to expect all students, especially ones of color to have to sit through a class in which the N-word is repeated over and over. (Greyson)

In the *New York Times* essay, "Why Read That Book," the author, who is African American, writes that as a teenager he suffered through reading *Huckleberry Finn* in high school with the, "White kids going out of their way to say 'N-word Jim,'" and with the tortured teacher trying unsuccessfully to explain the symbolism of the language. The author states that, "Whatever, I could live my whole life without reading that book again." He states that if teachers think that keeping those words in is worth the pain they will cause the students of color, he understands that as well, because it is about choice and not censorship. (Butler)

Alternate Book Choice

With all these complicated issues that need to be taken into account, assigning a book for students to read is clearly not a simple endeavor. Preparing for every scenario can lessen the anxiety felt by everyone involved. No matter how strongly a teacher feels about the merits of a book, students may not feel comfortable with it, or their parents may not feel that it is appropriate for their child to read. They have the right to request an alternate book. It is, therefore, an excellent idea on the book rationale itself to state this, so that everyone is aware of this option from the beginning and it is a part of the initial introduction to the book. On the rationale itself, you can write a note stating how you hope the information provided was helpful and that you realize that there may still be questions. Invite the parents to contact you for more information. Then state that if the parent is still not satisfied that the book is a good match, they may request an alternate book.

Pat Scales, a librarian and expert on intellectual freedom issues, states that, "We must allow them to reject such books in recreational reading, as well as in the curriculum. If a student or parent voices an objection to a particular novel, the teacher should offer an alternative novel without compromising literary quality." (Scales) The National Coalition Against Censorship provides information about censorship and assistance to teachers, authors, and librarians who are the recipients of book challenges, and also recommend that parents should be encouraged to request a specific remedy, such as an alternate assignment instead of demanding that no other students be allowed access to a book. It is only censorship if the parents ask for the book to be removed so that no other student can read it, and the book is removed without any organized, objective, and thorough review. (NCAC)

The best idea is to have a list of alternate books ready, so as soon as a parent asks for one, you are prepared. The best way to accomplish this is to know what assigned books are used in the curriculum. The decisions about what is being read usually occur in the spring or summer before the school year starts, which will give you plenty of time to obtain the list and prepare alternatives. Teachers are always looking for resources to help with locating interesting summer reading choices and welcome any professional assistance and suggestions. If it is possible, volunteer to be on the committee that selects the books, so that you can contribute to the selection process and so that you can also volunteer to prepare the lists of alternate books.

Selecting Alternate Books

The book you choose as the alternate does not have to match the storyline exactly but should match the feeling and overall context of the original book. I use the following criteria as a guideline to books that I choose to replace the original one.

Storyline	Tone	Characters	Genre	Location	Pace	Writing Style

Plot driven
 	
Character driven
	Funny
	
	Emotional
	
	Intense
	
	Bleak
	
	Upbeat
		Conflicted
		
		Weak
		
		Frightened
		
		Relationship with
		    Mother
		    Father
		    Sibling
			Science fiction
			
			Dystopia
			
			Mystery
				Country
				
				State
				
				Region
					Fast
					
					Relaxed
						Engaging
						
						Free verse
						
						Witty

Assignment: *I Know Why the Caged Bird Sings* by Maya Angelou

Poet Maya Angelou chronicles her early life, focusing on her childhood in 1930s rural Arkansas, including her rape at the age of five, her subsequent years of muteness, and the strength she gained from her grandmother and Mrs. Bertha Flowers, a respected African-American woman in her town.

Alternate selection: *A Thousand Never Evers* by Sheri L. Smith

As the Civil Rights Movement in the South gains momentum in 1963, and violence against African Americans intensifies, the black residents, including seventh-grader Addie Ann Pickett, in the small town of Kuckachoo, Mississippi, begin their own courageous struggle for racial justice. Like *I Know Why the Caged Bird Sings,* the main character struggle with prejudice through the strength of their character and perseverance.

Alternate selection: *Sparrow* by Sheri L. Smith

After the death of the beloved grandmother who raised her, high school student Kendall Washington travels to New Orleans, expecting to be taken in by her only living relative, an aunt, but the reunion does not go as planned. Like *I Know Why the Caged Bird Sings*, the main character is an African American girl struggling to find her place in a world that is not welcoming to her, but yet, she finds herself. Both main characters had strong relationships with their grandmothers.

Assignment: *To Kill a Mockingbird* by Harper Lee

This is a classic story of a girl, her beloved father, and prejudice in the South.

Alternate selection: *The Rock and the River* by Kekla Magoon

Even though both characters are African American boys in this book, each book consists of characters that, because of race and culture, learn something about themselves, their families, and their communities. The boys' relationship with their father and mother is strong and complicated.

Alternate selection: *Between Us Baxters* by Bethany Hegedus

This book is also about the close relationship between a girl and her father. The stories also each take place in the South amidst racial turmoil and segregation.

Assignment: *The Absolutely True Diary of a Part-Time Indian* by Sherman Alexie

This illustrated novel is told in the first person and is about a Native American teenager who is a cartoonist. He gets a chance to leave his reservation to attend a predominantly white school where he learns about himself and his place in the world.

Alternate selection: *American Born Chinese* by Gene Luen Yang

In this graphic novel, three characters, a Chinese American trying to participate in popular culture, a Chinese folk hero attempting to be worshipped as a god, and a teenager who is so ashamed by his Chinese cousin's behavior that he changes schools, feel as though they are outsiders. Each character has some innate talent or gift that he slowly discovers as he takes the time to learn about himself.

Alternate selection: *Surviving the Applewhites* by Stephanie S. Tolan

Talented sixteen-year-old Miles' first year at Culver Creek Preparatory School in Alabama includes good friends and great pranks, but is defined by the search for answers about life and death after a fatal car crash.

Assignment: *The Kite Runner* by Khaled Hosseini

Amir, haunted by his betrayal of Hassan, the son of his father's servant and a childhood friend, returns to Kabul as an adult after he learns Hassan has been killed, and attempts to redeem himself by rescuing Hassan's son from a life of slavery to a Taliban official.

Alternate selection: *Sold* by Patricia McCormick

This novel is told in vignettes, in which Lakshmi, a thirteen-year-old girl from Nepal, is sold into prostitution in India. This book is similar in that it showcases the desperation of the situation that some children find themselves in and still manage to survive, both physically and emotionally.

Alternate selection: *Camel Rider* by Prue Mason

Two expatriates living in a Middle Eastern country, twelve-year-old Adam from Australia and Walid from Bangladesh, must rely on one another when war breaks out and they find themselves in the desert, both trying to reach the same city with no water, little food, and nothing in common. I chose this book because of the close relationship between the two boys is similar to the bond that is shared between the boys in *The Kite Runner*. I also liked that the setting and cultures were similar.

Resources for Selecting Alternate Books

Often, you will come across books that seem to match with other books when engaging in collection development. When you need help, there are resources to use or to share with the teachers in your community.

1. BookBrowse: Your Guide to Exceptional Books. *http://www.bookbrowse.com*

   This site offers book club tips, author information, and best of all, read alikes based on individual books and authors.

2. Novelist. *http://www.ebscohost.com/novelist*

   This site can be used by subscription only. Most libraries already have access to it, but if they do not, you can go to the website and sign up for it. This is a wonderful site full of book discussion guides, booktalk tips, book lists, and each book you choose has an accompanying list of similar books.

3. ReadAlikes. *http://atn-reading-lists.wikispaces.com/Read+Alikes*

   This list was compiled by a collective of librarians who are dedicated to promoting libraries and reading. The list has many titles that you can click on to get a list of related books.

4. One Librarian's Book Reviews. *http://librariansbookreviews.blogspot.com*

   This site contains book reviews of young adult books and within the book reviews the reviewer suggests read alikes. The choice of books is not very comprehensive, but is still worth looking at when you are searching for read alikes.

References

"BookBrowse: Your Guide to Exceptional Books." *http://www.bookbrowse.com/reading_guides.* 18 August 2011.

Butler, Paul. "Why Read That Book?" *New York Times*, 06 January 2011. *http://www.nytimes.com/roomfordebate/2011/01/05/does-one-word-change-huckleberry-finn/why-bother-reading-huckleberry-finn.* 03 September 2011.

"Find a Bad Book." (PABBIS) Parents Against Bad Books in Schools. *http://www.pabbis.com.* 15 April 2011.

"The First Amendment in Schools: Resource Guide: Introduction: Avoiding Censorship in Schools." The National Coalition Against Censorship. *http://www.ncac.org/p.php?id=4269.* 10 July 2011.

Greyson. "Modernizing vs. Censoring: Where's the Line?" *Social Justice Librarian*, 04 January 2011. *http://sjlibrarian.wordpress.com/2011/01/04/modernizing-vs-censoring-wheres-the-line/.* 12 August 2011.

Kakutani, Michiko "Light Out, Huck They Still Want to Sivilize You." *New York Times*, 06 January 2011. *http://www.nytimes.com/2011/01/07/books/07huck.html?pagewanted=all.* 12 July 2011.

Lombardi, Ester. "Huckleberry Finn—Has *The Adventures of Huckleberry Finn* Been Banned? " About.com. *http://classiclit.about.com/od/huckleberryfinnfaqs/f/faq_huck_ban.htm.* 28 June 2011.

"Mission Statement." National Council of Teachers of English, 2011. *http://www.ncte.org/mission.*

NCTE. "A Smattering of Facts from NCTE's Past Sources Included." *http://www.ncte.org/centennial/resources/citations.* 12 March 2012.

Noll, Elizabeth. "The Ripple Effect of Censorship: Silencing in the Classroom." *English Journal.* 83.8 (1994): 59-64. *http://www.eric.ed.gov/ERICWebPortal/detail?accno=EJ494605 29.* May 2011.

Ravitch, Diane. "The Scream: Does Children's Literature Have to Be Scary." *Education Next.* 22 September 2005. *http://educationnext.org/thescreamdoeschildrensliteraturehavetobescary.* 05 February 2011.

Roberts, Gregory. "'Huck Finn' a Masterpiece or an Insult." *Seattle Post-Intelligencer,* 23 November 2003. *http://www.seattlepi.com/local/article/Huck-Finn-a-masterpiece-or-an-insult-1130707.php.* 19 July 2011

Scales, Pat. "Banned books: Q&A with librarian and educator Pat R. Scales." *Free Library,* 01 March 2002. *http://www.thefreelibrary.com/Banned+books%3A+Q%26A+with+librarian+and+educator+Pat+R.+Scales....-a097116843.* 14 February 2011.

CHAPTER 9
PARENTS AND CENSORSHIP

The parents who challenge books see themselves as concerned parents who are simply doing what they are supposed to do: Keep their children safe by being aware of the information with which they come in contact. In my experience as a parent and working with parents, my perception is that parents feel they know what is best for their children and that they should have the final decision as to what is appropriate for their children. The perception they have of themselves is not how they may be perceived by many others who view them as uninformed and controlling. Parents who want to censor books are often labeled as:

- ignorant

- narrow-minded

- motivated by fear

- want to control every aspect of their children's lives

- are uncomfortable with addressing controversial subjects and ideas with their children

- are more than likely to be resistant to new ideas and to the realities of the world their children face today

- not only interested in controlling the lives of their own children, but want to restrict the rights of other children as well

Some groups that promote censorship seem to conform to this singular depiction of parents who challenge books. Parents against Bad Books in Schools (PABBIS), is one such group that appears to fit these criteria. PABBIS targets books they decide are "bad" based on criteria that include factors such as "bad taste" and "controversial or objectionable material" and that are unfit for the classroom or school library. PABBIS targets the books they determine as bad by posting selected text from those books that contains words and scenes that they deem inappropriate. They also state that, as responsible parents who care about children, their mission is to educate and warn parents to be aware of the bad and unfit books children are being exposed to in their schools. They only want to inform other parents by raising awareness, and informing those parents that they have a choice. (PABBIS)

SafeLibraries.org is another organization of concerned parents who labels librarians as, "good or bad." Good librarians protect children from inappropriate content by restricting their access to books and other materials that are unsafe, and bad librarians believe in the "anything goes" theory and push books that are basically pornography, onto unsuspecting and vulnerable children. Their organization also focuses on the young adult authors they describe as, "porn pushers," because they write about topics that the group feels are inappropriate for teens. (SafeLibraries)

Despite the active and vocal role these groups and many other local groups play in appearing to target librarians and teachers and with challenging the books they disagree with, they dispute the label "censors," and instead, they state that they believe as parents, they have the right to monitor what their children read, and to refuse to allow their children to read any material that they feel goes against their sense of morality or values. They believe the problem is that schools seem to want to teach their students to have respect for each other, their teacher, and their parents, and yet, at the same time, they don't seem to realize by choosing books that contain profanity, sex, and violence, they are undermining the very foundation that would ensure the development of the very values they are trying to teach.

With the most extreme voices garnering most of the media attention, it is easy to see why some people view these parents as irrational and belligerent. Author Lauren Myracle experienced this perception herself when she attended a banned book read-aloud. Unexpectedly, when someone gave a speech where they stated that "The people who want to ban books are prudish, small-minded, and self-righteous, and they need to get over it," the statement made her pause, as she believes that pushing the "us versus them" theme takes away any chance of opening a dialog that would increase the understanding between the groups.

In fact, according to the ALA, the reality is that most parents are neither unreasonable nor angry. Many challenges are brought by anxious parents or citizens, who are concerned over the well-being of either their child, or other children in the community. What they may not understand is that although they have the right to decide what their children can read, they do not have the right to decide what other children read.

In addition, stereotyping all parents as those who believe in censorship clearly is not the answer, as not all parents believe that restricting reading is the best idea. This diversity is demonstrated in a Twitter post written by a mother and an author, Kemari, who is very anti-censorship and yet, understands the yearning parents feel to protect their children. She states that, "As a mother and a writer, I abhor censorship and its proponents. I understand that it is a parent's prerogative (and duty) to act as a gatekeeper for their children. But there is a difference in protecting our children from actual harm, and barring our children from experience and knowledge. Morality and intelligence is not borne out of what we read. It comes from our experiences, our mistakes (and the lessons we learn from them), and the values we bear witness of in those around us." (Kemari)

When trying to build relationships with parents or those in the community who criticize, it is helpful to ask, is it possible that their passionate stance stems not from intolerance but from their dedication and concern for the well-being of their children? Perhaps they are simply asserting their rights as parents to shield their children from knowledge that they feel is inappropriate or doesn't reflect their values. It is also possible that the motivation to censor does not come from a hateful place but from a personal, more thoughtful and painstaking process, based on an internal struggle about what is right and what is wrong for their children.

Influence of History and Culture

Parents who challenge books do so for a variety of reasons. Making an effort to understand those reasons can only help librarians to narrow the gap between what the challengers feel versus the right to read. Culture and history shape our thinking and our outlook on life and, of course, shape our opinions on what is appropriate and safe reading for our children. A challenge that took place regarding the book *Roll of Thunder, Hear My Cry* is an example of the impact that culture and history can have on book selection. This book was challenged by an African American parent in 2004, after it was assigned to be read by a middle school class. The parent contended that the children were too young to understand the racial material presented in the book, and that it might trigger racial tensions within the school. The parent also stated that mistreatment of African Americans in the book embarrassed her child and made him feel sad. She states that she does not agree with harsh details about black life during segregation or that the N-word is used repeatedly. She also states that her son is not unaware of racism, and that they discuss it at home, but she feels uncomfortable with the idea of studying it as a subject in a school setting. She would like for her son to read the book when he is older and at home where they can discuss it. The parents were offered an alternate title but rejected that offer, instead opting to request that the book be removed from the entire district, a request that was rejected. (Postal)

Influence of Societal Issues

In Denver, Colorado, a parent challenged the book *The Giver* in 1994, because he thought the book was dangerous because of its depiction of suicide, euthanasia, and infanticide in a positive light. He also pointed out that in Colorado, a state that ranked fifth in suicide rates, and in a school in the same district as Columbine High School, the choice of a book that takes on these particular sensitive issues was not appropriate or safe. He also states the school policy was to notify all parents when controversial issues are to be discussed in class, but he was never notified. Nevertheless, after review, the book was kept in the classrooms and in the school libraries. (Associated Press)

Point of view is clearly important and cannot be discounted when discussing censorship, as the passion and certainty that both parents felt in challenging each book's use in the classroom was equally matched by the passion and certainty that the schools felt in their decision to include it for students' assigned reading.

Book Ratings

After parents objected to four books that were chosen for classroom use—*Beloved* by Toni Morrison, *Kaffir Boy* by Mark Mathabane, *I Know Why the Caged Bird Sings* by Maya Angelou, and *Animal Dreams* by Barbara Kingsolver—because of the books' depictions of rape, sexuality, and profanity, they suggested that this issue might be avoided in the future if ratings or information clearly stating the sexual content, violence, or profanity was somehow made available to parents before the books were assigned. (Wallace)

The parents at Del Campo High School in Fair Oaks also requested that a joint group of parents and teachers develop a rating system to account for assigned books that contained "life issues" like abortion, birth control, and suicide or violence, and overt sexuality. This request came about after the books *Of Mice and Men, The Lord of the Flies,* and *I Know Why the Caged Bird Sings* were assigned and some parents were dismayed at the amount of profanity, sexuality, and disrespect for religion that were depicted in the books.

The overriding complaint that these parents seem to share is that they feel as though they are not receiving the information they need about the books their children are reading. Their request stems from the fact that young adult literature features stories that address the teen experience with honesty and outspokenness that is startling to some and provocative or controversial to others. Book ratings, similar to the ones applied to movies, are increasingly seen as a viable solution that would provide parents with a method of gaining information about the content of books before their children read them, purchase them, or are assigned them in a classroom, with the added benefit of lessening the need for book challenges.

Pat Scales, an expert on intellectual freedom who teaches about anti-censorship around the country, states that although ideas like these come from the best intentions, rating books in terms of their content raises some disturbing questions. She points out several issues regarding this idea: How will a consensus be achieved in regard to the ratings? Will they count the number of four-letter words, sex scenes, and acts of violence? How will they define violence? What kind of rating will complicated issues like abortion and torture receive? What about fantasy, science fiction, or new age books? (Scales)

According to the ALA, book ratings, because of their subjectivity and influence on public opinion, don't support the Library Bill of Rights which states that objective and neutral information should be the only information that libraries should provide. The ALA also states that labeling or making notes about the content of the books on the bibliographic record that refer to sexuality, violence, or profanity is also a violation of the Library Bill of Rights, because the assumption is that everyone shares the same view of what is distasteful. No one person should take responsibility for deeming what is offensive. (ALA)

Despite these misgivings, the call for a book content ratings system continues to become more and more popular. In *Pediatrics* magazine, a study was completed that found many parents don't understand why content ratings aren't used by all forms of media that would give them the information they need to guide and protect their children. The nearly seven hundred parents who were interviewed especially wanted specific details, such as warnings about profanity, physical abuse and torment, fight scenes with deaths, illegal drug use, and teen alcohol abuse. Sixty-eight percent said they'd like to have age-appropriate recommendations. Fifty-seven percent of parents wanted to have a universal rating system for all media.

Many librarians also express a need for, if not content ratings, at least some way to obtain more detailed information about the content of the books they are thinking of selecting. Librarians were interviewed about their thoughts regarding what would guide them in the complicated process of choosing books in the sensitive climate that they face. It was found that 25 percent of middle school and 20 percent of high school librarians thought when they felt hesitant about purchasing books containing sexual content, more detailed and specific age-appropriate guidance from book reviews, or possibly some kind of rating system might help their decision-making process; however, they were unsure if a formal content rating system, similar to the movie ratings, would be able to account for the maturity and variability of teenagers. They did feel as though traditional book reviews were not comprehensive enough to inform them about material that parents or children might find disturbing. They described their desire for more information to be used for book recommendations, or for "matchmaking" rather than "screening" books. (Biederman)

The *School Library Journal*, a well respected book review magazine for young adults, also reports that librarians are constantly asking for more detailed information in order to make more appropriate book selections. Brian Kenney, the editor of *School Library Journal*, states that librarians frequently bombard him with questions about why books are filled with curse words or bodily functions, or why graphic novels are so graphic. He reports that, "Some readers want ratings—akin to the system that the Classification and Rating Administration of the Motion Picture Association of America use to rate films."

He believes that the reason for this concern is because library collections are under such an intense scrutiny that librarians are understandably nervous about offending students, parents, school administrators, and community members. He states, "Reports of book challenges turn up every hour, it seems, and they are one of the toughest, and at times, scariest parts of your job."

Content Ratings Sites

The desire for information from both parents and professionals has become so intense, many organizations that are independent from publishers or traditional book review magazines have launched their own book review websites that offer book content ratings. Common Sense Media; the most well known of these sites, is an organization that was founded with the express purpose of fulfilling those information needs through their popular website that provides content reviews for movies, television, music, games, apps, websites, and books.

Common Sense Media: Media Sanity or Media Censorship?

Common Sense Media, in their mission statement, states that they are "dedicated to improving the lives of kids and families by providing trustworthy information, education, and the independent voice they need to thrive in a world of media and technology." Their goal is to support media sanity; not media censorship. They also firmly believe that parents should have a "choice and a voice about the media our kids consume." (Common Sense Media) Their website reviews a wide variety of books by looking at certain criteria that they think gives the parents information that they need the most.

Books are reviewed by examining a wide variety of information that includes sexuality, violence, consumerism, drugs and alcohol, educational value, and positive messages, along with other criteria. Onsite book reviews are conducted and independent reviews are solicited from parents, children, and teenagers to provide more opinions. Questions and issues that parents and children can discuss about the themes presented in the books under review are also provided to encourage discussion. The books are given a rating based on these criteria.

At the website there is a sample of the criteria that they use with examples:

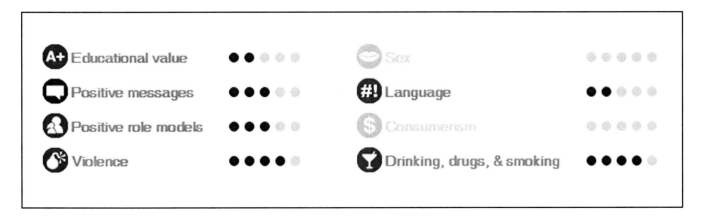

"Why we rate something ON, PAUSE, or OFF for an age: Right below our ratings, we have a list of specific content categories with icons that highlight content concerns, along with in-depth information. We have different icons for different kinds of reviews. If no icon is highlighted, that means the content isn't an issue. If three are highlighted, that means there's a fair amount, and five highlighted icons indicate there's lots of it." (Common Sense Media) Their primary method of rating books is determining if the books message is age appropriate using this system:

On: Content is appropriate for kids this age
Pause: Know your child, some content may not be right for some kids
Off: Not appropriate for kids this age
Not For Kids: Not appropriate for kids any age

Viewpoint: Common Sense Media is negative towards reading.

Many other organizations and professionals in the young adult literature field offer the following criticisms of the organization.

- *They promote a negative attitude toward books.* According to Brian Kenney, the constant search for what is wrong with the content of books makes the content appear dangerous and even frightening. Common Sense Media's approach makes parents and children think that instead of embracing and taking chances on unknown books that appeal to them, those books should instead be suspect and should be thoroughly examined before they are "safe" for enjoyment. He states that the "offending incidents" are presented without the context that would serve to explain those incidents within the greater meaning of the story.

- *Common Sense Media is imposing their subjective idea of what content is problematic.* By stating they are alerting readers to the violence or sexual content in books, Common Sense Media is telling their readers that they believe that those things are bad and negative instead of allowing the readers to use their own judgments to determine that for themselves.

- *Common Sense Media doesn't give children and teenagers the chance to determine on their own what books are best for them.* Children develop reading skills and ability by choosing books that interest them which encourages them to read. According to Pat Scales, children deserve to choose the books that they like and are very capable of rejecting the ones that they do not. They do not need adults help in making that decision.

- *Potential to encourage censorship.* This is the issue that critics of Common Sense Media are the most concerned with. The National Coalition Against Censorship, American Booksellers Foundation for Free Expression, American Library Association Office for Intellectual Freedom, International Reading Association, Association of American Publishers, PEN America Center, National Council of Teachers of English, Society of Children's Book Writers & Illustrators, and Authors Guild collaboratively wrote a letter of protest to the site regarding all the issues mentioned above and in particular about the dangers of enabling censors. (Kenney) The letter states that the focus on specific incidents of violence, sexuality, or profane words gives groups that are looking for reasons to censor certain books the ammunition they need to initiate challenges. Pat Scales agrees with this theory and states that a challenge has already been made in the Midwest as a direct result of a Common Sense Media book review.

Viewpoint: Common Sense Media has merit.

However, there are others within the young adult professional community who view Common Sense Media in a more positive light. Author Melissa Marr, who wrote the popular books *Wicked Lovely* feels positively toward Common Sense Media and wrote a letter thanking them in 2008. She states that her books do refer to sexuality and other issues she feels are better suited to older teens and that she personally feels uncomfortable when she attends book signings or public library events and sees elementary-age children reading her book. Because of this, she states that she was pleased at how her book was reviewed by the site and agreed with their opinion that her book should really be read by older teens. (Berman)

In *School Library Journal*, a personal opinion essay acknowledges the problems that Common Sense Media has, but also mentions the site's merit and usefulness as well. The librarian who wrote the essay believes that "Common Sense Media is simply a tool" and "as with any tool, it can be used to help or to harm, depending on the person wielding it." Age ratings are a problem within the site, because they are not always accurate and vary, but she points out so do traditional book reviews. However, what she finds valuable about Common Sense Media is the "straight talk about content" that enables her to choose and recommend books with all the information available to her. In addition, as someone who dealt with a book challenge before, if the books she chose were challenged again, she feels that she can respond that she carefully and thoroughly chose the books using all the information she could gather. (Lohmiller)

Common Sense Media collaborated with Netflix, the popular movie rental service that offers DVDs, Blu-ray, and online streaming, to help them choose family friendly content in order to provide a large selection of kid-friendly TV shows and movies to their new Just for Kids service.

Librarians Take Action: Help parents evaluate content rating sites.

The ALA states that although libraries should only offer objective reviews of library materials, it *is* acceptable to offer library users content ratings from an outside source so that library users can make *their own* choices, based on all the information available to them. The ALA also states that the way to develop relationships with parents and to educate them is to "build bridges" with them, by understanding what their needs are and by providing them with resources to help them meet those needs. In my experience, I believe if parents or students want more details about the books their children are reading, as an information provider, I need to supply them with that information. Giving people the information they require and also educating them and offering them objective reviews of what those information sources contain is the best assistance I can provide for them. The decision as to whether or not they find the information helpful is theirs.

Content Rating Site Evaluation Tool

This content rating tool is a way to provide parents with a clear idea of what content rating sites are and what they offer. This information can be provided in a presentation about helping parents find good books for their children. I would also make sure that the parents are informed about the more traditional book review magazines, like *School Library Journal* and *VOYA* that offer reviews on their website as well, that can supplement the content site reviews.

Criteria to Evaluate Content Rating Sites

1. Examine the purpose and intent of the organization that created the site. The reasons that any organization is founded are important to know so that the purpose and intention behind the opinions expressed are clear to all those who utilize the information.

   - Who founded the content rating site?

   - Does religion play an important part in the organization?

   - Does their site possess a mission statement?

2. Examine the rating system. When content is being rated, it is important to know how the ratings are calculated. Are they based solely on personal opinions or is there a guide or set criteria? Is the criteria easily found on the site and is it explained so that it can be understood?

   - Does the site offer a rating system?

   - How clearly is the rating system explained?

   - How are the ratings calculated?

   - What content areas are rated?

   - How did they come to the conclusion to rate some content areas as opposed to others?

3. Look for reviewers' credentials. Reviews don't have to be completed by professional book reviews to have merit. In fact, sometimes the best information about books is given by friends. This is why book review sites like Teen Reads.com are so popular because everyone values information obtained from people who are like them. It is important, however, to at least know some basic information about why they choose to review books, what experience or background they have in literature, and what motivates them to review books.

   - Who are the reviewers?

   - How are they chosen?

   - Do they have any experience in the field of literature?

   - What kind of credentials do they have?

   - What is their interest in young adult literature?

4. What types of material do they rate? Because content rating sites are operated by smaller organizations, they are often limited by the materials that they are able to review. It is important to know what limits they have or special areas they rate.

   - Young adult books

   - Children's books

   - Other materials like movies, music, television

5. Do they rate a wide variety of books? This is a very important aspect of any rating site. Because content rating sites are small, they often only review books that are interesting to them or that they feel need comment.

   - Multicultural books

   - LGBT books

   - How do they choose the books they review?

6. Who is invited to review books? The most positive aspect of content rating sites is that many of them offer parents, children, and teens the opportunity to provide their own opinions about the books that they read.

   - Are teens invited to review?

   - Are parents invited to review?

7. Is there a place to make comments or to discuss book related issues? Offering a place for anyone using the site to make comments or post opinions is a great way to share information and ideas that enable readers to feel more involved in the review/rating process.

   - Is there an attached blog or comment page?

8. Does the site make a statement about censorship? Whenever books and information are being discussed, it is important that the concepts of intellectual freedom and the potential for censorship be clearly understood and addressed directly, hopefully, in the site's mission statement.

   - Is there a statement about censorship?

   - Do they discuss the First Amendment?

   - Do they discuss intellectual freedom?

Popular Content Rating Sites

Squeaky Clean Reads. *http://www.squeakycleanreads.com/index.html*
   This site was started by two stay-at-home moms who wanted to find books that were free from "objectionable content." Their rating system assesses the following criteria: violence, profanity, sexual content, recommended age group, and mature themes. How they determine what merits a high or low level is not indicated. You can search by genre, title in alphabetical order, and by keyword searching.

   They also provide a list of squeaky clean books that possess minimal amounts of violence, profanity, sexual content, and mature themes. One issue with the site that I found is that there was little diversity in the books reviewed and after completing a general examination of the site I could not find any Hispanic, African American, or LGBT books.

Story Snoops. *http://storysnoops.com*

Story Snoops is a site that was founded by four moms in San Francisco who found that their children were reading books that they, as their parents, were not ready for them to read. They decided to provide a way for other parents to be more prepared for what their children are reading. They also want to help parents seek out books that reflect the interests, weaknesses, and strengths of their children. They offer a FAQ that gives information about their qualifications: They state that they don't provide literary reviews but look at books from a parent's perspective. They don't adhere to a values system, instead they just want to provide parents with information. They *do not* use a ratings system because they only want provide content information and allow the reader to decide if it is appropriate for them; however, you can search by content areas such as racial pride, safe sex, ethnic issues, and many other variables. They offer a blog where the site and reading topics can be discussed. They also review many multicultural books on a variety of cultures and a few LGBT books.

Parental Book Reviews. *http://sites.google.com/site/parentalbookreviews*

This site was formed by a group of parents, teenagers, and other adults who are interested in young adult literature. The purpose is to inform parents and teenagers about the content of books they are considering reading. Their reviewers consist of adults and teenagers. Their rating system includes extreme to none levels of profanity, sexual content, violence, and other notables that include underage drinking, smoking, drugs, and witchcraft. They have a blog where many topics regarding young adult literature are discussed with both adults and teenagers. They also feature a list of clean reads. After careful examination of the site, I could find little evidence of multicultural or LGBT books.

Novel Book Ratings. *http://novelbookratings.com*

Novel Book Ratings was founded by parents who wanted to find a way to examine the content of books so they could better choose books for their children and help other parents as well. They invite others to review books if they become members of the site. Their rating system is listed and explained in detail. They review the characterization, plot, and the overall impression of the book. The content ratings assess the sexuality, profanity, and violence in the books on a level of 0 to 3.

One Librarian's Book Reviews. *http://librariansbookreviews.blogspot.com*

This site was founded by a college librarian who wants to help teachers and parents locate appropriate books for their students and children. The rating system rates books for violence, profanity and the "mrg" factor" which equals "mature romantic garbage." There were only a few multicultural books and as far as I could see from my searching no LGBT books.

Bookalachi. *http://bookalachi.com*

Parents who were looking for a way to know the content of the books that their children were reading founded this site. They rate language, sexual content, alcohol/drugs, violence/disturbing, social/family, and religious and spiritual references. They don't have specific reviewers and invite everyone to review the books. They read the reviews before they post them until you agree to become a member, then your reviews are posted without any editing. One positive aspect of this site is that they are one of the few sites that review many children's and picture books. They make a note to mention that focusing on the content alone might take away from the overall context of the book and encourage all users of their site to read some books in entirety to counteract this.

This overview of sites can be used as a guide when recommending content ratings sites to your library users or if you want to use them yourself as a guide to keep current on what sites parents and other library users are accessing to learn about books. Each category is marked when the site meets the evaluation criteria.

Book Content Rating Site Evaluation Tool

	Common Sense Media	Novel Book Ratings	One Librarian's Book Reviews	Booklachi	Story Snoops	Squeaky Clean Reads	Parental Book Reviews
Purpose of site listed	*	*	*	*	*		*
Rating system explained	*	*			None		
LGBT books	*				*		
Multicultural books	*	*			*		
Reviewers' experience in Literature field			*		*		
Reviewers' credentials listed			*		*		
Teens invited to review	*						
Parents invited to review	*						
Attached blog or comment page	*						
Censorship mentioned							

Librarians Take Action: Form a parent and child book club.

Establishing a relationship with your parents, as well as your teen library students, or teen library users is a great way to enable them to feel a sense of trust in you, your judgment, and the book recommendations that you make. Starting a parent-teen book club provides an opportunity to further enhance that relationship. I recently started hosting a parent-teen book club as a way to get to know my parents on a more personal basis and to encourage communication between parents and their teenagers. I found that it is also a wonderful way to introduce the parents to the library and the services that I can offer to them. One particularly successful part of a parent-teen book club is that I arrange it so the parents and teens can choose the books. This allows for the parents to introduce everyone to the books that they think are important and that are meaningful to them.

Benefits of a Parent-Teen Book Club

1. Engages parents and teens in a discussion about books.

2. Encourages communication between parents and teens by having them read books that each group recommends.

3. Provides a chance to interact with parents in a relaxed environment where they can get to know you and become familiar with the services the library offers.

4. Provides a forum to discuss intellectual freedom issues.

5. Provides an opportunity to familiarize the parents with the book collection.

Advertise the Group

Advertising your events through local schools by sending out an informational flyer is a good idea for both school librarians and public librarians, because that is where your teens spend most of their time. School and public librarians with a good relationship can help advertise one another's events. I work closely with the public librarian in my town and we work together. For example, whenever she has an activity, and she asks me for help, I send her information to the students through our information system. After you have sent out your flyers a few times, it is also important to send parents a formal letter that indicates that the entire library is committed to the program.

The first step is to design a flyer for the parents with all the pertinent information on it. I start giving the flyer out in August before school starts, at the seventh grade and eighth grade orientations, where I collect names, phone numbers, and email addresses. I do this because I know that parents and teens start planning activities for the year in August. I advertise again by giving out the flyer in September at the Back to School Night. The first week of October, send a reminder letter with the date of the initial meeting.

Guidelines for Successful Book Groups

1. Have a meeting no more often than every three weeks.

2. Allow new parents and teens to join each month so that no one is ever turned away.

3. Allow the teens and the parents to choose the book each month so that each group gets a chance to introduce the other to books that they like.

4. Have a selection of different books ready for the group to pick from each month so that the book choosing process flows easily.

5. Have a small gift to give away each month—either by names in a hat or by the first parent teen group to arrive.

6. Make it fun—at least twice during the year, if possible, see a movie version of a book that you have read instead of discussing the book. For example, I attended the movie *Precious* with the high school book group after they read *Push* by Sapphire.

7. You can ask a different parent or teen to facilitate the group each time, but I prefer to lead the group myself so that the parents and teens don't feel pressure to prepare for it. Teens and parents often have so many activities to prepare for along with homework and extracurriculars that I don't want them to feel like they have yet another thing to prepare.

8. Keep it light. This is supposed to be relaxing discussion, not homework to stress over.

References

Associated Press. "Suicide book challenged in schools." *USA Today,* 20 July 2009. *http://www.usatoday.com/life/books/2001-07-20-the-giver.htm.* 21 May 2011.

Berman, Matt. "Look Who's Talking Common Sense: Melissa Marr." Common Sense Media. 12 March 2007. *http://www.commonsensemedia.org/new/look-whos-talking-common-sense-melissa-marr* . 15 January 2011.

Biederman, Lynn. "Young Adult Literature." TeenLitLab at ALA Annual Conference, 2009.

Bookalachi. *http://bookalachi.com.* 09 March 2011.

"Common Sense Media" 2011. *http://www.commonsensemedia.org.* 17 June 2011.

Gordon, Serena. "Parents Find Media Rating Systems Lacking." *USA Today: Health.* 21 June 2011. *http://www.philly.com/philly/health/topics/132458883.html.* 25 July 2011.

Kemari. "YA Saves: United We Stand." YA Saves: Paying Homage to Literature that Illuminates the Darkness. 05 June 2011. *http://yasaves.easilymused.com.* 31 Oct. 2011.

Kenney, Brian. "Fear Factor: Kids' Lit Style." *School Library Journal.* 01 July 2010. *http://www.schoollibraryjournal.com/slj/home/885494-312/fear_factor_kids_lit_style.html.csp.* 15 June 2011.

Kenney, Brian. "Sex, Drugs, and Reading Levels." *School Library Journal.* 06 January 2007. *http://www.libraryjournal.com/slj/printissuecurrentissue/863259-427/sex_drugs_and_reading_levels.html.csp.* 29 January 2011.

Lohmiller, Darcy. "Straight Talk: Does Common Sense Media have a place in the book selection toolbox?" *School Library Journal.* 01 January 2011. *http://www.libraryjournal.com/slj/printissuecurrentissue/888336-427/straight_talk_does_common_sense.html.csp.* 31 August 2011.

Myracle, Lauren. "Building bridges with the book-banners." *http://www.guardian.co.uk/books/booksblog/2010/sep/29/bridges-book-banners.*

Novel Book Ratings. *http://novelbookratings.com/*. 07 February 2011.

One Librarian's Books Reviews. *http://librariansbookreviews.blogspot.com.* 06 February 2011.

(PABBIS) Parents Against Bad Books in Schools. *http://www.pabbis.com.* 29 March 2011.

Parental Book Reviews. *http://sites.google.com/site/parentalbookreviews.* 10 February 2011.

Postal, Leslie. "Parents Ask to Take Book Out of Schools in Seminole." NCAC: On the Issues. National Coalition Against Censorship, 02 January 2004. *http://articles.orlandosentinel.com/2004-01-26/news/0401260240_1_drake-seminole-novel.* 10 August 2011.

Raby, Mark. "Netflix Just For Kids app launches on PS3." 12 March 2011. *http://www.slashgear.com/netflix-just-for-kids-app-launches-on-ps3-12217983.* 12 March 2012.

"SafeLibraries" 2008. *http://safelibraries.org.* 05 February 2011.

Scales, Pat. "Scales on Censorship: What's Going On" *School Library Journal.* 05 January 2008. *http://www.libraryjournal.com/slj/articlescensorship/859039-341/scales_on_censorship_whataposs_going.html.csp.* 15 April 2011.

Scales, Pat. "Weighing In: Three Bombs, Two Lips, and a Martini Glass." BookList Online. August 2010. *http://www.booklistonline.com/ProductInfo.aspx?pid=4341541&AspxAutoDetectCookieSupport=1.* 12 July 2011.

Squeaky Clean Reads! *http://www.squeakycleanreads.com.* 12 April 2011.

Story Snoops. *http://www.storysnoops.com/blog.* 06 January 2011.

Wallace, Brian. "Manheim Township Parents Want Warnings on Books." Lancaster Online, 21 March 2011. *http://lancasteronline.com/article/local/364957_Manheim-Township-parents-want-warnings-on-books.html.* 28 June 2011.

CHAPTER 10
TEENS AND CENSORSHIP

Young adults are at the forefront of the debate about the state of young adult books. Are the books that are being offered to them too dark, too violent and depressing, forcing negativity on vulnerable teens that are being taught to see the world as a lonely, desperate place? Or, are the books that young adults read accurately reflecting the way they view the world and maybe opening their eyes to other ways of life, while preparing them to become aware of issues and problems they might encounter on the journey to adulthood?

While this debate over what is best for teenagers rages on between parents, authors, librarians, and journalists in the blogosphere, through Twitter, newspapers, and the literary world, it is easy to forget the adolescents who are the focus of the controversy. This is a mistake because young adults, striving to understand who they are as individuals, as well as their place in the world, will demand the right to choose for themselves what they want to read and yet, they still require guidance from the adults in their families, schools, and communities who care about them and have their best interests at heart.

Teens Read!

Do teens really read today? The common perception is that teenagers are too busy playing video games or listening to music to care about reading. This stereotype is clearly not the case, as teens are reading more than ever. The *New York Times* bestseller list is dominated by young adult books such as Twilight and The Hunger Games series and sales of young adult books are up 25 percent, according to the Children's Book Council. Movies based on books that depict the lives of teenagers, like the *Diary of a Wimpy Kid* and *Precious* based on the book *Push*, have enjoyed incredible success, almost solely due to the interest of young adults. In response to this surge in popularity, every major publisher now has a young adult imprint. The literary world has also taken notice with the National Book Foundation now expanding their awards to include young people's literature as a category.

One of the simplest, yet most important, reasons that teen books became so popular is because bookstores moved the young adult books away from the children's section into a place that teens could feel proud of and call their own.

So what do teens enjoy about reading? In the article, "Generation R (R is for Reader)," one teen stated that "Unlike movies, you create the world in your mind. Books make me laugh, cry, and truly connect with the characters and provide an escape to a different reality." Another teen stated that she likes reading books because she can "experience someone else's life and understand different points of view. It provides a healthy escape from the real world to a world where everything is possible." (Reno)

How do teenagers experience reading? Teens read and share what they read in both traditional and non-traditional ways. In the 2007 Pew Report, *Teens and Social Media*, 59 percent of teens surveyed regularly participate in online creation activities, from reading, writing, and sharing fan fiction, to reading and posting to blogs, to remixing online music, images, and videos. (Lenhart)

YA Saves!

Teens showcased their ease with utilizing virtual methods of communication when they responded in unprecedented numbers to speak out in defense of the books they loved. An article in the *Wall Street Journal* derided what was described as the dark, depraved world of young adult fiction, where sexual abuse, eating disorders, and self-mutilation are the order of the day. (Gurdan) Author Maureen Johnson, author of the popular book *13 Little Blue Envelopes*, wrote a Twitter post in which she asked, "Did YA help you? Let the world know how! Tell your story with a #YAsaves tag." Fifteen hundred responses later, "YAsaves" became one of the top three trending topics in the United States on Twitter, with a record number of teens, notable authors, readers, and journalists responding in defense of young adult literature.

A serious and passionate discussion followed about whether or not young adult fiction was going in the right direction and what the stories meant to the lives of the readers. What surprised everyone was the sincere and thoughtful input about books from young adults, who clearly were able to articulate their points and ideas in a fashion that demonstrated just how sophisticated, capable, and confident they were.

One teen posted, "I've definitely read a lot of these kinds of books, and I don't cut myself or do drugs." Another teen, who writes stories on Figment.com, stated that she read books about teens who cut themselves and she does not see any reason why she would do it herself, but she did think that reading the novel made her understand why some teens do harm themselves. Another teen writer said, "Just as playing with Barbie dolls doesn't make girls become anorexic, reading about teens with problems doesn't make kids develop problems. Instead, it's beneficial. They understand it's not real."(Springen)

Teen blogger and the founder of WORD ("words worth reading and discussing for teens"), Nicole's response beautifully sums up the reaction of teens: "We (teens) are YA. Young adult is brilliant. It can be terrifying and dark and gritty and fantastic and wonderful and full of hope. It shows the darkest of the dark while letting us know that there will always be light. Just like our lives. We are the books we read. To attack them is to attack us."

Teens Speak

The battles against censorship that our children and teenagers wage today on behalf of the books that they love has its roots in First Amendment court cases fought on behalf of the rights of teens years ago.

Tinker vs. Des Moines was one of the most notable cases in which teens were found by the courts to possess First Amendment rights. On December 16, 1965, students agreed to wear black arm bands to their Des Moines schools to show their opposition to U.S. involvement in Vietnam. School officials learned of the plan and the Des Moines Independent School District rapidly made a rule that students who participated in such a protest would be suspended from school. Thirteen-year-old Mary Beth Tinker, her fifteen-year-old brother John, and fifteen-year-old Chris Eckhardt wore armbands anyway and were suspended. A local attorney agreed to take their case and told them he thought they had an important First Amendment principle at stake. For four years they pursued their case, as they lost at two lower courts and were finally heard at the U.S. Supreme Court, where they finally won. (ACLU)

The Supreme Court's opinion became famous as it articulated the relationship between the First Amendment, teachers, and students. "First Amendment rights, applied in light of the special characteristics of the school environment, are available to teachers and students. It can hardly be argued that either students or teachers shed their constitutional rights to freedom of speech or expression at the schoolhouse gate. This has been the unmistakable holding of this Court for almost fifty years." (Legal Information Institute)

The precedence that cases like this and the Pico vs. Island Trees case has enabled and emboldened teens to continue to advocate for their right to have their voices heard through the exercise of their First Amendment rights, which they have not hesitated to use in their fight against the censoring of the books they love.

When the Citizens for Literary Standards in Schools challenged several books in the Blue Valley School district, fifteen-year-old Sasha Mushegian wrote an editorial against the decision in the *Kansas Star* newspaper. The following is an excerpt of what she said: "Every book I have read has taught me something, even if it was just, 'This is what really bad writing sounds like.' I am fiercely passionate about books I like, and I react to an insult to a good book the way I would to someone picking on my little brother." (Mushegian)

Bless Me Ultima by Rudolfo A. Anaya has been at the center of controversy many times and has been challenged multiple times. In Norwood, Colorado, where the book was being taught in a local high school, the parents expressed concern due to the fact that the book referred to paganism and had a considerable amount of profanity. The superintendent censored the book by removing and even allowed the parents to burn them. The students were so offended by their actions that they staged an all-day sit-in to protest the removal of the book. (KidsSpeak)

In 2004, First Lady Laura Bush recommended *Bless Me Ultima* to *Seventeen* magazine as one of her favorite books. (Seventeen Magazine)

Probably the most famous exercise of these rights took place in 1999, when the Harry Potter books were banned from the classroom in Michigan. The first protests were not led by adults but by the fourth grade students who wrote letters to the superintendent in protest. Their efforts inspired both children and adults alike to organize a group called the Muggles for Harry Potter that caught on with both children and adults across the country. The group wrote letters, circulated petitions, and spoke at school board meetings to protest the banning of the books. (KidSpeak)

Clearly this portrait of teen readers demonstrates that contrary to the easily influenced, vulnerable stereotype that many who want to censor young adult books claim that young adults are teens, with their increasingly sophisticated reading habits and emotional maturity, are speaking about what they like to read and what influence it has on them, allowing and encouraging writers to push their own boundaries by writing about a wide variety of subjects to meet their needs. Librarians, who have always been advocates of First Amendment rights, have particularly been committed to advocating for the rights of our youngest library users, which is made clear by Article V of the Library Bill of Rights, "A person's right to use a library should not be denied or abridged because of origin, age, background, or views." The "right to use a library" includes free access to, and unrestricted use of, all the services, materials, and facilities the library has to offer. Every restriction on access to and use of library resources, based solely on the chronological age, educational level, or legal emancipation of users violates Article V.

Librarians Take Action: Give teens a voice with teen advisory groups.

Teens are anxious to have their voices heard and want to have a say about their school, their churches, and their libraries because these are these are institutions that are the most relevant to their social world. Libraries, with an emphasis on respecting the opinions and needs of young adults, as well as our commitment to valuing their opinions and judgment, can be the best places for teens to showcase their talents, skills, and their ability to confidently express their thoughts and ideas in welcoming and open environment. (Tuccillo)

Librarians can give their teen library users the opportunity to express their opinions by organizing a teen advisory group (TAG). By doing so, librarians can give teens a platform where they can shape their library experience to fit what is relevant to them and they can demonstrate to their community how capable and knowledgeable they are about the issues that affect them the most. TAGs consist of teenagers who support their local school or public library through volunteering for various activities and events.

TAGs Help Librarians

The group can do anything that fits the mission and purpose of the library. My group helps me to:

- Plan Teen Read Week

- Plan Read Across America

- Plan Banned Book Week celebrations

- Help with the Scholastic Book Fair

- Contribute to collection development

- Suggest books that should be purchased

- Write book reviews

- Provide book talks

My TAG is essential to the organization of my library. With all of the budget cuts and paring down of staff in the school library, the TAG is essential in my efforts to help the library function. The group is imperative in my efforts to keep the library collection current and relevant in terms of selecting books that are interesting to my library users. For example, almost my entire graphic novel and manga collection is chosen by my teen group because they know what is popular.

TAGs Help Teens

TAG members can:

- Learn organization skills.

- Learn how to work in a group.

- Learn the importance of involvement.

- Become lifelong readers.

- Appreciate libraries.

- Become an inspiration to other teens and younger children.

- Demonstrate to adults how knowledgeable teens are about the world around them.

- Gain confidence in their opinions.

- Showcase their skills and talents.

- Become educated about their First Amendment rights, intellectual freedom, and censorship.

In my experience, the main benefit that TAG members receive is the opportunity to have a voice in a decision making process that directly affects them. So many times, teens, especially at the middle school age, are still subject to rules when participating in groups. A TAG enables teens to develop skills and strategies that will sustain them as they continue to mature and take on more responsibilities. You also have the opportunity to teach an interested group about the First Amendment, intellectual freedom, and censorship. I achieve this by offering an educational aspect to my group where everyone is required to learn about these important issues and how it affects them personally, as well as their community.

TAGs Help Libraries

TAG members can:

- Become advocates for the library.

- Become advocates for the right to read.

- Become advocates against censorship.

- Educate others about intellectual freedom.

- Encourage other teens to read.

- Become role models for younger children.

- Showcase the library programs and book collection.

A great offense is often the best protection against censorship. Having teens who can proactively talk to the community, to parent groups, and to their teachers about the books that they like and inspire them is the best way to garner the attention of the community in a positive way. In addition, by reaching out to the teenage community, you can also engage and interest their parents in library programs and initiatives.

Start a TAG

- Advertise at your local Back to School Night.

- Advertise in local recreation newsletter.

- Advertise in school parent/teacher newsletter.

- Recruit teens that use your library regularly.

- Send out invitations to teens that have been recommended by other group members.

- Send out invitations to local groups.

- Contact local groups or schools who require teens to complete volunteer hours in their communities.

The size of the group does not matter; as long as you have at least two teens, more will follow as word of all the exciting activities and events that teens can participate in gets around. I advertise in all the ways that I have suggested, but the bulk of my volunteers just seem to appear and want to participate. Many of the teens that I have are not the traditional students. I have a mixture of National Honor Society students and advanced readers, with teens who are average students who like graphic novels, and students who just like to help unpack the Scholastic Book Fair boxes and check out books to other students. I find that an approach that welcomes all talents and interests is the best way to recruit and retain interested students who will feel as though they belong and matter.

YOU ARE THE LIBRARY!

WHO CAN JOIN?

WHAT DO YOU DO?

OFFER TEEN PROGRAMMING IDEAS AND SUGGESTIONS

READ TO YOUNGER KIDS

DISCUSS TEEN-RELATED BOOKS AND COLLECTIONS

PROMOTE LIBRARY SERVICES TO THE COMMUNITY

HELP PLAN AND PARTICIPATE IN TEEN PROGRAMS

ACT AS AN ADVISORY GROUP TO THE LIBRARY

EDUCATION OTHERS ABOUT FREE SPEECH

EARN VOLUNTEER HOURS

HAVE A LOT OF FUN!

WHERE AND WHEN?

WHO TO CONTACT

LIBRARIAN

LIBRARY ADDRESS

PHONE NUMBER

Fundraising for TAGs

- Grants

- Collaboration between school and public libraries

- Scholastic Book Fair

- Bookmark contest

- Bake sales

- Car washes

- Movie nights

Students embrace reading, interacting

Middle school students help read books to younger pupils

At left: Abigail Juarez, 5, listens and reacts to books read by Franklin Middle School students Collin Kane, 14, and Carlin Fernandez, 13, during Read Across America Day at Hillcrest Elementary School Friday March 2.

At right (top): Franklin Middle School student Carlin Fernandez, 13, reads a book to kindergarteners during Read Across America Day at Hillcrest Elementary School Friday March 2.

At right (bottom): Franklin Middle School student Collin Kane, 14, reads a book to kindergarteners during Read Across America Day at Hillcrest Elementary School Friday March 2.

PHOTOS BY TANYA BREEN/ STAFF PHOTOGRAPHER

The way I make money for most of my events in a school library is through the Scholastic Book Fair that I organize along with my TAG. Through this event, I also buy small prizes and books for book contests. Since this is not enough money for author and poet visits and other big events, I have found that collaborating with my public librarian counterpart is a great way to share expenses for events that benefit us both the most.

Grants are another way to earn money for larger events and programs. The first place to look is local organizations that donate money to local groups. Where I live, there is a an organization called the Franklin Foundation that invites local groups to apply for small amounts of money ranging from $50 up to $1000 for activities or programs that encourage learning among children and teenagers. The American Library Association also offers information on grants and is the next best place to start.

Organize fund raisers that meet the unique needs and interests of your community. Every year, I organize an annual bookmark contest that is very popular with my students. I get great participation from students from all economic and social groups, as well as regular and non-library users. The students vote on their favorite bookmark and then a local printing company prints them at a much reduced price. I give the winners gift certificates for the Scholastic Book Fair, which encourages my non-reading contest winners to buy and read books. I host a party for all the winners in the library with food and desserts, which allows me to introduce those who may not use the library to all the services and fun events that are offered. The bookmarks have become so popular with students and the local community, that we sell the bookmarks at local events to raise money for more reading programs.

TAG Activities

The group can plan any activities that they are interested in and that benefit the library's program. My TAG helps me to plan big events like Banned Book Week, author visits, Read Across America, and ongoing activities. Two of the most simple, and yet important, activities are training my group members to write book reviews and give book talks. In my experience, this is a great way for the students to show how important reading is to them, how articulate they are, how surprisingly insightful teens can be, how well-read they are, and, most important, to share their interests with their parents, peers, and the community.

Teen Book Reviews

Book reviews should include the following:

- An overview of the book

- Information about the genre

- The setting

- Interesting comments about the characters

- The pace and writing style of the book

- An overall impression of the book

Although this information is important, the best book reviews don't just involve the facts, but also describes what makes the book special, what is unique about the book, and whether or not the book was enjoyable to read.

Oh,
The
Places
You'll
Go!

- "The Cat in the HatTM &
© Dr. Seuss Enterprises, L.P. 1957, 2000.
All Rights Reserved

Design a *Bookmark* for your school

Design an original bookmark that promotes us and our school in an exciting way.

Use these themes:

Oh,
The
Places
You'll
Go!

- "The Cat in the HatTM &
© Dr. Seuss Enterprises, L.P. 1957, 2000.
All Rights Reserved

Reading

Harmony

Franklin Middle School

Reading book reviews written by other teens is a great way to introduce your TAG to how book reviews are written that are informative and interesting, while still remaining true to their unique voices. It also takes away some of the apprehension that your teens may have about their ability to write reviews when they see that other teens are successful at it. Find teen reviews:

- Teen Reads.com reviews popular young adult books, has interviews with well-known authors and solicits teen readers' opinions through surveys, newsletters, blogs, and polls.

- *VOYA* magazine has one of the most extensive teen book reviewing programs available. Teen book reviewers are paired with adults to learn how to write book reviews that are objective, interesting and informative.

- Reading in Color is a great readers' blog written solely by a young adult about the books that teens enjoy. The book review site focuses on multicultural books and authors, which is a wonderful resource for teen reviewers. The style of the book reviews is very conversational and honest and is a good example of how important it is to have the reviewer's unique point of view as a teen reader show through.

- Words for Teens is a book review blog written by a young adult who loves to read and wants to share her love of reading with others. The site focuses on fantasy, steam punk, and science fiction. The reviewer manages to cover all the basic elements of a book review while still allowing her voice as a teen that likes young adult books to show through.

Teens can submit book reviews to school and public library newsletters or create a review newsletter. The TAG can make a monthly or quarterly newsletter with a book review written from each genre to give readers an idea of all the different types of books that are available.

Many local newspapers offer a teen section where teens are invited to contribute their thoughts and ideas. A school newspaper is a great place to submit reviews, because it already has a built-in audience of readers who are interested in what their peers have to say. Many online library catalogs that serve young adults have an option where teens can submit book reviews. The catalog provides an easily accessible format where the reviews can be archived for future use.

Teen Book Talks

Talking to other people about the books that inspire and excite us is often the best way to excite others about books. The reason why book talks remain popular is because of the human element that connects the words with potential readers. The purpose of book talks is not to focus on the details but to communicate to others the reader's passion and commitment to the books he is describing, so that he can convince others to read them.

Teens can give book talks to school parent/teacher meetings, which are often requesting student presentations at their meetings. After the book talks, the teens can encourage and challenge the parents to read some of books they talked about. A few of the parents and teachers at our meetings always read the books, and at the next meeting we have a mini book discussion.

Friends of the Library are groups that exist to promote and advocate for libraries. Teens sharing what books mean to them and what books are popular and interesting to them, help the adults who make up these groups to understand just how important libraries are to teens.

Books about Censorship for Book Reviews or Book Talks

The following books are about censorship and how children and young adults experience censorship. Reading and promoting these books will introduce your teens to intellectual freedom and introduce and educate others about how these issues affect everyone, no matter what the age of the reader.

Avi. *Nothing but the Truth.* Orchard, 1992.
> Ninth grade student Philip Malloy is suspended from school for singing along to "The Star-Spangled Banner" in his homeroom because he causes a disturbance. Was he standing up for his patriotic ideals, or is it all just a misunderstanding?

Blume, Judy. *Places I Never Meant to Be: Original Stories by Censored Writers.* Simon & Schuster, 1999.
> This collection of short stories describes the authors' personal experience of censorship in their own words. Judy Blume, Norma Fox Mazer, and other young adult authors are profiled.

Bradbury, Ray. *Fahrenheit 451.* Ballentine, 1953.
> The classic dystopian book, written in 1953 tells the timeless provocative story of a future society where reading is outlawed and firemen start fires to burn books.

Brown, Marc. *Arthur and the Scare Your-Pants-Off Club.* Little, Brown, 1998.
> Arthur and his friends rush to their local library to get the newest book in their favorite scary book series. They are shocked to find out that the series has been banned. Arthur, Francine, Buster, and the rest of the gang make a plan to get the book back on the shelves.

Clements, Andrew. *The Landry News.* Atheneum, 2000.
> Cara writes a newspaper editorial about her burned out and dispirited teacher, Mr. Larson. The editorial energizes the teacher who starts teaching his students journalism, and his class starts a newspaper. The teacher then uses the proceedings as a real-life lesson on the First Amendment and the students rally to his support.

Crutcher, Chris. *The Sledding Hill.* Greenwillow, 2005.
> A small group of students and parents decide that the book *The Tales of Huckleberry Finn* is racist, sexist, and immoral and should be censored by removing it from reading lists and the school library. Barney, the editor of the school's paper, decides to print his story about previous censorship efforts at school with interesting results.

Garden, Nancy. *The Year They Burned the Books.* Farrar, Straus and Giroux, 1999.
> This story centers on Jamie Crawford, the editor of the high school paper, who takes on a conservative school board candidate who opposes the sex-education curriculum. The book also features a library book burning.

Reed, M. K. *Americus.* First Second, 2011.
> This novel, written in graphic novel format, tells a story about Christian activists who try to get a favorite fantasy series banned from the Americus public library. The main character, Neal, and the local young adult librarian lead the protest against censorship.

Advocacy Organizations for Teens

National Coalition Against Censorship (NCAC): This organization's mission is to protect free expression and access to information by providing resources that include information, advocacy and support to librarians, authors, schools, teachers, and students. They document censorship cases, write letters in defense of those who are censored, and provide detailed support. There are handouts to print and examples of methods to combat censorship in its many forms.

National Coalition Against Censorship: Young Adult Groups

Youth Free Expression (NCAC): This organization works directly with students, teachers and parents to support the efforts against censorship that occurs in schools. They advocate for public policies and laws that respect free speech. They write school administrators, legislators and library boards to educate them about the rights of young adults and they recruit activists to promote and defend the free speech rights of young adults.

KidSpeak.com (NCAC): KidSpeak is a great organization that offers teens and children the opportunity to speak out about censorship. They document book challenges that occur across the United States as well as children and teens efforts to act as advocates against censorship. They also help to educate and inform teens and children about intellectual freedom, the right to read and how censorship affects everyone.

References

ACLU. Tinker v. Des Moines (393 U.S. 503, 1969) 16 March 2007. *http://www.aclu.org/free-speech/tinker-v-des-moines-393-us-503-1969*. 14 May 2012.

Bush, Laura. "25 Books to Read Before You're 25." *Seventeen Magazine*. June 2004.

Gurdan, Meghan. "Darkness Too Visible." *Wall Street Journal*. 4 June 2011. *http://online.wsj.com/article/SB10001424052702303365740457635762592697038.html*. 17 July 2011.

KidsSpeak. "Students Fired Up over Book Burning". 03 February 2005. *http://www.kidspeakonline.org/news.html*. 14 May 2012.

Legal information Institute. "Tinker v. Des Moines Independent Community School District." *http://www.law.cornell.edu/supct/html/historics/USSC_CR_0393_0503_ZO.html*. 14 May 2012.

Lenhart, Amanda. "Teens and Social Media." Pew Institute. Pew Internet & American Life, 19 December 2007. *http://www.pewinternet.org/Reports/2007/Teens-and-Social-Media.aspx*. 05 March 2011.

Mushegian, Sasha. "I love books." Kansas City.com. 16 January 2005. *http://www.kidspeakonline.org/sasha.htm*. 20 June 2011.

National Coalition Against Censorship. *http://isites.harvard.edu/fs/docs/icb.topic786630.files/Teens%20Social%20Media%20and%20Health%20-%20NYPH%20Dept%20Pew%20Internet.pdf*. 29 April 2011.

Reading in Color. *http://blackteensread2.blogspot.com/.* 15 June 2011.

Reno, Jamie. "Generation R (R Is for Reader)." *Newsweek.* 13 May 2008. *http://www.thedailybeast. com/newsweek/2008/05/13/generation-r-r-is-for-reader.html.* 07 March 2011.

Springen, Karen. "Are Teen Novels Dark and Depraved — or Saving Lives?" *Publisher's Weekly.* 09 July 2011. *http://www.publishersweekly.com/pw/by-topic/childrens/childrens-industry-news/ article/47570-are-teen-novels-dark-and-depraved---or-saving-lives-.html.* 18 July 2011.

TeensRead. *http://www.teenreads.com.* 03 June 2011.

"Thoughts On: WSJ Article, YA Saves, and the YA Genre." Worthy of Reading and Discussion: Words for Teens. 05 July 2011. *http://www.wordforteens.com/2011/06/thoughts-on-wsj-article-ya-saves-and-ya.html.* 15 July 2011.

Tuccillo, Diane. *Library Teen Advisory Groups.* Scarecrow Press, 2004.

VOYA. http://www.voya.com. 10 June 2011.

Words for Teens. *http://www.wordforteens.com.* 11 May 2011.

CHAPTER 11
LIBRARIANS AND CENSORSHIP

Facing book challenges is probably the most stressful and upsetting aspect of librarianship, according to Joan E. Berlin of the National Coalition Against Censorship, who states that what adds to the emotional turmoil is that librarians are put in an impossible situation where those that censor, "claim a kind of moral high ground," where they are working towards protecting children, while those that oppose them are dangerous and don't care about protecting children. (Hill)

Librarian Dee Ann Venuto describes her experience with the negative effects of book challenges. She was a librarian for nineteen years when she experienced her first formal challenge. A group of community members challenged three titles that they found to be inappropriate. They wanted the books removed and wanted to know who purchased the books and why. The eventual result was that one book was removed and two remained. However, for Venuto, the resolution of the immediate issue was not the end for her. She felt that although she did receive some support, some colleagues definitely did not support her or, at the least, felt uncomfortable around her; a result that had a negative effect on her level of job and life satisfaction. The emotional toil that occurs when librarians experience book challenges is so stressful, that fear of facing another one can sometimes lead librarians to self-censor in order to avoid any potential controversy. (Hill)

Viewpoint: Fear of book challenges leads to self-censorship.

A study completed by the *School Library Journal* found that 70 percent of the librarians they spoke to said they would not purchase a controversial book because of the possible reaction by parents. Forty-nine percent of those librarians also reported that they had experienced at least one book challenge and that the experience had a definite impact on their collection decisions. (*School Library Journal*)

In 2008, the *School Library Journal* published a survey in which they asked school media specialists to identify what factors led them to self-censor. They sent the survey to 5,438 of their *SLJ's Extra Helping* subscribers and received 654 replies. Seventy percent of the respondents stated that they were terrified of how parents will respond to controversial material in their collection and 29 percent reported that they are afraid of the negative reaction by their school administrators. The reactions from students at 25 percent and community members were at 23 percent, while 21 percent of librarians were affected by personal values. (*School Library Journal*)

Personal Characteristics

With many personal issues clearly affecting collection development decisions, researchers also examined the personal characteristics of age and educational level, as well as external issues in terms of what type of institution, school or public library, to explore how these issues influenced selection. They surveyed 2,145 school librarians in the states of Arkansas, Delaware, and North Carolina. They found that high school librarians were the most likely to engage in self-censorship, and that school librarians as a whole were more likely to censor than public librarians. Age was also a factor, with the possibility of engaging in censorship increasing with age, and librarians between the ages of 60-69 censoring the most. Educational level was a factor in that the lower the educational level, the higher the possibility of censorship. Inversely, those with master's degrees or higher level certification or licensure had the lowest rates. (Rickman)

Content of Books

In the 2008 survey conducted by *School Library Journal*, they also examined the content that caused librarians to self-censor and found that sexual content was the reason most often given, with profanity and homosexuality also being very highly rated. Other studies and surveys also mirrored these results. Young found that self-censorship decisions were made on the basis of religion, sexuality, violence, and profanity. (*School Library Journal*)

- Sexual content, 87 percent

- Language, 61 percent

- Violence, 51 percent

- Homosexuality, 47 percent

- Racism, 34 percent

- Religion, 16 percent

Sexuality

The Teen Lit Lab studied the relationship of librarians' personal views on the sexual content of books and how that affected their selection decisions, and found that although they overwhelmingly were anti-censorship, they nevertheless experienced a great deal of personal conflict over the decision to purchase books that featured explicit content.

This conflict was also explored in 2007 by researchers who found that librarians were systematically not purchasing the most popular and well-reviewed LGBT young adult books. Researchers Jeff Whittingham and Wendy Rickman completed a study in which they checked the online library catalogs and asked a cross section of media specialists if their collections featured the most popular and well-reviewed gay-, bisexual-, lesbian-, and transgender-themed books that were published between 1999 and 2005. This list included *Rainbow Boys, Geography Club,* and *Boy Meets Boy,* among other titles. (Whelan) They asked a total of 499 librarians and only received thirty-seven replies, which they attributed to the high level of unease the librarians had with the subject matter overall. They found that about twenty-one percent of public libraries, nearly five percent of university libraries, and less than one percent of school libraries had any of the books on the list.

What is interesting about these results is that they essentially mirror the reasons listed for book challenges by the ALA. Librarians, like everyone else, struggle with balancing the needs and interests of their young adult readers with the rapidly expanding teen book market. Figuring out a proper balance between maturity of the readers in terms of profane language or sexuality is a difficult process at best. Combine that with the expectations of the community or school system makes an objective approach to collection development decisions even more difficult.

Selectors vs. Censors

Understanding the difference between selecting materials and censoring materials is the key towards adhering to that commitment; selectors and censors approach collections differently. Selectors are inclusive, positive, and see balance, while censors seek exclusivity and control. Selectors seek to promote reading and education, while censors seek to inhibit reading and the freedom that inspires learning. Keep this approach in mind when selecting books as the best way to ensure that your collection is diverse in terms of multiculturalism, books that represent LGBT teens, and religion.

> Cynthia Grant, the author of *White Horse*, a popular young adult book about heroin addiction, states, "The best collection is one that always makes you feel slightly uneasy. In other words, if you're doing your job, somebody won't be happy." (Coley)

Librarians and Self-Censorship

The selection of books is supposed to be an objective process that is shaped solely by the needs of the library users that we serve. However, due to outside criticism and influences as well as personal values and culture, this seemingly simple activity becomes complicated. Self-censorship occurs when you restrict a reader's access to books for reasons that are subjective, such as worrying what might happen, or to circumvent any objections that might occur, you are acting as a censor. Self-censorship is that simple and that complex, as it is one of the least understood and most complicated issues that librarians face today.

Self-Censorship Scenarios

- *Placing a book in a locked cabinet or behind glass*: Some librarians might take a controversial book and lock it away where it can be seen, but not touched without permission. Restrictions such as these are frustrating, says author Coe Booth, who knows of a few libraries where her book *Tyrell* has been put in glass display cases or locked behind the librarian's desk instead of in the teen section. Her disappointment lies within the idea that these restrictions are being put into place in anticipation of a challenge and not in reaction to any actual complaints.

- *Moving a book meant for children into the adult department*: Books that are written and intended for young adults or children are moved into the adult collection or nonfiction collection because they are considered too controversial for young adults or children to have open access to them. In 2000, the books *Heather Has Two Mommies* and *Daddy's Roommate*, children's picture books that were written for very young children about the subject of children who have gay and lesbian parents, were removed from the children's section of the library by the town council and moved to the adult section after a religious group complained and challenged the books. The courts eventually ruled against the decision and the books were replaced. (NCAC)

- *Requiring young adults to have permission to check the book out*: When certain books are considered controversial, sometimes librarians will require that students get permission from their parents before they are allowed to read it in order to avoid any problems. One of the first court cases that dealt with this issue occurred in 2002, when the school board decided to place the Harry Potter book series on a restricted borrowing list that would require parental permission in order for the children to check them out. The parents argued that creating this restriction stigmatized the books and their readers. The court ruled in favor of the parents, stating that requiring permission implied that the books and readers were evil.

- *Purchasing the book and then removing it without any due process*: After a book is purchased and the librarian, parents, or administrators read it, they then decide that they made a mistake and want to remove the book. However, a book can't just be removed without a process of an objective review taking place.

- *Not buying the book*: Not purchasing a book because it might cause controversy or because it might be challenged is probably the most prevalent way that self-censorship occurs. Barry Lyga, the author of *Boy Toy*, explains in an interview for *School Library Journal,* that this manner of censorship has the potential to be the most destructive because of its insidious nature. When he finished *Boy Toy*, a well-reviewed novel about a twelve-year-old who has sex with his seventh grade teacher, he expected parents to be incited, letters to local papers, and complaints to the school board. But instead, nothing happened and the book sold fewer copies than his previous books. After casual conversations with librarians, who told him that they loved the book but that there was no way they could buy it, and noting that several bookstores had it shelved in the adult department, he realized that there were no complaints because young adults were not getting the book. "The book just didn't get out there," says Lyga, "Kids weren't getting the book because adults weren't letting them get the book." (Whelan)

What Is the Cost of Self-Censorship?

Book challenges are blatant and provoke an immediate and visceral response that is characterized by passionate public discourse that serves to inform and educate all of us. An individual or a group objects to the content of a book that contains sexuality, violence, or profanity, among other complaints. Letters or formal complaints are written and submitted, usually followed by school or library board meetings where everyone can give their opinions with an eventual decision being made.

Intellectual freedom is at risk with self-censorship that is subtle, quiet, and occurs under the radar with only the librarian as the sole witness. This secrecy has the effect of creating an imminent risk to the intellectual freedom of us all because everyone is denied the opportunity of even knowing that the ideas exist and are perhaps controversial to some, denying the opponents and supporters the chance to have an open discussion about their beliefs. Students who are denied the freedom to read lose out on their opportunity to expand their minds and outlook on life when the literature that they read is so sanitized that their critical thinking skills are impaired.

Finally, the dilemma is this, if our collections are so free of any material that could possibly upset anyone or inspire thought or debate, than our libraries will soon have nothing of interest to offer anyone. Allowing materials to easily be noticed and accessed by library patrons is the goal of all librarians, however, in our zeal to provide the kind of access that everyone wants, it can be just as easy to forget to be aware of restrictions slowly encroaching upon intellectual freedom.

Viewpoint: Leveled reading in libraries equals censorship.

The goals of educators in schools, school libraries, and public libraries are for their students to read with fluency and comprehension, and have the ability to critically evaluate what they have read. To achieve this goal, reading levels have been implemented, and in some cases mandated, in many public schools. Reading levels are based on word frequency, or how often the same words appear in a passage of text; and syntactic complexity, or the average sentence length in a passage of text. Students are assessed by their classroom teachers based on their ability to recognize words and their ability to assign meaning to the story. Reading levels are then assigned to children based on those levels. (Manna) Many parents who are aware that their children are being taught and evaluated through these various programs request leveled books in their public libraries. Parents, teachers, and administrators also often request that school librarians design their collections around this concept.

This may seem to be a problem that mainly occurs in elementary libraries; however, middle school and high school literature classes also assess for reading capabilities and assign reading levels to their students. This presents a particular problem for young adult librarians who, when guiding more independent readers, need the flexibility to let them assess for themselves what type of book engages their desire to read. The dilemma for all librarians is that no matter what the age of the child, restricting access to library materials based on age or grade level does not acknowledge or respect the individual needs, interests, and abilities of users and violates the Library Bill of Rights. The problems are:

1. That readers may feel, or actually be, compelled by teachers to only choose books from their reading level, thus restricting their access to books with other reading levels that they might otherwise enjoy.

2. Relying only on the age or grade level of the students does not take into account their maturity level, social experiences, culture, or other miscellaneous factors that make up their overall reading level.

3. Relying totally on the level of books selected solely by computerized selection does not utilize all the elements that make up a comprehensive library collection.

This has inadvertently created some censorship problems that were most likely preventable. In 2005, the ALA reported that the book *The Perks of Being a Wallflower* was challenged due to a page in the book about date rape. The problem was that the book was assigned a fourth grade reading level by the Accelerated Reading program and had been placed in elementary schools. The book, which received excellent reviews and is popular among teenagers, is designated for young adult readers, and most likely, is not a book that a trained library collection specialist would have selected for elementary students. When asked whether or not challenging the book was censorship, Pat Scales stated that no, questioning a book's relevance based on the maturity and emotional level of the students is not censorship. The fault lies in depending on a computerized system without the additional checks and balances found in collection development policies. (*School Library Journal*)

A similar incident occurred in Jefferson, Indiana, where *Tyrell*, a book recommended for grades nine and up, was placed on elementary books shelves because the Accelerated Reading program stated that fourth grade was the appropriate reading level. The author Coe Booth, when asked about the controversy, stated that the book is written for and marketed for teenagers and although she knows that some younger children do read it and appreciate it, she did not write it with that age group in mind. The school did have a book policy in place and eventually decided to remove the book from the elementary schools and leave it in place in the high school. (*Chicago Tribune*)

Viewpoint: Book labeling equals censorship.

Providing labels for books is a great way to help guide young adults to the genre and type of writing that they are the most interested in. The labels must correspond to a genre and also be neutral in viewpoint. You also want to avoid segregating books into a certain area that would make them appear to be something too controversial or strange to be included with the rest of the books. For example, I label and place the entire graphic novel and manga collection close to the checkout desk on easily accessible shelves, so that my students can run in between classes and check them in and out quickly.

Labeling Christian books with Christian labels is considered to promote censorship because libraries that mark books as Christian or religious fiction, might be construed as preferring Christianity over other religions. The preference for any religion is a violation of church and state that is prohibited by the First Amendment and the Library Bill of Rights. What you can do is label the books as inspirational fiction, which covers a wide range of books that promote inspiration and life affirmation.

In 1950, the famous Harlem Renaissance author Zora Neale Hurston wrote about the segregation of books written by African American authors in her article, "What White Publishers Won't Print." In this article, she said, "For various reasons, the average, struggling, non-morbid Negro is the best-kept secret in America." (Hurston)

Labeling multicultural books, while seemingly making them more accessible, also can appear to mark them as being segregated into a multicultural section that is set aside for one group of people and not for others. Coe Booth makes reference to this issue when discussing some librarians' reaction to her book *Tyrell*. She finds it "infuriating," because it seems as if, "any book with an African American character on the cover is quickly labeled street lit, regardless of the subject matter or the setting of the book." (*School Library Journal*) Bernice McFadden is the critically acclaimed author of debut novel, *Sugar*, her debut novel. She has gone on to write several more successful adult novels that are also popular with older teenagers. She points out that there are no labels for "British Literature, White American Literature, Korean Literature, or Pakistani Literature." She coined the term, "seg-book-gation" to describe the marginalization that she and other African American writers use to describe what they feel is the labeling and segregation of their work into separate sections that they feel announce to other readers that their books are "not for them." (McFadden)

Viewpoint: Recommended book lists equal censorship.

When a local school has a required summer reading list, and the library pulls the titles from the general collection and places them together, is that considered viewpoint-neutral? Yes. Lists, such as those for summer reading or to assist with collection development, help to provide books that will be in high demand for teen library users. Selections should be accessible to all users and not limited to the target audience.

However, it also important to be aware of possible biases that can occur in ready made lists that could potentially cause unintended censorship. An unintended bias is exhibited in formal lists that professional groups prepare for librarians to utilize for collection development. YALSA studied award winning book lists and popular book lists to determine the level of diversity they represented. The lists were chosen because many busy librarians select the books to purchase from them. The award winners list, the popular lists, and the lists made by teens were deficient in various areas of representation of diversity. Many did not feature non-white, religious, and LGBT protagonists, and those who lived in urban areas. All of the lists did not adequately represent Hispanics. The lists are still useful, but it is important to recognize that bias is everywhere. Expand your search criteria to ensure that the collection you create respects an open-minded, objective view. (Rawson)

Librarians Take Action: Address the issues of reading levels.

1. Most library OPACS have a built-in reading level option. If it does, you can instruct parents, teachers, library administrators, and young adults how to use it.

2. Most of the reading programs have lists of books by reading levels that can be checked to see if your library carries them.

3. Offer to do a workshop for parents on reading advisory and its relationship to reading levels.

4. Offer to do a workshop for school administrators and teachers on reading advisory and reading levels.

Librarians Take Action: Use careful consideration when labeling books.

Labeling by rotating trendy sections is the best practice. Feature popular series, like The Clique, Kimani Tru, and Pretty Little Liars books on the same shelves, or feature popular sports authors, like Paul Volponi and David Lubar together.

1. Be aware of how limiting some labels can be.

2. Don't label by ethnicity or gender.

3. Labels are helpful when they are grouped by overall interests, for example:

    - vampire stories

    - love stories

    - mysteries

    - fantasy

Open Communication with Colleagues

Blogs and FAQs are great places to obtain information.

1. The ALA provides a FAQ on intellectual freedom and censorship that helps librarians find the answers that they need to alleviate some of the doubt and confusion that they may have. I also refer to questions and answers that I have gathered from discussions with other librarians, as well as questions that I found debated on library blog sites. The issues that concern librarians are discussed in these open forums.

2. Pat Scales offers a column that provides librarians with practical advice in the *School Library Journal.* One such article referenced a librarian who was wondering if she should purchase *The Lovely Bones* for her middle school students. Pat Scales answered that the best idea was to refer to their selection policy and what it said about adult books and teen readers. She also said that just because a student asks for a book, it does not mean that they are mature enough to read it. That is what professional reader's guidance is all about. (*School Library Journal*)

3. The Cooperative Children's Book Center offers an online intellectual freedom question and answer website where librarians post questions and trained experts in intellectual freedom answer the questions. This is a great place to ask difficult questions. (CCBC)

Speak openly and honestly with librarians and other colleagues.

1. Encourage other librarians to share their fears and concerns without judgment.

2. Talk openly with colleagues about the barriers that can influence selection policy.

3. Create an environment where librarians feel comfortable and supported.

4. If you are in a leadership position, make the first move in encouraging discussion. (Schliesman)

References

CCBC. "Intellectual Library." University of Wisconsin, 2011. *http://www.education.wisc.edu/ccbc.* 15 March 2011.

Coley, Kenneth. Moving Toward a Method to Test for Self-Censorship by School Library Media Specialists. AASL. December 2002. *http://www.ala.org/aasl/aaslpubsandjournals/slmrb/slmrcontents/volume52002/coley.* 14 May 2012.

Gonzalez, Michael. "Gary takes closer look at 'Tyrell'." *Chicago Post Tribune.* 04 August 2011. *http://posttrib.suntimes.com/news/3742086-418/gary-takes-closer-look-at-tyrell.html.* 05 September 2011.

Grogan, David. "Arkansas Lawsuit Says Restricting a Book Counts the Same as Banning It." American BookSellers Foundation for Free Expression. 07 March 2003. *http://news.bookweb.org/news/arkansas-lawsuit-says-restricting-book-counts-same-banning-it.* 05 April 2011.

Hill, Rebecca. "The Problem of Self Censorship." *School Library Monthly*. November 2010. 9-12.

Hurston, Zora Neale. "What White Publishers Won't Print" *Negro Digest*, April 1950. *http://mahogany-books.com/blog/2010/06/what-white-publishers-wont-print-by-zora-neale-hurston*. 14 May 2012.

Manna, Ruth. Leveled Reading Systems: Mysteries Revealed. 2012. *http://www.scholastic.com/teachers/article/leveled-reading-systems*. 14 May 2012.

McFadden, Bernice. "Black Writers in the Ghetto of the Publishing Industry Making." *Washington Post*, 26 June 2010. *http://www.washingtonpost.com/wp-dyn/content/article/2010/06/25/AR2010062504125.html?hpid=opinionsbox1*. 20 March 2011.

NCAC. "Heather Has Two Mommies and Public Library access policies." *http://www.thefileroom.org/documents/dyn/DisplayCase.cfm/id/356*. 23 May 2011.

Rawson, Casey. "Are All Lists Created Equal? Diversity in Award-Winning and Bestselling Young Adult Fiction." *Journal of Research on Libraries and Young Adults*. 1.3 (2011): *http://www.yalsa.ala.org/jrlya/2011/06/are-all-lists-created-equal-diversity-in-award-winning-and-bestselling-young-adult-fiction/*. 08 August 2011.

Rickman, Alan. "A Study of Self-Censorship by School Librarians." American Association of School Librarians, 2006. *http://www.ala.org/aasl/aaslpubsandjournals/slmrb/slmrcontents/volume13/rickman*. 7 November 2011.

Rickman, Wendy. "A Study of Self-Censorship by School Librarians." American Association of School Librarians, 2006. *http://www.ala.org/aasl/aaslpubsandjournals/slmrb/slmrcontents/volume13/rickman*. 18 November 2011.

Scales, Pat. "School Library Media Centers and Intellectual Freedom." *Intellectual Freedom Manual*, 2009. *http://www.ala.org/ala/aboutala/offices/oif/iftoolkits/ifmanual/fifthedition/schoollibrary.cfm*. 18 May 2011.

———. "Success Stories: It's tough to remove labels, but it's not impossible." *School Library Journal*, 2010. *http://www.libraryjournal.com/slj/articlescensorship/856649-341/success_stories_ itaposs_tough_to.html.csp*. 11 January 2011.

Schliesman, Megan. "Self-Censorship: Let's Talk About It." Children's Cooperative Book Center. Spring 2007. *http://www.education.wisc.edu/ccbc/freedom/selfcensorship.asp*. 10 May 2011.

Whelan, Debra Lau. "A Dirty Little Secret: Self-Censorship." *School Library Journal*. 1 February 2009. *http://www.schoollibraryjournal.com/slj/home/886066312/nj_library_citing_ child_porngraphy.html.csp*. 22 Feb. 2012.

———. "Gay Titles Missing in Most AR Libraries." *School Library Journal*. 1 January 2007. *http://www.schoollibraryjournal.com/article/CA6403256.html*. 15 February 2011.

———. "SLJ Self-Censorship Survey." *School Library Journal*. 01 February 2009. *http://www.schoollibraryjournal.com/article/CA6633729.html*. 04 June 2011.

Chapter 12
The Selection Policy

A good selection policy can help prevent the potential for self-censorship because following it helps librarians guide their choices based on predetermined goals that are objective and not subjective. A good selection policy is also essential because it is the best defense against book challenges and potential censorship. A *great* selection policy is about more than protecting yourself and your decisions from potential challenges. It is an opportunity to put on paper your vision of the type of library you want to offer to your library users.

The policy should reflect the individual mission, goals, and overall values of your library and create a clear, comprehensive plan that you can refer to if anyone has questions about materials that you have purchased. It also demonstrates to anyone who examines it just how committed you are to meeting the needs of all library users. Great selection policies only come about after a complex process takes place that includes an in-depth internal and external work that must be addressed.

Explore Your Personal Issues

Before you start writing your selection policy you first need to openly and honestly explore your personal characteristics, thoughts, and values to determine what affect, if any, they have on your collection decisions. The collection development process has been characterized as a logical and rational activity that is characterized by objectivity and impartiality. In fact, most of the literature that discusses collection development and selection policies only discuss the mental process and not the affective or emotional process that accompanies it. However, the influence of our personal values and characteristics, our internal debates, as well as our questions and concerns about the appropriateness, in terms of issues like sexuality and profanity in young adult literature, and the impact of external criticism and the potential for book challenges, all can affect how we choose books and other materials for our libraries.

There are so many elements that develop and define your approach to developing selection policies that match your library users and your community. Clearly, self-awareness is essential to successfully navigating that process. "Self-knowledge is critical to a library media professional. You need to know yourself and your bias. Your values can influence your decisions. Your personal stand on issues such as abortion, capital punishment, or drug abuse can have an impact on everything from the materials you select to the topics you use as examples." (Lamb)

Issues Affecting Selection Decisions

- *Cultural Background*: Be aware of how your cultural background influences your selection choices and personal approach. As an African American person who loved to read as child, I can distinctly remember how disappointing it was to never see any books about teenagers like myself in libraries or bookstores. As a result, now that there are so many books available that feature multicultural themes and protagonists, I feel that it is my duty to ensure that my collection reflects the experiences of all of my library users.

- *Educational Philosophy:* When the TeenLitLab interviewed librarians to gain their professional perspective on sexuality in young adult literature, a discussion ensued regarding whether or not librarians should differentiate between purchasing books that examined teen sexuality in an explorative or an exploitative way. Some librarians thought that regardless of the context, any sexual acts that might be gratuitous should not be purchased, while others thought that librarians should at the least be informed of any objectionable content and be prepared to discuss it with the library user. Still another librarian did not see the need to distinguish between the two at all, because, in her professional opinion, "Just like in real life, the experience of reading about sexuality for teens could be exploratory or exploitative, and still be educational for them." (TeenLitLab)

- *Parental Status:* Point of view is everything when it comes to how questions regarding censorship are debated, as Kelly Burgess, a journalist and a mother, soon discovered. She was assigned to cover a story about censorship in which a mother was fighting to get a book she considered inappropriate removed from her local public library, and a young adult librarian was fighting equally hard to keep it in. The book in question was *Lilly a Love Story,* a romance that takes place in 1883 between a young girl and an outlaw. As a librarian who specialized in objectivity, she didn't expect to have any particular reaction to the story. However, as she became more familiar with the sections of the book that were sexually explicit in nature and depiction, she surprisingly found herself becoming sympathetic to the mother who wanted the book removed. As a mother, Burgess was forced to admit that she would have been appalled if her seven-year-old daughter were a few years older and had happened to come across that book and read those passages in her local library. A few years later her daughter turned thirteen, and Burgess's perspective evolved again, as her daughter was reading books that years earlier she could not imagine that she would have ever allowed her daughter to read. Today, she and her now sixteen-year-old daughter read many of the same books and openly discuss the issues that the books reveal. As she looks back on the story she covered years ago and its impact, she finds that she can look at the experience with a new perspective and understanding of the powerful influence that life experience has on shaping our views and the perceptions of the boundaries between those personal perceptions and censorship. (Burgess)

- *Other Issues*: Take the time to think of other issues that impact your philosophy and values system, or that are "hot button issues" for you in terms of collection development, and include guidelines for those issues in your selection policy. The School Media Center site for librarians suggests that you choose at least three issues that particularly stand out in your mind and explore your true feelings about them. They suggest a few topics and I have added some more in the following table.

Political viewpoints	Angels	Abortion	Racism
Evolution	The Koran	Children's rights	Witchcraft
Graphic novels	Profanity	Violence	Fantasy books

Diversity and Inclusivity

Before you begin to write your selection policy, you also need to ensure that you are meeting the criteria of the Library Bill of Rights, which ensures the rights of every library user to have access to information that reflects their experiences and their world.

The ALA offers this Interpretation of the Library Bill of Rights to explain the commitment to diversity in collection development,

> "Library collections must represent the diversity of people and ideas in our society. There are many complex facets to any issue, and many contexts in which issues may be expressed, discussed, or interpreted. Librarians have an obligation to select and support access to materials and resources on all subjects that meet, as closely as possible, the needs, interests, and abilities of all persons in the community the library serves.
>
> "Librarians have a professional responsibility to be inclusive, not exclusive, in collection development and in the provision of interlibrary loan. Access to all materials and resources legally obtainable should be assured to the user, and policies should not unjustly exclude materials and resources even if they are offensive to the librarian or the user. This includes materials and resources that reflect a diversity of political, economic, religious, social, minority, and sexual issues. A balanced collection reflects a diversity of materials and resources, not an equality of numbers."

Diversity incorporates a wide variety of variables that interact to define and shape individuality that include:

1. *Gender*
2. *Race and Nationality*
3. *Religion*
4. *Family Status*
5. *Sexual Orientation*
6. *Socioeconomic Status*
7. *Disability*

Multiculturalism

Diversity is welcomed and promoted within the library community and yet, the personal stereotypes and lack of awareness of multicultural experiences, lifestyle, and culture, either unconsciously or consciously, can still influence how books are selected for our collections, leading librarians to subjectively reject or ignore books that do not reflect the experiences that they are accustomed to, or believe are appropriate and necessary.

Multicultural Resources

When selecting multicultural books and other materials, the traditional resources are very helpful. *VOYA*, *School Library Journal*, and *Multicultural Review* offer a large variety of book reviews and featured articles on multicultural authors and subjects. However, bloggers who live, breathe, and write about multicultural books nonstop offer real time, first hand information that is eye-opening, fascinating, and are essential resources for teen librarians.

1. The Brown BookShelf. *http://thebrownbookshelf.com*

    The Brown Bookshelf focuses on bringing an awareness of African American authors and books to the public through its book lists and links to authors' websites. They feature a special yearly program called "28 Days Later," a campaign to showcase a different African American writer every day during Black History Month.

2. Reading in Color. *http://blackteensread2.blogspot.com/p/reading-poc-me.html*

    Reading in Color is a book blog site featuring book reviews, booklists, and showcases book challenges. What distinguishes this book blog site from others is that it was founded by a teenager who is dedicated to encouraging multicultural teens to blog about multicultural books. The blog also advocates for diversity throughout the publishing industry by supporting initiatives that take a stand against the predominance of young adult book covers that don't feature multiracial characters. The site recently won the award for best teen blog site from the Black Weblog Awards.

3. Black Books Direct. *http://www.blackbooksdirect.com*

    Black Books is a Yahoo store that distributes the most current and difficult to locate books, DVDs, and audio books about African American culture. The books are separated by teen and children's categories and also feature Christian books and graphic novels, as well as other materials.

4. DiversityinYA.com. *http://www.diversityinya.com/category/blog*

    Diversity in Young Adult Fiction is a readers' and writers' blog from a wide variety of backgrounds that want to encourage diversity in fiction. The blog was founded by two new YA authors, Malinda Lo, the author of *Ash,* and Cindy Pon, the author of *Silver Phoenix*. They feature such specials as Diversity Roundup where they focus on topics like biracial characters in teen literature, the Demonization of Complexity, in which they discuss "why we feel obligated to pick a side between two races, or two religions, or cultures." They want to use their site to remind everyone to diversify their reading.

5. Bowllan's Blog. *http://blog.schoollibraryjournal.com/bowllansblog*

    Amy Bowllan educates, informs, and advocates for diversity in all aspects of young adult literature in her *School Library Journal* blog, Writers against Racism. She tackles such diverse issues as the Irish soldiers of Mexico, boys and reading for pleasure, and Invisible Children, an organization that seeks to inform readers about the struggles of girls of color around the world who fight for the right to go to school.

Research studies, journal articles, and personal anecdotes all refer to the abundance of literature that feature LGBT teen protagonists and the issues that shape how they experience adolescence. The issue used to be, as with books about multicultural characters, that there was little or no reference to any gay characters that was positive, if they were mentioned at all. Now there are books available, but incredibly, the books still aren't getting to their intended readers.

Young Adult Selection Policy

Young adult literature, with its specific focus on the interests, issues, and problems that are unique to young adults, can be playful, controversial, and inspirational all at the same time. And yet, most libraries, unless they are school libraries, are relegated to a paragraph or two in many libraries' selection policies. Young adult fiction, like the young adults who read it, is characterized by its constant evolution, volatility, and unique ability to inspire; all characteristics that merit, and even demand, its own selection policy. Having a separate young adult selection policy is essential because it is your best defense against book challenges and potential censorship.

Basic Elements of the Selection Policy

- *The mission of your library*: This section should provide a brief overview of what your library wants to accomplish and goals for library users. A brief statement regarding intellectual freedom and the Library Bill of Rights should be included.

- *Responsibility for selection of library resources*: This section should list who is involved in the selection process and what their exact role is. It should also describe the commitment to selecting in an objective manner that rejects censorship.

- *Purpose of young adult literature*: This section should describe the characteristics of young adult literature that make it unique and special. Adolescent development and how it relates to the selection should also be mentioned, along with some mention of the topics and subjects of the books that will be explored when making selections.

- *Description of the elements that comprise your collection*: Fiction, non-fiction, graphic novels and comics materials, magazines, gifts.

- *Objectives to be met by the selection process*: This section will provide the overall specific goals that the selection process strives to achieve.

- *Specific criteria used to meet the selection goals*: This section will describe in detail the specific elements that will be used to choose resources.

- *Weeding process should be described*: Many people become concerned to see library materials being thrown away. A description of why and how to dispose of your resources will help alleviate those concerns.

- *Resources used for the selection process*: This section should describe what journals and websites you use to find the resources that will be selected.

- *Selection policy and special endeavors*: In the policy special selection, issues should be addressed. For example, diversity in literature, especially in terms of multiculturalism should be a goal that is described and worked towards to ensure that your collection is inclusive. LGBT teens are an underserved group in many public and school libraries in regards to literature that enables them to have avenues to explore their interests, as well as educating and introducing others to their world. Recognize areas that are specific to your library. For example, if you buy adult literature for your more mature teen readers you should describe what criteria you use.

- *Selection policy and controversial issues*: A detailed explanation as to what issues are considered controversial and how these issues are recognized and addressed through the selection process should be included. The library's definition of censorship and a statement on how all efforts to censor will be rejected should be made here. A statement regarding what the response of the library will be if parents or community members have questions or concerns about any materials the library has should also be included.

Sample Selection Policy

Your Library Selection Policy
Library Mission

The mission of the Library is to serve all the teen library users in the community by offering them services and reading material that meets their cultural, recreational, social and educational needs through open access to all resources as specified in the Library Bill of Rights and supported by our commitment to Intellectual Freedom.

Responsibility for Selection of Library Resources

All decisions related to book selection will encourage diversity and inclusivity as indicated in the Library Bill of Rights. The selection of Library materials shall be a collaborative process where the library staff, administrators, teachers, students, parents (school library), and community members (public library). The library director or administrator is responsible for giving final approval of all materials selected for the library. The young adult librarians have the responsibility of locating resources that are diverse, inclusive, popular, and relevant to young adult library users.

Purpose of Young Adult Literature

The purpose of young adult literature is to provide adolescents with books that recognize that they have transitioned from children's literature to novels that reflect their unique interests and needs as adolescents who are in the midst of developing their sense of self and personal identity. Teens in this developmental stage are interested in books that mirror their efforts to shape their evolving sense of self such as coming of age stories, dating, friendships, sexuality, self esteem, school, parent, sibling relationships and problems with unique significance to teens such as eating disorders, bullying, drug usage, body image and gangs among other issues.

Fiction: The fiction collection is comprised of titles meeting the recreational and educational needs of students in seventh through twelfth grades. Books are selected to meet the varying reading interests and reading abilities of the diverse community. Series and genre fiction are included as well as novels about the problems of contemporary teens that cover a wide range of subjects, themes, and life situations. A work of fiction may be purchased despite the use of an occasional unpleasant word or incident, provided that the total impact of the book meets other selection criteria.

Selection of fiction is made with reference to one or more of these criteria:

- It should provide pleasant reading for recreational and creative use of leisure time.

- It should contribute positively to the individual's educational needs, awareness of self, community, and cultural heritage and awareness of self in terms of mind, body, and health.

- It should promote an awareness of a wide variety of societies, cultures, ethnicities, and races.

- It should match and represent the developmental level of its teen readers in terms of emotional, social, and psychological maturity.

- It should contribute to the value of the library's collection as a whole by representing all types and styles of literature.

Non-Fiction: Non-fiction titles should include readability, authenticity, existing library holdings, and community interest. Non-fiction titles should provide a balance between popular and high interest titles.

Graphic Novels and Comics: Manga, graphic novels, and comics are selected based upon the age appropriateness of the text and illustrations. The collection may also include non-fiction and classics in graphic format. Selections are based upon professional reviews, customer requests, and the popularity of styles, authors, characters, and series.

Audio Materials: Audio materials that meet the selection criteria for fiction and non-fiction materials are purchased in a variety of formats to meet the listening needs of the teen community. Preference is given to popular titles and titles that appear on the summer reading lists.

Magazines: Basic popular and general informational magazines of interest to teens are selected to supplement the book collection and meet the recreational reading needs of teens.

Gifts: Gifts will be accepted and judged on the same basis as purchased materials. The inclusion in the collection will be based upon the condition of the material, literary merit, duplication, and available space. Gifts not added to the collection will be placed in the library's book sale or disposed of as the library sees fit.

Objectives to Be Met by the Selection Process

1. To provide materials that will enrich and support the varied interests, abilities, learning styles, and maturity levels of the teens served; this means that resources that meet the varied reading levels and abilities of all teens will be actively sought.

2. To provide materials that will stimulate growth in factual knowledge, literary appreciation, aesthetic values, and societal standards.

3. To provide materials on various sides of controversial issues so that teens may have an opportunity to develop the ability to critically analyze and make informed judgments about the information they receive.

4. To provide materials that represent the many religious, ethnic, and cultural groups and that contribute to our national heritage and the world community.

5. To place principle above personal opinion and reason above prejudice in the selection of materials of the highest quality in order to assure a comprehensive collection appropriate to the school community.

6. Library resources will meet high standards of quality in factual content and presentation.

7. Library resources will be selected to help students gain an awareness of our pluralistic society.

8. Library resources will be selected for their strengths, rather than rejected for their weaknesses.

Specific Criteria Used to Meet the Selection Objectives

Literary Quality: Literary quality relates to style of writing or the arrangement of words and sentences that best expresses the dominating theme. It includes sentence structure, dialogue, and vocabulary. Literary quality is not affected by format or illustration.

Storyline: Character driven, action packed, intricately plotted, issue oriented, plot driven.

Tone: Funny, suspenseful, romantic, upbeat, emotionally intense, serious, dark.

Writing style: Dialogue rich, attention grabbing, engaging, witty, compelling, descriptive.

Genre: Genre fiction, also known as popular fiction, is a term for fictional works (novels, short stories) written with the intent of fitting into a specific literary genre in order to appeal to readers and fans already familiar with that genre.

Types of Genre Used for Selection

Realistic fiction, fantasy, horror, humor, mystery, suspense, science fiction, graphic novels, and romance.

Multiculturalism

Books and other resources that address the experience of all library users will be selected to ensure that the diversity of every teen's experience—that includes multiculturalism, ethnicity, and sexual orientation—will be equally represented.

General Requirements

1. Contribution the subject matter makes to the interests of the students.

2. Popularity with teen library users.

3. Award winning literature.

4. Parent, community member, teen recommendation.

5. Price relevant to budgetary needs.

6. Favorable reviews found in standard selection sources.

7. Reputation and significance of the author, producer, and publisher.

8. Validity, currency, and appropriateness of material.

9. Contribution the material makes to breadth of representative viewpoints on controversial issues.

10. High degree of potential user appeal.

11. High artistic quality and/or literary style.

12. Quality and variety of format.

13. Value commensurate with cost and/or need.

Resources Used for the Selection Process

The journals and websites used to find the resources that will be selected include:

1. Amazon.com. *http://www.amazon.com*

2. *School Library Journal. http://www.schoollibraryjournal.com*

3. *VOYA. http://www.voya.com*

4. *Teacher-Librarian. http://www.teacherlibrarian.com*

5. *Library Journal. http://www.libraryjournal.com*

6. Barnes and Noble. *http://www.barnesandnoble.com*

7. Coretta Scott King Award Home. *http://www.ala.org/template.cfm?template=/CFApps/ awards_info/award_detail_home.cfm&FilePublishTitle=Awards,%20Grants%20and%20 Scholarships&uid=A3F20048C4DAB6F2*

8. Follett TITLEWAVE. *http://www.titlewave.com*

9. Multicultural Book Reviews. *http://www.mcreview.com/*

10. Newbery Medal Home Page. *http://www.ala.org/alsc/awardsgrants/bookmedia/newberymed-al/newberymedal*

11. Teen Reading (YALSA). *http://www.ala.org/yalsa/teenreading/trw/trw2011/home*

12. Other non-traditional resources that are unique to the library

Weeding

The teen collection undergoes systematic weeding and withdrawal in an attempt to keep the collection relevant and accurate. Materials may be withdrawn because of unnecessary duplication, poor condition, biased content, obsolete content, or disuse. Evaluation techniques are used to measure collection usefulness in terms of scope and depth, as well as strengths and weaknesses. Materials are evaluated for deletion based upon:

• Age and condition of item

• Comparison of the collection with accepted core collection lists

- Circulation

- Relevance to observed and anticipated community needs and desires

- Long-term or historical significance or interest

Selection Policy and Special Endeavors

Diversity in Literature. Inclusivity and recognition of multiculturalism will be addressed by actively seeking materials that reflect the complexity and entirety of the multicultural experience is reflected in the collection.

LGBT Issues. LGBT teens are an underrepresented group in many public and school libraries in regards to literature that speaks to their existence and experience in their communities as evidenced by anecdotes and a growing body of research. This collection will actively search for literature that reflects their interests as well as educating and introducing others to their world.

Selection Policy and Controversial Issues

Profanity. Authors use profanity in young adult novels to reflect the reality of the manner that some teens express themselves, because it depicts the lifestyle of the characters their family or their community, or perhaps because it demonstrates the character's personality, emotions, or state of mind. The standard for what language is considered appropriate and what is inappropriate varies due to culture, values, family, and community standards and the characters depicted in young adult novels reflect this variety.

Sex. The controversy surrounding sexuality in young adults books is usually centered around the depiction of the physical act, however, sexuality as it is written about is not only about the physical act of sex but represents the entirety of the adolescent sexual experience that includes puberty, health issues like sexually transmitted diseases, teen pregnancy, and abortion. Other issues include abstinence, body image, healthy and unhealthy relationships, sexual orientation, and sexual abuse

Controversial Materials and Request for Reconsideration

The Library does not exclude titles, other than by budgetary constraints or failure to meet selection criteria. The Library upholds the American Library Association (ALA) Library Bill of Rights. Library staff believes that the parent or guardian holds the final responsibility for the material that their children borrow from the library.

The Library makes an attempt to judge materials on the whole, not as an isolated part. Any patron who feels that an item is inappropriate is encouraged to first speak to the librarian in order to discuss their concerns and hopefully find an acceptable resolution. If no resolution can be made, then the library user is free to ask for a "Request for Reconsideration of Library Materials" form from a staff member. The item will be reviewed by a staff committee that will take into consideration professional reviews. The committee will submit its recommendation to the Library Director/Principal/English Curriculum Supervisor. It is the responsibility of the Library Director/Principal/English Curriculum Supervisor to determine the Library's official response.

References

American Library Association. "An Interpretation of the Library Bill of Rights." Diversity in Collection Development. American Library Association, 02 July 2008. *http://www.ala.org/Template.cfm?Section=interpretations&Template=/ContentManagement/ContentDisplay.cfm&ContentID=8530.* 10 May 2011.

Bonner, Cindy. *Lily a Love Story*. Algonquin, 1992.

Burgess, Kelly. "Age-Appropriate Themes for Your Teen's Reading: How To Carefully Consider the Reading Content for Your Teen." Family.com. 1994. *http://family.go.com/parenting/pkg-teen/article-767139-age-appropriate-books-for-your-teen-s-reading-t/.* 06 April 2011.

Lamb, Annette. "Information Access & Delivery: Issues. What are Your Perspectives and Philosophies?" *The School Library Media Specialist*, September 2010. 12 January 2011.

Teen Lit Lab. *http://presentations.ala.org/images/f/f6/Sex_in_Young_Adult_Literature_ALA_Conference_Final.pdf.* 15 December 2011.

Chapter 13
Intellectual Freedom

*We are not afraid to entrust the American people with unpleasant facts,
foreign ideas, alien philosophies, and competitive values. For a nation
that is afraid to let its people judge the truth and falsehood
in an open market is a nation that is afraid of its people.*

—John F. Kennedy

This statement is a testament to the ideals that American libraries have committed themselves and for which they have advocated. Librarians firmly believe that intellectual freedom is the right of every individual to seek and receive information from all points of view without restriction. This belief should be front and center, to promote awareness and understanding among all library users.

An intellectual freedom policy should be displayed prominently in the library and should be attached to your selection policy so any time there is a question about a book choice, you can immediately access it and use it as a part of your discussion about the questioned material.

Intellectual Freedom Policy

The intellectual freedom policy that you develop should reflect how your library understands and commits to the principle of intellectual freedom that ensures your library users will be afforded the best and most efficient service, founded on the principles of the constitutional rights, democracy, and respect for human rights that we all share. This statement should be succinct, clear, and written in a jargon-free, easy-to-understand context. Your statement should include the following elements:

- *A Mission Statement.* The opening statement on your intellectual freedom policy should reflect your library's commitment to intellectual freedom and how you will ensure that those principles will be respected and promoted. The policy should include a statement on the library's position against censorship. Links to the Freedom to Read Policy and the ALA Freedom to Read Statement should also be included in the library's website and in print as a part of the selection policy. (ALA)

- *Definition of Intellectual Freedom.* Library users may protest materials and resources because they are upsetting or offensive to them and they believe that they are protecting others. Provide a clear explanation as to why the library believes that their views are important and how the library is also committed to protecting the views of others, as well. This explanation may help them to understand how the First Amendment and the free access of information goes together.

- *Access*. Every policy should have a statement regarding the idea that all people are welcome in the library and that everyone has a right to have free and open access to all library materials without any hindrances.

- *Children's Rights*. Every policy should address the needs and rights of children in their statement because this is the main area where there is much confusion and misunderstanding. The issue revolves around the role of the library in protecting and guiding children while providing services to them. A statement that clarifies the rights of parents to guide their children in making appropriate choices is very necessary and helpful, as it affirms to parents that their role is important and clearly recognized.

- *Confidentiality*. Acknowledge that confidentiality is a right of all library users and clearly state how the library will protect those rights.

- *Facility Use*. The library's commitment to free access does not just involve the library resources materials, but extends to every aspect of the library including its physical presence. (ALA)

Virginia Woolf on intellectual freedom:

"Therefore I would ask you to write all kinds of books, hesitating at no subject, however trivial or however vast. By hook or by crook, I hope that you will possess yourselves of money enough to travel and to idle, to contemplate the future or the past of the world, to dream over books and loiter at street corners, and let the line of thought dip deep into the stream."

Sample Intellectual Freedom Policy

This sample policy demonstrates how a policy should be written. It clearly shows what the mission of the library is and how that mission relates to intellectual freedom. Every policy should contain these basic elements while reflecting the ideals of your library.

Your Library Intellectual Freedom Policy

Mission Statement

Your Library will promote all efforts to ensure that Library users have free and open access to information and materials and will ensure that those resources offer a broad range of ideas that are available in an atmosphere of respect and with regard for confidentiality. Therefore, your Library opposes censorship and restrictions on access to the full range of constitutionally protected materials and speech. This statement is derived from the Library Bill of Rights and The ALA's Freedom to Read statement.

Intellectual Freedom

Intellectual freedom is the right of every individual to both seek and receive information from all points of view without restriction. It provides free access to all expressions of ideas through which any and all sides of a question, cause, or movement may be explored.

Why Is Intellectual Freedom Important?

Intellectual freedom is the basis for our democratic system. We expect our people to be self-governors. But to do so responsibly, our citizenry must be well-informed. Libraries provide the ideas and information, in a variety of formats, to allow people to inform themselves. Intellectual freedom encompasses the freedom to hold, receive, and disseminate ideas.

Access

The Library will provide free access to and unrestricted use of all the services, materials, and facilities the library has to offer. A person's right to use a library should not be denied or abridged because of origin, age, background, or views.

Rights of Children

The Library will provide children with the same rights to have free and unrestricted access to all the services, materials, and facilities the library has to offer. Every restriction on access to, and use of, library resources, based solely on the chronological age, educational level, literacy skills, or legal emancipation of users violates the Library Bill of Rights that is derived from the First Amendment rights that all citizens share. The Library does recognize and respect the right of parents to guide their children and only their children in their use of library resources.

Confidentiality

The Library is committed to providing strict confidentiality in terms of circulation records, overdue notices, registration information and notification of reserved materials.

Facility Use

The Library promotes intellectual freedom in terms of free and open access for all residents to utilize the library building use. To facilitate this usage a designated person will be responsible for assisting library users in the use of library space in terms of meeting space, display space and bulletin boards.

George Orwell on intellectual freedom:

"If large numbers of people believe in freedom of speech, there will be freedom of speech, even if the law forbids it. But if public opinion is sluggish, inconvenient minorities will be persecuted, even if laws exist to protect them." (Orwell)

Librarians Take Action: Respond to a book challenge.

Any institution that is committed to upholding the principles of intellectual freedom is sure to face challenges. Having a detailed selection policy and intellectual freedom policy are the necessary tools to answer those challenges.

An essential part of a librarian's defense is having a plan set for addressing those challenges with detailed responses and solutions that are easily accessible and that acknowledge the library's stance in support of intellectual freedom.

Complaints and Library Users

When one thinks of people who want to challenge a book, the picture is often one of people with signs, shouting, and fervently marching into the library demanding all copies of the books. Challenges are usually much more subtle than this scenario and can occur in a variety of ways.

Types of Complaints

The ALA describes the following types of complaints:

- Expression of Concern. An inquiry that has judgmental overtones.

- Oral Complaint. An oral challenge to the presence and/or appropriateness of the material in question.

- Written Complaint. A formal, written complaint filed with the institution (library, school, etc.), challenging the presence and/or appropriateness of specific material.

- Public Attack. A publicly disseminated statement challenging the value of the material, presented to the media and/or others outside the institutional organization in order to gain public support for further action.

- Censorship. A change in the access status of material based on the content of the work and made by a governing authority or its representatives. Such changes include exclusion, restriction, removal, or age/grade level changes. (ALA)

Types of Questions and Suggested Responses

Here are examples of the type of questions you might receive and how you might answer them. Have a copy of your intellectual freedom policy in your hand and a copy for the person for every question or complaint. You can weave the concepts of the document that clearly explain the library's mission into the conversation. (ALA)

Expression of Concern: *I was looking through this book that my daughter checked out and I am unsure if this type of book should be available to children.*

Response: This person is questioning and unsure as to what he wants to do about the book. He is not sure how he feels, but he is seeking advice and information from you because he respects and values your opinion. Try to discover what elements bother him the most about the book so that you can guide him to read the book in its entirety or suggest some other books by the same author or suggest alternative books that have a similar theme. Don't forget about the teenager who chose the book. Ask the parent what the teen's opinion was of the book and ask if the parent wants to bring the teen in so that they can both choose some books together.

What to do step-by-step:

1. Welcome the person and thank them for coming to talk to you.

2. Gently ask him what, exactly, are his concerns about the book.

3. Commend him for taking the time to bring his concerns to you.

4. Let him know how much you appreciate parents who want to discuss books and their children. Validate his opinion by agreeing with his right as a parent to state his concern. You might say, "Yes, I can understand why this scene or those words might make you feel uneasy."

5. Explain about intellectual freedom and how it relates to why you chose the book and how you choose books overall.

6. If you have read the book and are familiar with it, discuss the:

    - themes of the book

    - character descriptions

    - the context of the scenes or words used

    - the author, their background, and why he or she wrote the book

    - book reviews written by teens and those in library journals

7. If you have not read the book:

    - Don't panic!

    - You have probably read something else by the author and can use that as reference.

    - If it is a first novel, then honestly state that it is a new book by a new author that sounds promising.

    - Explain that you have not read the whole book yet but will do so right away and encourage the parent to read it as well.

    - Invite him behind your desk and pull up a chair for him while you use a computer to look up book summaries and book reviews about the book with them.

Engaging the person with these tactics will indicate to him that you don't view him as the enemy, but that you value his opinions and view him as your partner and your equal, and that you both share the goal of ensuring that all of your teen library users have access to good books.

Oral Complaint: *I am shocked and disappointed that a book like this would be made available for young adults and I would like to request that it be removed from the library as soon as possible.*

Response: This person may be angry and upset and may not be willing to listen to you because she has made up her mind. However, you should make every effort to try to establish a relationship with this person by emphasizing the common goals you share in caring for young adults—wanting to enhance their intellectual development and caring about their overall well being. If she is willing to discuss the book, you can use the same steps that are previously explained when someone comes to you with an expression of concern.

What to do step-by-step:

1. If this person is not willing to discuss the book with you, you can take the following steps:

    -   Begin by deescalating the situation.

    -   Be as polite as possible to the person.

    -   Invite her into your office or to sit down somewhere so she can have your full attention.

    -   Commend her for taking the time to bring her concerns to you.

    -   Let her know how much you appreciate parents who want to discuss books and their children.

    -   Validate her opinion by agreeing with her right as a parent to state her concern by saying, "Yes, I can understand why this scene or those words might make you feel uneasy."

2. Apologize that the contents of the book have made her so upset.

3. Ask her what specifically is upsetting.

4. Ask if the book upset her child and if it did, apologize for that.

5. Ask her if they read the whole book and, if they did not, what parts did they read.

6. Explain about the First Amendment and intellectual freedom and how it relates to why you chose the book and how you choose books overall.

7. Explain to the person how the First Amendment guarantees that other parents and teens can make the same choice that she has to not read the book, but that it also means that others might choose to read the book and that they should be given that opportunity.

Public Attack: *The complainant or group of complainants goes directly to the media through the local newspaper, public school board meeting, or television to complain about the books in your library.*

Response: At this point the person or group of people is not interested in discussing their concerns and the challenge will have to be handled by your library administrator or director. You can:

1. Share any information you have with your director or administrator if you know the person or group.

2. Give your administrators all the information you can about the book.

3. Research past challenges and court cases from around the country with the results.

4. Collect book reviews from teens and professional journals.

5. Provide book rationales that you have prepared.

6. Provide all information about the First Amendment, intellectual freedom, and the library bill of rights.

Advice from the American Library Association:

1. Have one spokesperson for the library. Make sure that reporters, library staff, and the members of the board know who this is. Make it clear that no one other than this spokesperson should express opinions on behalf of the library.

2. Prepare carefully for any contacts with the media. Know the most important message you want to deliver and be able to deliver it in twenty-five words or less. You will want to review your library's borrowing and collection development policies and the American Library Association's Library Bill of Rights.

3. Keep to the high ground—no matter what. Don't mention the other side by name, either personal or corporate. Speak in neutral terms. Name calling and personalization are great copy for reporters but create barriers to communication.

4. Do not let yourself be put on the defensive. Stay upbeat, positive—"Libraries are vital to democracy. We are very proud of the service our library provides." If someone makes a false statement, gently but firmly respond: "That's absolutely incorrect. The truth is the vast majority of parents find the library an extremely friendly, safe place for their children. We receive many more compliments from parents than we do complaints."

5. Be prepared to tell stories or quote comments from parents and children about how the library has helped them.

6. Be strategic in involving others. For instance, board members, friends of libraries, community leaders, teachers, and other supporters can assist by writing letters to the editor or an opinion column and/or meeting with a newspaper editorial board or other members:

If they still don't want to accept your explanation:

1. Thank them for coming to see you and state how sorry you are that they have been upset or confused by any material that is in the library.

2. Explain to them what the process is to challenge a book in your library.

3. Offer them the recommendation of reconciliation form and ask them to fill it out and bring it back as soon as possible.

4. Give them your rationale packet to take with them.

5. Or if you don't have one for that book, print out some books reviews for them to take. Use formal book reviews, as well as teen book reviews by teens and parents. I have found that this type of information is more reassuring than any other documentation that I provide to them.

Librarians Take Action: Respond to book challengers with a formal letter.

School classroom teachers, school librarians, and public librarians are the recipients of book challenges. Each group is committed to the goal of adhering to the First Amendment rights of their students or their young adult library participants by allowing them to read the books they choose to read. Each group has issues that are unique to their teaching and learning environment that should be addressed.

Draw from your library's selection and intellectual freedom policies to draft a letter that incorporates the policies along with the mission of your library. The following sample letters to challengers incorporate the issues while also recognizing the special mission of each type of library.

1. Sample letter for books challenged that are a part of the school curriculum:

Dear _____,

Thank you for expressing an interest in your child's educational process and be assured that you will be contacted as soon as possible to discuss this matter further. We welcome input from all parents who want to participate in this most important endeavor. We recognize that parents understand their child's needs the best and we can work together to meet your child's needs.

Our mission as an educational institution is to ensure that our students' First Amendment rights, which protect their freedom to read without constraints, are met, while adhering to the fact you, as parents, have the ultimate authority to make all educational choices for your teen. We realize that some texts may or may not represent your values or behaviors that you may not accept. By reading about the ways in which others live, conduct their lives, or even make mistakes creates an awareness of other realities.

The books chosen for your teen to read have been selected carefully by a group of committed educators to meet criteria that is diverse in all areas, intellectually challenging, and that encourage critical thinking.

We hope that this information will help you to understand why this particular book was selected and will assist you in making the decision that best meets the needs of your child.

If you still have concerns, please fill out the request for reconsideration form to have the book reviewed further. Please be aware that you can request an alternative selection if you are not satisfied with what your child is reading. You may:

1.   Request an alternate version of the book if there is one available.

2.   You can request an alternate book that is similar to one the students have been assigned to read. A list of books will be provided to you.

Sincerely,

[Name]

2. Sample letter for books challenged in a school library:

Dear _____ ,

Thank you for expressing an interest in your teen's school library and be assured that you will be contacted as soon as possible to discuss this matter further. We welcome input from all parents who are interested in what their teens are reading and why the material was chosen. We recognize that you as the parent understand your teen's needs the best and we can work together to meet his or her needs.

Our mission as a school library is to ensure that our student's First Amendment rights, which offer them the freedom to read without constraints, are met, while still adhering to the fact you as their parents have the ultimate authority to make all educational choices for your teen. We realize that some texts may or may not represent your values or represent behaviors that you accept. By reading about the ways in which others live or conduct their lives an awareness of other realities is created.

The books chosen for your teen to read have been selected carefully by a group of committed educators, parents, and students to meet criteria that is diverse in all areas, intellectually challenging, and that encourage critical thinking. While we understand that you may not choose for your teen to select a certain book, other parents do approve of their teens reading certain books and we cannot deprive them of their choices.

If you still have concerns, please fill out the request for reconsideration form to have the book reviewed further. The school library is available for both students and their parents. Please feel free to schedule an appointment with the school librarian if you would like to see some of the resources that are used to select books. In addition, you are welcome to accompany your teen to the library so that you can discuss the books that are available to the students.

Sincerely,

[Name]

3. Sample letter for books that are challenged in young adult collections in a public library:

Dear _____ ,

Thank you for expressing an interest in our public library and be assured that you will be contacted as soon as possible to discuss this matter further. We welcome input from all parents and community members who are interested in what their teenagers or other young adults are reading and why the books were chosen. We recognize that you as the parent understand your teenager's interests and which books are appropriate for their emotional and mental developmental level.

Our mission as a public library is to ensure that the First Amendment rights of all our young adult library users are met. We achieve this by ensuring that we offer books that speak to the culture and lifestyle of all young adults and that address the wide variety of issues that young adults face. We realize that some texts may or may not represent your values or represent behaviors that you accept. By reading about the ways in which others live or conduct their lives, young adults develop an awareness of other realities.

The books have been selected carefully by a group of librarians, parents, teens, and other community members to meet criteria that is diverse in all areas, intellectually challenging, and encourage critical thinking. While we understand that you may not choose for your child to select a certain book, other parents do approve of their children reading certain books and we cannot deprive them of their choice.

If you still have concerns, please fill out the request for reconsideration form to have the book reviewed further. The public library is open to everyone and we welcome your participation. Feel free to schedule an appointment with the young adult librarian if you would like to see some of the resources that are used to select books. In addition, you are encouraged and welcome to accompany your teen to the library so that you can discuss the books that are available to the young adults in this community.

Sincerely,

[Name]

Librarians Take Action: Offer a reconsideration of materials form.

When the person with the concerns remains unsatisfied with your responses and information that you have provided, your only alternative is to encourage him to take his concerns to another level. This can be achieved by giving the person the library's reconsideration of materials form. When constructing a reconsideration of materials form:

1. Make sure the form is simple and easy to read.

2. Make all the questions simple and easy to understand.

3. Ask or suggest that the person read the entire book, but also give him the option to simply read as much as he can.

4. Offer yourself as the contact person who can help him with answering the questions and to help lead him through the process.

5. Inform the person verbally and in writing about the length of time he should expect for the process to take place.

6. Inform him verbally and in writing what person or committee will review the form.

7. Along with the form, give him a book rationale if you happen to have one, and always give them a copy of your Library Bill of Rights and Intellectual Freedom information.

Sample Reconsideration Form

Your school district and your school board have established that the task of selecting library resources falls to the curriculum committee who selects resources based on a comprehensive and objective selection policy. Any concerns regarding those resources will be forwarded and addressed by the curriculum and reconsideration committee which consists of parents, students, the library staff, and school administration.

We would like to thank you for your participation in the ongoing conversation about books and the needs of our community. Your library is committed to selecting books and other materials that serve the needs of all library users. Books and other materials are selected based on the library's collection development policy. If you believe that a specific item is not appropriate for the library, please fill out this form and return it to the library at your earliest convenience in order to proceed further with your request for further discussion.

Title _____

Author _____

Publisher and Date _____

Please check the type of material you are concerned with

Book _____ Textbook _____ Video_____

Magazine _____ Library Program _____ Display_____

Your name _____ Phone _____

Address _____

_____

Are you a:

Parent_____ Concerned citizen_____

A member of an organization (name) _____

1. What brought this resource to your attention?

2. Please summarize your reasons for requesting reconsideration of the work:

3. Are your objections based on age of the potential user or to the point of view expressed?

4. What do you believe is the theme or intent of this work?

   What do you feel might be the result of reading this work?

5. Are you aware of judgments of this work by reviewers or critics?

6. What action would you like the library/school to do with this work?

   Do not assign/lend it to my child

   Return it to the staff selection committee/department for re-evaluation
   Other (Explain): _____

7. What work would you recommend that would, in your judgment, be more appropriate?

If you have any questions about how to fill out the form please don't hesitate to contact me at (999) 555-4444 ext. 333 or at librarian@yourlibrary.org.

What happens to this form once I have completed it?

The request goes to the Director of Literature curriculum who will review the request and schedule a meeting with the Request for Consideration committee. The members are: the librarian, a parent representative, a school principal, a student council representative, a teacher representative, the director of literature, and a school board representative. You will be contacted in no less than two weeks with the outcome of the decision.

What happens if I am still not satisfied with the explanation and the outcome of the reconsideration?

If you continue to not be satisfied with the result the challenge will be taken into consideration at the next school board or library board meeting.

Thank you very much for informing us of your concerns and please don't hesitate to contact us with further questions.

Challenges at School or Library Board Meetings

School library and public library board meetings are similar in nature and organization. They both take place monthly unless there are special sessions, and are usually announced in advance to the public so that the public may attend and offer their opinions. (ALA)

In my community, all school board meetings occur monthly and are public except those that are noted in advance as closed session meetings. All library board meetings are also open to the public. The meeting schedule is sent home at the beginning of the year and they are always announced in advance in the local newspaper, on the school website, and usually on the radio. In the city that I live in all school board meetings are videotaped and are shown on our local access school channel.

Typical Board Meeting

The meetings usually take place in a local school auditorium or gym or library meeting room so that the public is accommodated. The board members may be seated in chairs on a stage with microphones in an auditorium or at the same level as the audience members in a library or gym.

The meetings usually begin by members discussing old business from the last meeting and then they move on to talk about new issues. This is the time that they would discuss any issues regarding book challenges if they reach the level where the board has to comment on it.

At this point of the meeting, they will announce that they are opening the meeting for public comment and will ask if anyone wishes to speak. Anyone is invited to speak—parents, community members, young adults, and children.

When the public wishes to speak, the following parameters are usually followed, although you should check with your school or library board to see how public speaking is addressed.

1. Anybody who lives in the town or city can speak. This includes children under 18 and adults.

2. People usually get in a line at the podium where they will speak. A microphone is provided at the podium.

3. A time limit is given of three to five minutes.

4. The speaker will be asked to state his name and address for the record—children and adults alike.

5. The speaker will be allowed to speak or ask questions and usually most people just make a statement.

6. The speaker is not asked questions but may ask questions of the board members.

Speak Effectively

Although I have not had any book challenges go before the school board, there have been many times when the library budget or librarians were in danger of being eliminated where my library students and their parents have spoken in defense of the library at school board meetings. If you have an issue going before the board, help your students, parents, and community members prepare for the task of speaking at one of these meetings with these tips.

1. Prepare a statement before the meeting.

2. Remember that you will have to state your address with the zip code. Write it down with the statement so if you are nervous, you have it all on paper.

3. Know the length of time you will have.

4. Be aware that there could be a small number of people or hundreds of people attending.

5. Be aware that you will be speaking into a microphone.

6. State what you want to happen.

7. Speak slowly and clearly.

8. Keep your tone pleasant and low.

9. Do not become angry.

Librarians Take Action: Write a letter in support of the book.

You can write letters but it is much more effective if you can encourage others to write letters for the challenged book. Try to encourage teen library users, parents, community members, anti-censorship organizations, or authors to participate. Authors, in particular, are very happy to help out and write a letter, or even make an appearance on behalf of their books. Pat Conroy and Chris Crutcher wrote letters to various school boards where their books were challenged. (Random House) The Kurt Vonnegut Library even supplied students and families with free copies of *Slaughter-House Five* when it was banned at a school in Missouri.

Sample Letter from the Judy Blume Resource Guide

Dear _____,

I am writing to express concern about efforts to remove _____ from the [Course Name and/or grade level] curriculum at [School Name]. I understand that the book has been challenged because of objections to _____.

I strongly urge you to keep this book in the curriculum at [School Name] and to uphold the freedom to read for all students in our community. The views of those seeking removal of the book are not shared by all. The challengers have no right to impose their views on others or to demand that the educational program reflect their personal preferences.

[Briefly address the challengers' objections, and urge the consideration of the book as a whole.] If parents do not want their children to read a particular book, then they are free to request an alternative assignment. But they may not infringe on the rights of others to read the book or to tell other parents what their children may read in school.

In addition, removing the book will only teach children to remain silent instead of asking questions for fear of addressing "offensive" or "inappropriate" topics. They will learn that the way to deal with difficult speech is to avoid it, and that fear and ignorance supersede the quest for knowledge. Reading is the safest way for kids to learn about the world in which they are growing up and to help them anticipate real-life problems.

Sincerely,

[Your Name]

Sample letter from the (NCAC) National Coalition Against Censorship

Dear _____:

I am writing to express concern about efforts to remove _____ from the [Course Name and/or grade level] curriculum at [School Name]. I understand that the book has been challenged because of objections to _____.

I strongly urge you to keep this book in the curriculum at [School Name] and to uphold the freedom to read for *all* students in our community. The views of those seeking removal of the book are not shared by all. The challengers have no right to impose their views on others or to demand that the educational program reflect their personal preferences.

[Briefly address the challengers' objections, and urge the consideration of the book *as a whole.*] If parents do not want their children to read a particular book, then they are free to request an alternative assignment. But they may not infringe on the rights of others to read the book or to tell other parents what their children may read in school.

In addition, removing the book will only teach children to remain silent instead of asking questions for fear of addressing "offensive" or "inappropriate" topics. They will learn that the way to deal with difficult speech is to avoid it, and that fear and ignorance supersede the quest for knowledge. Reading is the safest way for kids to learn about the world in which they are growing up and to help them anticipate real-life problems.

Sincerely,

[Your Name]

Remember that you are not just defending a book but the principles that this country was founded upon. The thorough and friendly procedures you use to work through the complaints demonstrate those principles to everyone involved. You are also not alone, as the relationships you have built among the teenagers that frequent your library, their parents, your colleagues, and other friends of the library, as well as organizations that are advocates for intellectual freedom are strong enough that you will find support in many places.

References

ALA. "Challenges to library materials." *http://www.ala.org/ala/issuesadvocacy/banned/challengeslibrarymaterials/index.cfm.* 10 July 2011.

ALA. "Essential Preparation." *http://www.ala.org/ala/issuesadvocacy/banned/challengeslibrarymaterials/essentialpreparation/index.cfm.* 10 July 2011.

ALA. "Intellectual Freedom Basics." *http://www.ala.org/Template.cfm?Section=basics&Template=/ContentManagement/ContentDisplay.cfm&ContentID=164089.* 15 April 2011.

ALA. "Quotations and Links." *http://www.ala.org/template.cfm?section=bbwlinks&template=/contentmanagement/contentdisplay.cfm&contentid=87403.* 12 March 2012

ALA. "What You Can Do To Oppose Censorship." N.p., n.d. *http://www.ala.org/Template.cfm?Section=basics&Template=/ContentManagement/ContentDisplay.cfm&ContentID=24792.* 02 January 2011.

Blume, Judy. "Book Censorship in Schools: A Resource Guide/Toolkit." Judy Blume on the Web. *http://www.judyblume.com/censorship/toolkit.php.* 13 July 2011.

"Book Censorship Toolkit." Kids Right to Read Project. National Coalition Against Censorship. *http://www.abffe.com/KR2R.pdf.* 09 July 2011.

Grant, Cameron. "President John F. Kennedy" The President's UFO. 01 August 2009. *http://www.presidentialufo. com/john-f-kennedy.* 21 May 2011.

Orwell, Gorge. "Freedom of the Park." 07 December, 1945. Tribune, GB, London. *http://www.georgeorwell.org/Freedom_of_the_Park/index.html.* 14 May 2012.

Woolf, Virginia. *A Room of One's Qwn.* Harvest Books, 1929. EBook. *http://ebooks.adelaide.edu.au/w/woolf/virginia/w91r/chapter6.html.*

CHAPTER 14
CELEBRATE BANNED BOOKS

The Official Banned Book Week website, *http://www.bannedbooksweek.org*, is the best place to begin planning your banned book celebration. The site, sponsored by the American Booksellers Association, American Society of Journalists, and the American Libraries Association, among others, offers a banned book celebration handbook, activities, ideas, and event suggestions that are helpful and inspiring.

They offer virtual ways to celebrate that really make the week long event interactive and exciting. Those that celebrate can load videos of themselves reading banned books that can be uploaded to FaceBook at *http://www.facebook.com/bannedbooksweek*.

A new endeavor offered through the organization has come about through their collaboration with Google, which for the first time is offering an interactive Google map (*http://www.bannedbooksweek.org/mappingcensorship*) that shows the locations of banned books across America. The information is drawn from cases documented by ALA and the Kids' Right to Read Project, through a collaboration of the National Coalition against Censorship and the American Booksellers Foundation for Free Expression.

Banned Books Week

In 1967, the ALA founded the Office for Intellectual Freedom (OIF). The mission of this office was to support intellectual freedom as described in the Library Bill of Rights. This included challenging censorship and resisting abridgement of free expression and free access to ideas. At that time, there was no celebration of Banned Books Week. However, librarians and those in the publishing industry began to recognize that more needed to be done to educate and inform the public about the effects of censorship on their communities and society. In 1982, Judith Krug, librarian and First Amendment advocate, along with the American Booksellers Association, founded Banned Books Week to honor and promote Americans' right to read whatever we choose, a right guaranteed by the First Amendment.

Since 1982, banned book celebrations have occurred all across the country with events and activities, both simple and elaborate, organized to bring attention to the importance and relevance of our First Amendment rights. Following are some examples.

Celebrations in America

Northern States
- Ocean County Free Library, Ocean City, NJ: hosted a First Amendment Film Festival that showcased movies of books that have been banned or censored.

- New Castle County Library, New Castle, DE: hosted a Parental Advisory teen dance party with formally banned music and read "racy" children's books.

- River Run Bookstore, Portsmouth, NH: invited local celebrities and others to read from banned books and their own books.

Southern States
- Main Library, Jacksonville, FL: presented *Fahrenheit 451* as a banned book play in a multimedia format.

- University of South Florida: student group displayed posters and books that have been banned in schools and libraries across the country.

Midwestern States
- American Library Association, McCormick Tribune Freedom Museum and the Newberry Library, Chicago, IL: joined together to host a Banned Books Week read out.

- University of Indiana-Purdue University, Indianapolis, IN: put books in especially designed bamboo bird cages.

- Harry W. Schwartz Bookshop, Milwaukee, WI: roped off a section of the library and only let customers who had tickets enter the area where the books were.

Western States
- MADCAP Theatre, Tempe, AZ: hosted a free movie night and showed the Monty Python movie *The Life of Brian,* which has been criticized and banned in several countries.

- Tattered Cover Book Store, Denver, CO: Offered discounts on banned books and some of the proceeds went to a charity and to the ACLU in honor of Banned Books Week.

- The University of New Mexico Bookstore, NM: displayed banned or challenged books in a small black "jail" that they had made for the purpose of Banned Books Week with the red and black censored signs woven throughout the prison doors.

Celebrating Books Around the World

Countries around the world also celebrate Banned Books Week to draw attention to the effects of censorship worldwide. Books, writers, and ideas are not just banned in the United States but occur everywhere because of differing ideas of what is inappropriate or appropriate or ideology. Banned books share, no matter where they are, the result in the inability to speak freely.

Canada recognizes the importance of reading and accessing information freely through Freedom to Read Week. The Freedom to Read Week is organized by the Book and Periodical Council's Freedom of Expression Committee, "a group committed to promoting intellectual freedom in Canada." Since 1978, the Freedom of Expression Committee has worked with educators, librarians, and the community at large to provide information that addresses censorship and book and magazine challenges in Canada."

Amnesty International also celebrates Banned Book Week. As a global organization they make it their mission during the week to recognize and educate the world about the international plight of those who have been jailed or arrested for writing, speaking, reading, and printing information that is considered controversial in their perspective countries.

 The Southern Vampire series by Charlene Harris is one of the most often banned and challenged series of books in Canada.

Librarians Take Action: Try these ideas and activities from the American Library Association.

The ALA has compiled a comprehensive list of activities and ideas from libraries and other organizations in order to share ideas and to generate new ones. The following are some of their suggestions.

DISPLAY books on and by persons who valued intellectual freedom—Thomas Jefferson, Benjamin Franklin, Maya Angelou, John Peter Zenger, Henry Thoreau, Judy Blume, James Baldwin, Thomas Paine, Frederick Douglass, Susan B. Anthony, John Thomas Scopes.

DEMONSTRATE the inaccessibility of banned books by roping off a section of the bookstore or library and allow into the area only those customers or patrons with an entry ticket. The Harry W. Schwartz Bookshop in Milwaukee, Wisconsin, found this to be very effective.

INTRIGUE customers or patrons by painting a display window almost entirely black, leaving only a small peep hole; then paint the word "caution" in large red letters, which will encourage them to peer in and see books that have been banned or challenged in the past.

DISPLAY the dust jackets of banned books with accompanying cards explaining the challenged and listing a favorable review. The School of Library Science at the University of North Carolina found this to be a very effective display for their bulletin board.

CREATE a bulletin board display using a top ten list as used by David Letterman. Use this book to compile a list or try the following suggestions.

Ten most far-fetched (silliest, irrational, illogical) reasons to ban a book.

1. "Encourages children to break dishes so they won't have to dry them." (*A Light in the Attic* by Shel Silverstien)

2. "It caused a wave of rapes." (*Arabian Nights*, or *Thousand and One Nights* by Anonymous)

3. "If there is a possibility that something might be controversial, then why not eliminate it?" (*Bury My Heart at Wounded Knee* by Dee Brown)

4. "Tarzan was 'living in sin' with Jane." (*Tarzan* by Edgar Rice Burroughs)

5. "It is a real 'downer.'" (*Diary of Anne Frank* by Anne Frank)

6. "The basket carried by Little Red Riding Hood contained a bottle of wine, which condones the use of alcohol." (*Little Red Riding Hood* by Jacob Grimm and Wilhelm K. Grimm)

7. "One bunny is white and the other is black and this 'brainwashes' readers into accepting miscegenation." (*The Rabbit's Wedding* by Garth Williams)

8. "It is a religious book and public funds should not be used to purchase religious books." (*Evangelical Commentary on the Bible* by Walter A. Elwell, ed.)

9. "A female dog is called a bitch." (*My Friend Flicka* by Mary O'Hara)

10. "An unofficial version of the story of Noah's Ark will confuse children." (*Many Waters* by Madeleine C. L'Engle)"

Librarians Take Action: Celebrate with these quick and easy activities.

- Make posters in a publishing program with quotes from banned book authors and place them around the school.

- Make announcements of banned book facts and trivia every day that week.

- Make banned book displays and cover them with yellow caution tape.

- Collaborate with the art teacher. Students make masks that they wear while reading banned books.

- Send a flyer home with the students with all the local events regarding banned book celebrations on them.

Librarians Take Action: Form a banned book reading club.

This is an activity that I have offered many times for the parents of my students. It can also work in a public library setting or is another great way that local public librarians and school librarians can offer a joint program together.

Starting a banned book reading club for adults featuring the classics is a great way to explore the books that are distinguished by the fact that they have captivated readers for generations. It is a wonderful way to bring the issue of censorship into the present as people discover that books that have been challenged or banned in the past for specific reasons continue to be banned today for the same reasons. Seeing first hand how the past and the present are connected makes the issue of censorship more relevant to everyday life. It is also a great way to reintroduce what the First Amendment is and how it relates to intellectual freedom. That understanding will hopefully lead to encouraging the group to recognize the dangers of censorship, including the negative and restrictive affect it can have on learning and critical thinking, perhaps encouraging them to become advocates in the fight for the freedom to read.

Reading banned books is also a wonderful way to revisit books that your group may not have read since high school or college or perhaps never got around to reading and now have a great reason to do so. Finally, reading banned classic books is an education in history, values, and culture and how these elements, when put together, can manage to invoke passionate discussion and debate even today.

Choose the Book

There are several lists of classic banned books available. At the first meeting, provide the members with a list and let them vote on at least two of their favorites. This is a sample list of classic books that have been challenged or banned:

- *The Great Gatsby* by F. Scott Fitzgerald
- *The Catcher in the Rye* by J.D. Salinger
- *The Grapes of Wrath* by John Steinbeck
- *To Kill a Mockingbird* by Harper Lee
- *The Color Purple* by Alice Walker
- *Ulysses* by James Joyce
- *Beloved* by Toni Morrison
- *The Lord of the Flies* by William Golding
- *1984* by George Orwell
- *Their Eyes Were Watching God* by Zora Neale Hurston

Schedule

The best time to start a group like this is in September and end in October, because it encompasses Banned Book Week on September 24th. From my experience, August is a difficult month to get lots of participation due to vacations and parents who are getting their children ready for school. Advertising it all summer and starting it in September is a better idea.

Goals

The goals are the same in that the group will want to thoroughly examine the books to learn everything they can about it so that they can get an idea of what the overall themes are and why the book has captivated readers for decades. Explore:

1. The themes of the book.

2. What the author wanted to accomplish through writing the book.

3. What motivated the author to write the book.

4. Why the time the author lived in influenced what the author wrote.

5. Why the book is considered a classic.

Discussion Topics

You want to educate everyone about First Amendment issues and how they relate to the book club. This can be achieved by making sure you begin by discussing and answering questions about these important issues so you can constantly draw the discussion around these topics. Explain and discuss with the group these issues:

1. The First Amendment.

2. Intellectual freedom.

3. The Library Bill of Rights.

4. The definition and difference between censorship, book challenges, and book banning.

5. Specific book challenges and book banning incidents to gain an understanding about why the book ignited such strong reactions and why those same reactions continue today.

6. The role that censorship has played in influencing the perception of the book throughout the years.

7. Explore the book through the guise of the various viewpoints, both positive and negative, that have shaped public opinion of the book over time.

The Social and Cultural Atmosphere

Explore the underlying social and cultural atmosphere that existed during the time the book was written to understand why the book initially generated controversy. Examine the social and cultural elements of today to see if they remain the reasons for the book's continued ability to generate controversy.

1. Why is the content of the book considered to be controversial by some?

2. Does the book contain content that could be controversial to some people?

3. Has the culture and society changed since the book was written or is it the same?

4. Are people worried about the book for the same reasons they were before?

5. Discuss why the book has been banned recently in public schools.

6. At what grade, if any, is the book appropriate to be read?

7. Would you want your child to read the book?

Censorship and the First Amendment and Teens

Apply what has been learned and explored about the effects of censorship to teens to help parents understand that censorship effects children and teens and children and teens have rights that are protected by the First Amendment.

1. Discuss the First Amendment and how it relates to teens.

2. Do children have the right to read?

3. What rights do parents have?

4. Would you want to read this book with your teen?

5. Should the book be considered a classic?

6. What is the definition of a classic?

The Last Meeting

The meeting should be treated as something important and special because it is the culmination of all the weeks of exploration and discussion. Some ideas:

1. Host a read-along of banned books during Banned Book Week and have them participate.

2. If you read a book that was made into a movie, offer to screen the movie for the group.

3. Have a final party for the group with food and drinks.

4. Contact your local university to find an expert on your book or an author who can visit the group and offer new insight about the book.

Librarians Take Action: Present a Banned Books Week Proclamation.

On the last day of Banned Books Week, it is a great idea to end with a memorable event. I have found that after all the excitement associated with the week, it is even more appealing to have a simple, but meaningful, activity close the last day. Reading the Banned Book Proclamation provided by the ALA is a wonderful and simple way to achieve this. The ALA offers this proclamation for libraries and other organizations to use freely in order to provide a common message for all those who support the First Amendment to speak with the same voice.

. . . RESOLVED, that the _____ Library celebrates the American Library Association's Banned Books Week, and be it further . . .

WHEREAS, the freedom to read is essential to our democracy, and reading is among our greatest freedoms; and

WHEREAS, privacy is essential to the exercise of that freedom, and the right to privacy is the right to open inquiry without having the subject of one's interest examined or scrutinized by others; and

WHEREAS, the freedom to read is protected by our Constitution; and

WHEREAS some individuals, groups, and public authorities work to remove or limit access to reading materials, to censor content in schools, to label "controversial" views, to distribute lists of "objectionable" books or authors, and to purge libraries of materials reflecting the diversity of society; and

WHEREAS, both governmental intimidation and the fear of censorship cause authors who seek to avoid controversy to practice self-censorship, thus limiting our access to new ideas; and

WHEREAS, every silencing of a heresy, every enforcement of an orthodoxy, diminishes the toughness and resilience of American society and leaves it less able to deal with controversy and difference; and

WHEREAS, Americans still favor free enterprise in ideas and expression, and can be trusted to exercise critical judgment, to recognize propaganda and misinformation, and to make their own decisions about what they read and believe, and to exercise the responsibilities that accompany this freedom; and

WHEREAS, intellectual freedom is essential to the preservation of a free society and a creative culture; and

WHEREAS, conformity limits the range and variety of inquiry and expression on which our democracy and our culture depend; and

WHEREAS, the American Library Association's Banned Books Week: Celebrating the Freedom to Read is observed during the last week of September each year as a reminder to Americans not to take their precious freedom for granted; and

WHEREAS, Banned Books Week celebrates the freedom to choose or the freedom to express one's opinion even if that opinion might be considered unorthodox or unpopular and stresses the importance of ensuring the availability of those unorthodox or unpopular viewpoints to all who wish to read them; now, therefore, be it

RESOLVED, that the _____ Library celebrates the American Library Association's Banned Books Week, (Insert Dates Here), and be it further

RESOLVED, that the _____ Library encourages all libraries and bookstores to acquire and make available materials representative of all the people in our society; and be it further

RESOLVED, that the _____ Library encourages free people to read freely, now and forever.

Adopted by the _____ Library
Date
City, State

References

"Banned Book Week." National Booksellers Association. *http://www.abffe.org/banned2010.htm.* 15 September 2011.

Banned Books Week." American Library Association. *http://www.ala.org/ala/issuesadvocacy/banned/bannedbooksweek/index.cfm.* 20 September 2011.

"Banned Books Week." Amnesty International. *http://www.amnestyusa.org/our-work/issues/prisoners-and-people-at-risk/censorship-and-free-speech/banned-books-week-2011.* 10 September 2011.

"Banned Books Week Ideas and Resources." American Libraries Association. *http://www.ala.org/ala/issuesadvocacy/banned/bannedbooksweek/ideasandresources/index.cfm.* 15 September 2011.

"Freedom to Read Week." Book and Periodical Council. *http://freedomtoread.ca.* 10 September 2011.

CHAPTER 15
NOTED INTELLECTUAL FREEDOM FIGHTERS

"The principles of intellectual freedom—the idea that a democracy is dependent upon free and open access to ideas—are hallmarks of the library and education professions. These values that are expressed in Library Bill of Rights affirm and defend the First Amendment rights of: speech, the press, religion and assembly, as they pertain to librarians, libraries, library users and beyond."

—American Library Association

The principles that American libraries uphold—free and open access to all people, regardless of their age, education, ethnicity, language, income, physical limitations or geographic barriers—are the envy and inspiration of people all around the world and have set the standard for library service worldwide.

While advocating for freedom is always the right choice, it is not always the easiest choice. The following librarians did not hesitate to act in support of intellectual freedom because of their appreciation of the First Amendment and their commitment to its support, even when faced with difficult decisions that were sometimes praised and other times met with disdain, anger, and even violence. Nevertheless, they made the choice that they instinctively knew was the right one, even sometimes at the expense of their social standing within their communities, their economic interests, emotional well-being, and at times, their personal safety.

Ruth Brown

In 1950, Ruth Brown, a well-respected librarian at the Bartlesville Public Library in Bartlesville, Oklahoma, decided to have lunch at Hull's drugstore with two of her friends, Mary Ellen Street and Clara Cooke, who were teachers. The problem was that Street and Cooke were African American and were not allowed to be served at the same counter as Brown and the other white patrons. In fact, as soon as they arrived and asked to be seated, Miss Brown and her friends were asked to leave, reportedly doing so quietly and with dignity. This simple act that occurred before the term "sit in" was even recognized would soon be repeated across the country as civil rights activists both young and old began to protest against segregation. However, in the small town of Bartlesville, their simple request shocked the townspeople and would set in motion events that would eventually cost Brown her job and solidify her place in history as a steadfast advocate for intellectual freedom. (Robbins 54)

It may seem surprising to think of American libraries as a significant part of the civil rights struggle. When one thinks of the civil rights movement, antiquated pictures of black and white drinking fountains, lunch counters, and schools come to mind, along with magnificent marches and larger than life heroes and heroines fighting for justice. Many who opposed inequality did so quietly and without fanfare, because they knew it was the right thing to do.

In the early 20th century, public libraries did not allow African Americans to enter the library, or at best, offered segregated services. In fact, the daughter of librarian E.J. Josey, who was a former president of the ALA in 1984, recounts a dinner party her father attended with Dr. Martin Luther King in the 1950s. Dr. King asked him about how the desegregation of libraries was progressing. "My dad said in response that he was going to be working on that." (Chute)

Miss Brown, throughout her tenure as the director of the Carnegie Bartlesville Public Library, was a tenacious advocate for the First Amendment as she quietly fought against segregation, civil rights violations, and censorship at every opportunity. She was an early advocate for equal use of the library for African Americans. As early as the 1920s, library records show a listing of library borrows in which some patrons were identified as "colored." Even though it was segregated, she made sure that African American children were provided with a story hour and she initiated taking story time to Douglas School, which was the local public school for African American children.

Miss Brown also firmly believed in ensuring that equitable library services were provided to all library users that were suited to the needs of the community. In the 1930s during the depression, she put that belief into practice by encouraging her colleagues to "reduce to a minimum worry about lost books and other red tape so that the library during the hard and difficult times would be available to all." (Oklahoma Library Legends)

In 1946, she began to recognize the inequity of African American soldiers who fought in the war to defend the rights of others, being denied rights at home. She joined the Committee on the Practice of Democracy to help improve relations among the races. The organization then decided to join with the Congress of Racial Equality (CORE), an organization that became synonymous with challenging racial inequality throughout the South. (Bartlesville Public Library)

By the 1950s she began to push to totally integrate the library which was immediately discouraged by her library board. Not to be deterred, she organized an exhibit on African American history titled, "Negro Culture from Africa to Today" and began subscribing to *Ebony* magazine and *Negro Digest*. She also took a personal interest in promoting equality among the races by inviting her African American friends to attend her segregated church, to the dismay of her fellow churchgoers. (Robbins)

Today her actions may seem mundane, but at a time when Senator McCarthy's war on communism was gaining in popularity, Miss Brown's activities were considered radical and dangerous by the Bartlesville citizens. In 1950, a citizen's council was appointed to fire Miss Brown from her position by charging that she was supplying subversive materials and engaging in subversive activities. The library board was asked to investigate, but found that they could not fire her based on her civil rights activism that occurred on her personal time. They could not find any evidence of subversive materials or teachings. (Oklahoma Library Legends)

On March 9, 1950, however, the *Bartlesville Examiner* published a story with pictures of two subversive magazines that had been subscribed to by the library for years: *The Nation*, *The New Republic*, and *Soviet Russia Today*. Two books were also shown: *The Russians, the Land, and Why They Fight,* and another book that was undetermined. The library board immediately moved the magazines into locked storage to "deflect the attack." It was found that the books pictured were never actually owned by the library and no one to this day knows when the picture of the materials displayed in the library was taken.

The library board was fired and on July 25, 1950, Miss Brown was called before a newly appointed board for questioning. She refused to verbally answer questions about her private life because there was no one there recording her testimony. Instead, she wrote down responses to those questions. When asked about the subversive materials in the library, she replied that the magazines mentioned were only three out of seventy five other magazines. She also stated that she did not believe in censorship and that she could not restrict what her public chose to read. Nevertheless, despite their inability to find her actions subversive, she was fired that same day. (Robbins 78)

Miss Ruth Brown became nationally recognized as the first librarian in the United States to receive help from the Intellectual Freedom Committee of the American Library Association. A movie called *Storm Center*, starring Bette Davis, was made in 1956 that drew from Miss Brown's story. A 1956 edition of the *American Libraries* magazine did a feature story on the movie. (Hawkins) On March 11, 2007, the Bartlesville Women's Network and the Friends of Miss Brown presented a commemorative bust of Miss Brown to the Bartlesville Public Library. Text on the memorial reads:

Ruth Winifred Brown, 1891-1975

Miss Ruth Brown was Bartlesville's librarian for over thirty years.

As a librarian, she believed in universal access to the wisdom—and the foolishness—of the ages.

Juliette Hampton Morgan

Montgomery, Alabama, in the 1960s was quickly becoming the epicenter of the civil rights movement, as the tension grew between African Americans who were determined to end segregation and inequality and white southerners who were determined to maintain the status quo. Juliette Morgan, librarian and unlikely civil rights activist, in the midst of this turbulent and volatile time, wrote a series of eloquent and insightful letters expressing her support for the struggle of African American citizens, despite the condemnation of her friends, family, and colleagues.

The right to freedom of thought and expression of thought is one of the most basic tenets of intellectual freedom and article 19 states that: "Everyone has the right to freedom of opinion and expression; this right includes freedom to hold opinions without interference and to seek, receive, and impart information and ideas through any media and regardless of frontiers." (Article 19)

As a librarian, Morgan firmly believed in this right and was certain that librarians "had a responsibility to promote and protect intellectual freedom."(Stanton) Her beliefs stemmed from the words of Andrew Carnegie, who said, "There is not such a cradle of democracy upon the earth as the free public library, this republic of letters where neither rank, office, nor wealth receive the slightest consideration."

Juliette Morgan was an only child of a wealthy white southern couple whose family was held in high regard by the white community. The Morgan family, with their wealth and status, was considered to be a part of southern aristocracy. Morgan was the direct descendent of a Confederate general on her mother's side and a state senator on her father's side. Morgan grew up in comfort and safety and attended the best schools in Alabama, eventually graduating Phi Beta Kappa in 1934, with a degree in English literature and political science from the University of Alabama in Tuscaloosa. She completed a master's degree there in 1935. She was a public school teacher, a librarian in Montgomery's Carnegie Library and later became the director of research at the Montgomery Public Library. (Southern Poverty Law Center)

These advantages did not keep her from being keenly aware of the discrimination that many African Americans suffered on a daily basis. Like most Southerners, she was familiar with the practice of lynching African Americans and those who did not accept their unequal status. She also knew that African Americans were not allowed the right to vote, so that they could actively participate in making their lives better. They were instead subjected to a poll tax, which meant they had to pay a fee or pass unfair tests in order to vote. Miss Morgan inherently knew that these things were wrong and began to be politically active. She soon joined the democratic club where she wrote letters to support federal anti-lynching legislation and the poll tax. It was at this time that she began to become even more involved in advocating for civil rights and she joined an interracial prayer group that was forced to meet at black churches, because integrated groups were not allowed to meet at white churches. (Stanton)

The Montgomery Bus Boycott of 1955 was famous for bringing the issues of equality and civil rights to the attention of the world due to the heroism of and bravery of every day citizens who risked their lives to fight for their freedom. (Stanton) In 1952, before the bus boycotts began in earnest, Morgan had already written the first of many letters regarding the mistreatment of African Americans on the city buses. Morgan suffered from a nervous condition that did not allow her to drive. Because of her disorder, unlike most white citizens of her stature, she rode the city buses frequently. She became increasingly dismayed by what she observed. She described an incident where a black woman paid her bus fare at the front of the bus and then walked to the back of the bus to enter, as was the custom. The bus driver drove off in an attempt to leave the woman behind. Miss Morgan became so angry that she pulled the emergency brake so that the driver had to stop the bus and let the woman on. (Stanton)

In a letter to the local newspaper, she wrote about her observations: "Are people really naïve enough to believe that Negroes are happy, grateful to be pushed around and told they are inferior and ordered to 'move on back'? They may take it for a long time, but not forever." (Stanton 128)

She wrote many more such letters to the local papers in support of local civil rights groups and their activities. However, her letters incensed the townspeople and began to turn her neighbors, friends, and colleagues against her and even question her mental health. One such letter that she wrote in 1957 was so eloquent that the publisher asked her if he could publish it in the local paper. The following is an excerpt from the letter.

> "There are so many Southerners from various walks of life that know you are right . . . . They know what they call 'our Southern way of life' must . . . change. Many of them even are eager for change, but are afraid to express themselves—so afraid to stand alone . . . . I had begun to wonder if there were any men in the state—any white men—with any moral courage." (Teaching Tolerance)

The letter was published in January of 1957 and by July of the same year, her family and friends had become so infuriated by her actions that she was shunned by everyone that was dear to her, including her own mother. She even began to receive threatening phone calls and hate mail. Due to her refusal to stop writing letters and the angry response of the local white citizens to her words, the mayor of Montgomery wanted to have her fired from her position in the library. The library trustees, citing her First Amendment rights, would not fire her. Nevertheless, many white library users tore up their library cards in protest and decided to boycott the library as long as she remained working there. (Tapestry of Faith)

The tensions between Morgan, her colleagues, and the townspeople grew so intense that on the night of July 15, 1957, someone burned a cross on her lawn. Morgan quit her library position that next day and committed suicide that night with an overdose of pills. In her suicide note she wrote these final words. "I am not going to cause any more trouble to anybody." (Stanton)

Despite the fact that Morgan was eventually silenced, her words continued to inspire those that read them. The Reverend Martin Luther King Jr. recalled Juliette Morgan's influence on him and the Civil Rights Movement in his book, *Stride toward Freedom: The Montgomery Story*. Dr. King pointed out that Morgan was the first person to draw an analogy between the boycott and Gandhi's practice of non-violent civil disobedience. King wrote, "About a week after the protest started, a white woman who understood and sympathized with the Negroes' efforts, wrote a letter to the editor of the *Montgomery Advertiser* comparing the bus protest with the Gandhian movement in India. Miss Juliette Morgan, sensitive and frail, did not long survive the rejection and condemnation of the white community, but long before she died in the summer of 1957, the name of Mahatma Gandhi was well known in Montgomery." (King 71)

Hampton's funeral was attended by both black and whites, however, after the black attendees were asked to sit separately from the whites, many of them left. (Stanton) In 2005, Juliette Hampton Morgan was inducted into the Alabama Women's Hall of Fame and, on November 1, 2005, the Montgomery City Council voted to rename the main public library after Morgan.

E. J. Josey

Today, freedom of access is such an essential part of each and every library in the United States that most libraries weave the concept into their selection and collection policies and mention their commitment to equal access in their library mission statement. The acceptance of open access as the standard for all libraries came about as the result of the hard work and sacrifice of many forward thinking librarians, as well as the library profession's willingness to engage in intense introspection and honest examination of the inequalities that existed amongst them. Librarian and civil rights activist E. J. Josey was one such leader. In the 1960s, his insightful and forward thinking leadership encouraged his fellow librarians to implement the ideas of equality and equal access, as he advocated for the desegregation of library professional organizations. "My father, having witnessed all the wrongs, being a student of history and what our founding documents stood for, always believed in working in the system even if it meant fighting against the system."

E. J. Josey was born in 1924 in Portsmouth, Virginia, where he grew up in a segregated society, complete with separate facilities for blacks and whites. It was this experience that made him want to make a difference and work for equality. He joined the army and went to school on the GI Bill where he first attended Howard University and earned a master's degree in history from Columbia University in 1950. After graduating with what were notable credentials, he found that no university would hire him. When asked about this part of his personal history, Mr. Josey stated, "New York City hadn't let down its barriers." (Pattak)

His use of the Columbia journalism library during his education led him to look there for a job. He eventually found one as the supervisor of the library news clipping collection. As his enthusiasm for libraries grew as a result of his position, he earned a master's degree in information science at the State University of New York at Albany. He became the director of the library at Delaware State College, in Dover, Delaware, from 1955 to 1959, and from 1959-1966 he was chief librarian and associate professor at Savannah State College in Savannah, Georgia.

During his time at Savannah State, he became very active in the civil rights movement on campus, where he served as the youth advisor of the Savannah State College NAACP Chapter. He was also a member of the executive committee of the Savannah, Georgia, branch of the NAACP. Josey was also active in the American Library Association. In addition, the library received the prestigious John Cotton Dana Award for exemplary public service in 1962 and 1964. Despite his work with the students and his excellent leadership of the library, Mr. Josey was denied entry into the Georgia State Librarians' Association because they did not allow African Americans to join their organization. This was despite the 1954 Supreme Court decision that called for an end to segregation in schools and libraries. Three other state library associations—Alabama, Louisiana, and Mississippi—also did not allow African Americans to join their organizations. (Pattak)

In 1964, when he attended the American Libraries Association Conference, there is no evidence that these particular transgressions were on his mind. "I really didn't go there for a fight," he recalled in an interview. "I went there for the National Library Week program, which I was using as a vehicle to encourage students at Savannah State to use the library." He had recently become more and more aware of the sacrifices that African American students were making to pursue their rights. He noticed to his dismay, that students were being beaten as they tried to integrate lunch counters, even those at Savannah State, the university where Mr. Josey was a librarian. This was what he thought of as he attended the various meetings at the convention. In an interview about the events that occurred at the conference, he stated, "When

I saw the courage that those students exhibited, I said to myself, 'I have to do the same thing. I needed courage to challenge my professional organization on its segregationist and racist behavior." (Pattak)

All these underlying emotions regarding the tumultuous events that were unfolding in society were brought to the forefront for Mr. Josey in the midst of a simple meeting. The ALA passed a resolution honoring the Mississippi Library Association for their National Library Week Activities, even though they had withdrawn from the ALA due to their refusal to follow the ALA's recommendation to allow African American librarians to join their state library organization.

In his groundbreaking book, *The Black Librarian*, Josey states, "I just exploded." He writes that in his mind was also the recent tragedy of the three young civil rights workers—Andrew Goodman, James Chaney, and Michael Schwerner—who had been murdered on June 21, 1964, somewhere in Mississippi, with their bodies not yet discovered.

Josey immediately protested the resolution but was dismissed and told to write a letter regarding his feelings. Josey went to the closest public library and wrote the protest letter on the spot, offering it to the organization on the last day of the convention. In what was referred to as, "The shot heard round the library" he introduced a resolution to forbid ALA officials from associating with state library associations that refused to open membership to people of all races.

As Josey describes the ensuing scene, "All hell broke loose" as the issue was passionately debated. Looking back on the scene, he reflected on the thought that his resolution could have died right there but for the support of Ruth Walling from Emory University who was member of the Georgia State Library Association and who stated that she was ashamed to be a member of the group when one of her colleagues had been denied membership. After her statement, other white librarians from the Northern and Southern associations also pledged their support, causing the measure to unanimously pass. (Pattak)

This resolution marked the beginning of the full-scale integration of the American professional library associations and eventually all of America's libraries. Josey became the first African American librarian to be admitted into the Georgia Library Association, although they still exhibited some misgivings as they admitted him, but did not officially notify him of their decision. (Chute)

In the spirit of a true activist for intellectual freedom, Mr. Josey continued throughout his career to engage his colleagues in remembering the library's role in social activism. In 1970 he led three hundred of his fellow librarians in a protest against the Vietnam War in which they all walked about the conference to protest the defeat of a resolution condemning the war at the Annual ALA conference. In the 1980s he led his colleagues in an effort to maintain sanctions on South Africa in protest of the country's participation in the apartheid system of official segregation and inequality." (*Savannah Tribune*)

Josey also was instrumental in forming the Black Caucus of the American Library Association, in an effort to increase minority representation in the ALA and to push diversity to the forefront of the organization. Through his leadership, he was also essential in establishing the Spectrum Initiative Scholarship program; a scholarship geared towards encouraging multicultural students to consider enrolling in library school. In 1984, he was elected president of the American Library Association, and he used his inaugural address to begin a quest to ensure that all library users were given equal opportunities to have access to technology. (Pattak)

After his death on July 3, 2009, ALA president Jim Rettig had these words to say about his exemplary service:

"Few have brought about more significant change in librarianship than the late Dr. E.J. Josey," said ALA President Jim Rettig. "Through his leadership, he opened doors to segregated library associations and acted as librarianship's conscience, encouraging the field to live up to and operate by fundamental American principles of justice and equity."

Françoise Beaulieu-Thybulle

Libraries and librarians around the world have taken the message of intellectual freedom to heart as they struggle to provide library services to their library users. In no place is this message taken more seriously than in Haiti. I had the pleasure of interviewing Françoise Beaulieu-Thybulle, director of the National Library of Haiti in September of 2011, seven months after the earthquake that devastated Port au Prince.

Beaulieu-Thybulle attended library school at Columbia University in 1980 and then returned to Haiti where she worked in the Foreign Affairs Ministry library and then as the director of the National Library in 1981. She began her position right after the disastrous hurricanes of 1977 and 1978, so she had some experience with natural disasters, but nothing as horrendous as the earthquake she would experience in Haiti.

Beaulieu-Thybulle remembers that fateful afternoon like it was yesterday. It occurred on January 12, 2010, at around 5:30 p.m. Her immediate reaction was one of shock at the randomness of the devastation. The school next to the library collapsed, with many students and teachers losing their lives, and yet the library stood, although many shelves and computers fell down. Haiti has only sixteen libraries to serve ten million people and twelve of those libraries suffered severe damage.

The loss of the libraries was particularly hard for the Haitian communities whose poorest members rely on the local libraries for children's and adult services, and are often the only place for hundreds of miles where families can have access to books. In addition, with the severe loss of life and need for basic services, the top priority was first to provide for the basic needs of shelter, food, and clothing.

Beaulieu-Thybulle and her colleagues sprang into action right away, bringing what aid they could to their neighbors and the community. They also began to personally assist in the library recovery by joining the construction workers, by donning helmets and other protective gear to salvage what books and equipment they could from all of the damaged libraries. (Auguste)

The next step was to continue the library's mission of providing services to the library users. The problem was, however, that the libraries were inoperable. Beaulieu-Thybulle and her colleagues, in the true spirit of intellectual freedom, did not let that deter them and decided if the people could not come to the library, that they would instead bring the library to the people.

Many Haitian residents and their families were living in tent cities immediately after the earthquake and even continue to live there today. Beaulieu-Thybulle and a host of other literacy volunteers brought books and other reading supplies, including paper, pencils, and crayons to the children and their families in the tents. Daily story hours, books talks, plays, and sing-alongs were held on the dirt floors, outdoors under the hot sun, and in extra tents when available. The stories and good times were extremely helpful to children who had lost their homes and their families. In addition, with many of the schools being closed indefinitely, the librarian's reading sessions allowed them to have the only education they would receive for weeks, until their schools were rebuilt and restocked with supplies. (Auguste)

Judith Krug

The tributes, positive messages, and overwhelming admiration offered by those who remember librarian extraordinaire and dedicated intellectual freedom advocate Judith Krug, speak volumes about the high level of personal regard that everyone had for her, both professionally and personally.

Jerry Berman, the director of the Center for Democracy & Technology and advocate for free speech on the Internet, wrote upon her death, "Her legacy rests in the constitutional challenge that secured the free speech rights for the Internet that we exercise today." (American Library Association)

John N. Berry, the editor of the *Library Journal,* recounted the many vigorous discussions he had with her about First Amendment issues. In an open letter he wrote to her after her death he fondly remembered one such discussion that took place many years ago when the Internet was an unknown entity and many people were unsure of its negative or positive effects on children. He thought that it was not unreasonable to limit access to the Internet for children ages thirteen and under for their own safety and that limiting their access would make it easier to open access to adults. Krug, with her typical tenacity, vehemently disagreed with his position and explained that children have the right to access any information they think is necessary and that she could think of many instances when they would need to access many types of information, regardless of their age. Her eloquent arguments changed his mind and forever shaped his thinking on the subject. (Berry) He writes these words about their many disagreements: "Despite a few battles with her, I have always admired Judith Krug. Her service to intellectual freedom, without a doubt ALA's most important cause or, if you like, core value, has been tremendous."

As the Internet became more and more influential in the 1990s, Krug's innate understanding of the relationship between the public and new emerging technologies like the Internet and its interaction with the First Amendment became very important, as she led the way to ensuring that library users, both children and adults, had free and open access to the Internet and its resources.

Librarians had always been accustomed to carefully selecting the best and most appropriate resources for their library patrons, however, the vast amount of resources that were available on the Internet enabled the library patron to select their own materials. She understood that the idea of the public that includes children and teens having complete and unfettered access to all types of information made many people nervous and uncomfortable. According to Krug, laws like the Communications Decency Act were a well-intentioned, but misguided, attempt to control the Internet through legislation. Under Krug's leadership, the ALA challenged the law all the way to the Supreme Court. In 1997, the Supreme Court ruled against the indecency provisions of the Communications Decency Act of 1996.

Krug was the director of the Office of Intellectual Freedom since its inception in 1967 until her death and was instrumental in initiating several of the most popular and enduring of intellectual freedom initiatives that promoted and defended intellectual freedom around the country and even around the world.

She initiated the Freedom to Read Foundation in 1969 as an organization that could defend the First Amendment under any circumstances. Since its inception, it has provided the funding to help librarians who have lost their jobs because they spoke up for their own or others' intellectual freedom, as well as helped in the defense of banned and censored books around the country.

She also helped to develop Banned Books Week, in order to promote the right to read stories and express opinions without interference from censors. This celebration of the First Amendment in the United States has also inspired celebrations around the world.

All these initiatives began to fight against the erosion of civil liberties and were equally important to Krug, who remained true to her principles throughout her career. Krug once told Caldwell-Stone that the importance of her work was made clear when she read *And Tango Makes Three* to her granddaughter's class. "The book is often the target of censors because it's about two male penguins that 'adopt' an unclaimed egg. When she was finished, a girl, she later learned was being raised by two women, stood and applauded." (Jenson)

Patricia Martin, who studies consumer culture, remembers Krug as a tireless champion of the First Amendment. She relates that only a few years ago, Krug contacted her because she was very concerned about digital privacy and information and thought that it was important that something be done about it. Martin fondly described Krug as both "friendly and fierce" in her approach and demeanor when it came to defending those rights, no matter what the circumstance, as she remembers the plans they made to support the issue of digital rights at a lunch meeting a few years before her death. "We conjured a national strategy. We landed funding. And we embarked. That's how it worked with Judith Krug. Ever vigilant about protecting Americans' Constitutional rights, Krug liked to snuff out First Amendment powder kegs before they exploded in people's faces." (Martin)

Deborah Caldwell Stone, the deputy director of the Office of Intellectual Freedom simply remembers Krug this way: "She was a force of nature, fiercely determined to make sure that censorship wouldn't triumph in the library or the larger world." (Jenson)

Dorothy M. Broderick

Dorothy M. Broderick was an advocate for young adults who dedicated her life to ensuring that teens' voices were heard and acknowledged. She was a children's and junior high school librarian and then became a professor where she taught in many library schools, published in journals and wrote books. Broderick served on the American Library Association's Intellectual Freedom Committee and in 1987, she won the prestigious Robert B. Downs Intellectual Freedom Award. She also was awarded the Freedom to Read Foundation Roll of Honor Award in 1998.

Broderick's experiences and affection for her young library users inspired her to become committed to the idea that adults should act as advocates for teens. She believed that teens were perfectly capable of speaking up for themselves, but that for the most part teens were "politically disenfranchised" and that they needed adults who had political power and access to work alongside them to express their needs. (Hannigan)

She also firmly believed in the self-efficacy of teens, in that they were very affective in deciding what books and resources were best for them and censoring their choices, no matter how inappropriate those choices seemed to adults, not only violated their First Amendment rights, but also impeded their ability to learn to think critically about the material they read. To make this point, Broderick reflected on a book review she wrote about the book *Voices* by Beatrice Sparks in 1978. She thought that the book, which was written by the author of *Go Ask Alice*, was basically trash. She stated that, "We hope that young people will recognize trash, when they see it . . ." but that they have to have the chance to read what they like and make up their own minds. She goes on to make a profound statement about censorship. "And we remind librarians that if we are to fight censors by telling them libraries must contain items they find offensive, occasionally we have to add items we find offensive." (*VOYA*)

This innovative way of thinking led Broderick and her partner, Mary K. Chelton, to launch *Voice of Youth Advocates* (*VOYA*) magazine in 1978 as a vehicle in which to offer young adults a platform in which to share their ideas with the literary community and as a place where librarians could work with young adults to assist them in advancing those ideas.

Mary K. Chelton, in an essay for *VOYA* magazine, wrote about how the magazine came about. In the 1970s she and Broderick were involved in various children services committees. They both worked with an ALA committee that published a journal about children's services that was to also include services for young adults. However, they found that the needs of teens were getting lost within the push for younger children's services. Chelton explains that Broderick felt that, "Without a voice of our own, YA services could not survive, and the idea for *VOYA* was born!"

The first issue, as Chelton describes, was put together basically on their kitchen table by friends and was a simple seventy pages total. Since its beginning, *VOYA* has received great reviews and has become the only book review magazine that showcases the direct opinions of teens themselves by giving teens the chance to write their own books reviews and opinion pieces. In her final reflection about the launch and success of the magazine, Chelton states, "In retrospect, we were very stupid about what it takes to produce a magazine, especially a review magazine, but it needed to be done to prove a point about the vibrancy and diversity of YA services and the important differences between child and adolescent development." (*YOYA*)

Amy Bowllan

Amy Bowllan began her career as a television investigative producer and reporter for WCBS-TV NY and KNXV in Phoenix, Arizona. She has received two Emmy awards for her work in broadcast journalism, as well as several Associated Press awards. In addition, Bowllan has taught grades K through 12 and has hosted television shows for PBS. Bowllan is probably most well-known to librarians and other book lovers through her popular blog that appears on the *School Library Journal* website. The blog is fun, entertaining, and informative; it is her chosen focus on multiculturalism, however, that makes it one of the most important and essential of the library blogs that exist today. She introduces her readers to stories that would most likely not get the attention they deserve.

Bowllan's decision to channel her resources towards multicultural resources promotes the values that intellectual freedom encourages, ensuring that resources offered to the public reflect a diversity of political, economic, religious, and cultural thought. Through her exclusive focus on multicultural issues and books, authors found a place to showcase their unique diverse literary perspective. Bowllan has brought these stories to the forefront through the Writers Against Racism (W.A.R.) program that introduces writers who have written young adult and children's novels that deal with diversity in all forms, as a way of combating racism by sharing diverse ideas and ways of life. (Bowllan)

Bowllan explains that she was inspired to support this project after she had worked as a reviewer and blogger for years. She came to realize there was a lack of books and stories about teens and children of color available through the classroom, school, and public libraries. She noted reading lists rarely included any multicultural authors or stories. For example, her son's reading list was "devoid of any authors of color except for Maya Angelou." She was stunned when she consulted with Dr. Zetta Elliot, a specialist in multicultural literature, who informed her that this was true nationwide and that this deficit also included GLBT authors and stories as well.

She also came to recognize that, as a book reviewer, the majority of the books she reviewed were that of white authors. She loves the books she reviews, along with their authors, but remained concerned about the lack of inclusion and also began to examine her own deficiencies in advocating for more diversity.

This commitment has lead Bowllan to write one of the most interesting and informative blogs in the young adult literary world. One of my favorite postings took place a few years ago. Bowllan profiled a young girl who had decided to recreate the famous doll experiment that was initially created in the 1960s. This study by Kenneth and Clark offered African American girls the choice of black and white dolls with which to play. The girls chose the white doll and referred to the black doll as "bad" and a toy that they did not want. The experiment, while not conducted by professionals, offered insight and introspection about the mindset and feelings of multicultural girls and the dilemmas they still face today.

Bowllan's December 2011 blog featured new author April M. Whitt, who has written a mystery series that features a wheelchair-bound smart and intrepid detective. Whitt, who has taught disabled children for years, decided to take the initiative to write the stories for her students that they always asked for but could never find. Bowllan provided exposure for her important work as her debut series, *Private Eye, Romeo Riley*, was launched in bookstores and libraries. (Bowllan)

In an interview with Multiculturalism Rocks!, a book review site that features multicultural books and authors, Bowllan reflects on her hopes for the future and the place that books have in it:

"My hope for the future lies in our young people. I want them to walk into their classrooms knowing that their teachers are providing them with a full menu of literary works from across the globe, and from people of ALL ethnic backgrounds. This will help to ensure a global interconnectedness that will bridge cultural gaps, and get people talking about the lives of everyday people. When we learn about others, we reach an understanding of others in ways beyond our wildest dreams. Bigotry, racism, and judging, washes away."

Dee Ann Venuto

"Our profession requires us to provide information that reflects all the varied needs and interests of our patrons and I will continue to do so." (Habley)

Intellectual freedom and the right to read are not just lofty ideals to Dee Ann Venuto, a high school librarian at the Rancocas Valley High School in New Jersey. She put these ideals into practice when, in the midst of a difficult and volatile book challenge, she steadfastly defended her students First Amendment rights. For her efforts, in 2010 she was honored by the National Coalition against Censorship (NCAC) and was the winner of the 2011 American Association of School Librarians (AASL) award for Intellectual Freedom:

Bonnie Grimble, the committee chairperson for the AASL made this statement about Venuto:

"The Intellectual Freedom Awards Committee applauds all school librarians who, on a daily basis, seek to uphold the principles of intellectual freedom. This year's award winner was chosen for her determined efforts in facing a challenge. Dee is an excellent model in demonstrating the teaching opportunities educators should grasp when faced with challenging hurdles. From the questions and doubts raised in the challenge, our winner created lessons that brought forth understanding and growth." (Habley)

Venuto states that, "Professionally, I truly believe it is discriminating to keep materials from young people who want to read, but do not always have access to the public library or the purchase of books." She does, however, realize that in the climate that exists today in libraries, that this commitment is not always easy or free from personal and professional conflict. In fact, she describes how throughout the years she has questioned herself many times when trying to objectively evaluate books that her students want her to purchase. In an interview she granted for the National New Jersey Library Association, she recalls interlibrary loaning a copy of the *Anarchist's Cookbook* for a student very early in her career; something she is not sure she would do today. She has also alternately agreed and disagreed with her student's requests to read such popular adult authors such as Eric Jerome Dickey and Zane. (Bruder)

Working through these professional conflicts familiar to many librarians only served to strengthen her resolve and ability to put aside personal opinions and objections when objectively selecting the books that engage her students. When the time came to test this commitment, Venuto did not hesitate to put her values and beliefs about intellectual freedom into practice.

On February 23, 2010, Beverly Marinelli spoke in front of the Rancocas Valley School board to challenge three books that were in the Rancocas Valley High School library that she considered inappropriate. The books that were to be removed from the library were: *Revolutionary Voices*: *A Multicultural Queer Youth Anthology* edited by Amy Sonnie (Alyson, 2000); *Love and Sex: Ten Stories of Truth* edited by Michael Cart (S & S, 2001); *The Full Spectrum: A New Generation of Writings about Gay, Lesbian, Bisexual, Transgender, Questioning, and Other Identities* edited by David Levithan and Billy Merrell. (Knopf, 2006)

Marinelli stated that she found the books on a list put together by the by the Gay, Lesbian, and Straight Education Network (GLSEN), which was founded by Kevin Jennings, who is now director of DOE's Office of Safe and Drug Free Schools. She explained that, in her way of thinking, "This issue has nothing to do with gayness or straightness." She was bringing the challenge because the reading list promotes the sexualization of children, regardless of their orientation. She then gave board members a packet of information about the books that contained the statement, "I feel that any books related to Mr. Jennings are detrimental to schoolchildren." The result was that the books were all removed from the library.

At the same time, Marinelli also challenged the book *Revolutionary Voices,* which was shelved in the adult section of the Burlington County Public Library System, where it was quickly removed, without following their own reconsideration policy. Follow-up research conducted by American Civil Liberties Union of New Jersey through a Freedom of Information Act discovered library emails showing that the library director referred to the book as "child pornography" and ordered all copies of the book to be removed. (Barack)

When faced with the same situation, school librarian Dee Ann Venuto knew that defending the books would be difficult and that her response, whatever it was, could have an adverse effect on her life, both professionally and personally. The easiest resolution to the problem would have been for her to remain silent and allow the books to be removed from the library without any due process. Instead, Venuto remained true to her beliefs in intellectual freedom and in her students' right to read. She decided to approach the challenge objectively and with reason, so that she could present to the school board, her colleagues, students, and the community the facts surrounding the challenge enabling them to be able to make an informed decision.

Venuto first thought about how she would encourage her students to approach such a situation. In doing so, she realized that the lessons she taught them about the importance of critical thinking and thorough research were the necessary tools to gather the information necessary to present to the school board.

Venuto began by reviewing the packet of information that Marinelli provided. She then found an article about a Republican effort to discredit Ken Jennings, President Obama's appointee, and a link to a video entitled *Radical Obama's Appointees*. She continued her research with an Internet search that uncovered a message board of the Burlington County Chapter of Glenn Beck's 912 Project, a conservative group formed to focus on American values. Her findings led her to conclude that "This wasn't just a parent who was upset, but a group that was much more organized." Venuto continued: "I could see that they were systematically planning to target school libraries in the county, and that if this is happening in New Jersey, there is probably a good chance it could happen in other places." She then took the difficult step of presenting her findings to the school board. (Goldberg)

The school board decided to place *Love and Sex: Ten Stories of Truth* and *The Full Spectrum: A New Generation of Writings about Gay, Lesbian, Bisexual, Transgender, Questioning, and Other Identities* back on the library shelves and to remove the book *Revolutionary Voices*. The decision to remove the book *Revolutionary Voices* was protested by the National Coalition against Censorship, who wrote this letter to the school board on behalf of their decision:

> No one has to read something just because it's on the library shelf. No book is right for everyone, and the role of the library is to allow students to make choices according to their own interests, experiences, and family values. Some parents prefer to keep their children from reading about sex; others may strongly disapprove of teen sexual activity and still not censor their children's reading. Some parents appreciate books that delve into the subject of sexual orientation, because they can create opportunities for adults and teens to talk about the topic. Even if the books are too mature for some students, they will be meaningful to others. (SLJ Staff)

The ALA Office of Intellectual Freedom also assisted Venuto in opposing the ban, which helped to draw even more public attention to the controversial decision. The controversy also inspired local artists and students to stage a series of readings from the book.

In her acceptance speech at the National Coalition Awards presentation, Venuto had this to say to *School Library Journal* about her ordeal:

> In the wake of school library closures across the nation and an increase in challenges to young adult literature, it is also admirable that this organization has chosen to focus on young adults and school libraries at their annual celebration. The challenge certainly presented a situation where one learns by living the experience, which is why librarians, administrators, and citizens will benefit from transparency. (Rocco)

Resources

Article 19. Universal Declaration of Human Rights. *http://www.un.org/en/documents/udhr/index. shtml#a19*. 14 May 2012.

Auguste, Margaret . "Li, Li, Li, Libraries Rebuild." *Faces: People, Places and Cultures*. September 2011: 34-35.

Barack, Lauren. "NJ Library, Citing Child Pornography, Removes GLBT Book." *School Library Journal*. 27 July 2010. *http://www.schoollibraryjournal.com/slj/home/886066-312/nj_library_citing_child_ pornography.html.csp*. 04 January 2012.

Berry, John. "E. J. Josey, Legendary Activist Librarian and Leader, Dies at 85." *Library Journal*. 2009. *http://www.libraryjournal.com/article/CA6669152.html*. 04 January 2012.

Berry, John. "She convinced ALA to put its money where its mouth is." *Library Journal*. 15 July 2005. *http://www.libraryjournal.com/article/CA606394.html*. 04 January 2012.

Bowllan, Amy. "Writers Against Racism." Bowllan's Blog. *School Library Journal*. 04 January 2012. *http://blog.schoollibraryjournal.com/bowllansblog*. 04 January 2012.

Bruder, Patricia. "Teen Lit: Edgy or Over the Edge?" New Jersey Education. 01 February 2010. *http:// www.njea.org/teaching-and-learning/classroom-tools/toolbox/teen-lit-edgy-or-over-the-edge*. 04 January 2012.

Chute, Eleanor. "E.J. Josey Pushed for Integration." *Pittsburgh Post Gazette*. 08 July 2009. *http://www. post-gazette.com/pg/09189/982402-122.stm*. 04 January 2012.

"E.J. Josey Passes Away." *Savannah Tribune*. *http://www.savannahtribune.com/news/2009-07-08/ Front_Page/EJ_Josey_Passes_Away.html*. 04 January 2012.

Goldberg, Beverly. "Obama's 'Safe Schools Czar' Targeted in New Jersey Challenge." *American Librar- ies*. 10 March 2010. *http://americanlibrariesmagazine.org/news/03102010/obamas-safe-schools- czar-targeted-new-jersey-challenge*. 04 January 2012.

Habley, Jennifer. "School librarian stands against organized challenge, receives AASL Intellectual Free- dom Award." *American Libraries*. 19 April 2011. *http://americanlibrariesmagazine.org/news/ala/ school-librarian-stands-against-organized-challenge-receives-aasl-intellectual-freedom-awar*. 04 January 2012.

Hannigan, Jane. "A Feminist Analysis of the Voices for Advocacy in Young Adult Services." Library Trends. Spring,1996: 852-875. *http://www.ideals.illinois.edu/bitstream/handle/2142/8049/librarytrends v44i4k_opt.pdf?sequence=1*. 04 January 2012.

Hawkins, Valerie. "Stormcenter." *American Libraries*. 2010. *http://americanlibrariesmagazine.org/ ask-ala-librarian/storm-center*. 04 January 2012.

Jenson, Trevor. "Judith F. Krug dies at 69; advocate for librarians battled censorship." *Los Angeles Times*. 15 April, 2009. *http://www.latimes.com/news/obituaries/la-me-judith-krug15-2009apr15,0,520939. story*. 14 May 2012.

Josey, E.J. *The Black Librarian in America*. Scarecrow Press, 1970.

"Judith Krug, Librarian, Tireless Advocate for First Amendment Rights, Dies." American Libraries Association.13 April 2009. *http://www.ala.org/news/news/pressreleases2009/april2009/oifkrug*. 04 January 2012.

"Juliette Hampton Morgan." Tapestry of Faith. 27 October 2011. *http://www.uua.org/re/tapestry/ children/windows/session11/sessionplan/stories/143771.shtml*. 01 January 2012.

"Juliette Hampton Morgan: A White Woman Who Understood." Teaching Tolerance: Southern Poverty Law Center. *http://www.tolerance.org/activity/juliette-hampton-morgan-white-woman-who-understood*. 04 January 2012.

King, Dr. Martin Luther. *Stride toward Freedom: The Montgomery Story*. Beacon Press, 1958. 71-73.

"Mary K. Chelton and Dorothy M. Broderick." VOYA Online. 29 March 2010. *http://www.voya. com/2010/05/17/cheltonbroderick/*. 04 January 2012.

Martin, Douglass. "Judith Krug, Who Fought Ban on Books, Dies at 69." New York Times. 14 April 2009. *http://www.nytimes.com/2009/04/15/us/15krug.html*. 14 May 2012.

"Miss Ruth Brown." Bartlesville Public Library. 2009. *http://www.bartlesville.lib.ok.us/aboutlibrary/ missbrown*. 04 January 2012.

Mvondo, Natalie. "Monday Interview: Award Winning Journalist, Author, Blogger & Educator Amy Bowllan." Multiculturalism Rocks. 21 February 2001. *http://multiculturalismrocks.com/2011/02/21/ monday-interview-award-winning-journalist-author-blogger-educator-amy-bowllan/*. 04 January 2012.

NCAC. "NCAC defends challenged GLBTQ books in NJ school library." 04 May 2010. *http://www.ncac. org/book-challenges-in-New-Jersey-school-library*. 14 May 2012.

Pattak, Evan. "E.J. Josey: Firing the Shot Heard 'Round the Library World". University of Pittsburg. *http://www.chronicle.pitt.edu/media/pcc010226/josey.html*. 14 May 2012.

Robbins, Louise. *The Dismissal of Miss Ruth Brown: Civil Rights, Censorship, and the American Library*. University of Oklahoma Press, 2000. 55-90.

Rocco, Staino. "NCAC Honors Myracle, School Librarian as Defenders of Free Speech." *School Library Journal*. 14 December 2010. *http://www.schoollibraryjournal.com/slj/newslettersnewsletterbuck etextrahelping2/888482-477/ncac_honors_myracle_school_librarian.html.csp*. 04 January 2012.

"Ruth Brown." Oklahoma Library Legends. *http://www.library.okstate.edu/dean/jpaust/legends/people/ brown.htm*. 04 January 2012.

SLJ Staff. "Free Speech Groups Protest GLBT Book-Banning at NJ School District." *School Library Journal*. 19 May 2010. *http://www.schoollibraryjournal.com/article/CA6728872.html*. 04 January 2012.

Stanton, Mary. *Journey toward Justice: Juliette Hampton Morgan and the Montgomery Bus Boycott*. Georgia University Press, 2006.

Stanton, Mary. "Juliette Hampton Morgan." *Encyclopedia of Alabama*. 2011. *http://www.encyclopedia ofalabama.org/face/Article.jsp?id=h-2981*. 04 January 2012.

Teaching Tolerance: Southern Poverty Law Center. "Juliette Hampton Morgan: A White Woman Who Understood." *http://www.tolerance.org/activity/juliette-hampton-morgan-white-woman-who-understood*. 04 January 2012.

INDEX

ABOUT THE AUTHOR

As a family therapist, Margaret Auguste frequently utilized books and stories as a therapeutic device. After witnessing the positive affects that reading brought to her clients, she earned her MLS degree at Indiana University in 1999, and began her library career as a library technology instructor and as a public services and technology librarian in New Jersey. She currently works as a school librarian at a middle school in Somerset, New Jersey.

Auguste shares her experiences and knowledge of libraries through writing. She has written for *Teacher Librarian* magazine, where she shared her experience transitioning from one career into another as an alternate route librarian. She has written for *FACES: People, Places and Cultures* about the plight of Haiti's libraries. She contributed to *VOYA* magazine about her experience collaborating with other librarians to bring authors into her school. She is a book reviewer for *School Library Journal* and *Multicultural Review* magazines.

Auguste is a leader in bringing technology information and skills to the community. As a software trainer, she traveled around the country and Canada teaching librarians and teachers how to implement and integrate technology into their workplaces. She taught Internet searching skills, website evaluation, and website design to the community. She also collaborated with local law enforcement to develop Internet safety information classes for parents, to educate them about how to keep their children safe when using the Internet.

Auguste has also brought the issues of diversity, culture, and race to the forefront through essays written for the anthologies *Hair Power Skin Revolution* (Troubador, 2010) and *Maternal Pedagogies: In and Outside of the Classroom* (Demeter, 2011), in which she writes about the psychological and social impact of skin color in America, and the historical and sociological impact of African American teachers on their students.

An American Libraries Association 1998 Spectrum Scholarship winner, she is a member of The Motherhood Initiative for Research and Community Involvement, a member of the New Jersey Association of School Librarians, and a member of the New Jersey Librarians Association.

CPSIA information can be obtained at www.ICGtesting.com
Printed in the USA
BVOW051659251012

303924BV00005B/3/P